WAITING TO DIE

WAITING TO DIE

One Man's Journey on Death Row

Feltus Taylor, Jr.

**Edited by
Monique Morrison**

BLOOMSBURY ACADEMIC
NEW YORK · LONDON · OXFORD · NEW DELHI · SYDNEY

BLOOMSBURY ACADEMIC
Bloomsbury Publishing Inc, 1359 Broadway, New York, NY 10018, USA
Bloomsbury Publishing Plc, 50 Bedford Square, London, WC1B 3DP, UK
Bloomsbury Publishing Ireland, 29 Earlsfort Terrace, Dublin 2, D02 AY28, Ireland

BLOOMSBURY, BLOOMSBURY ACADEMIC and the Diana logo are
trademarks of Bloomsbury Publishing Plc

First published in the United States of America 2026

Cover design: Sally Rinehart
Cover image © iStock.com/underworld111

A catalog record for this book is available from the Library of Congress.

ISBN: HB: 979-8-7651-5729-9
       ePDF: 979-8-7651-5731-2
      eBook: 979-8-7651-5730-5

Typeset by Integra Software Services Pvt. Ltd.
Printed and bound in the United States of America

For product safety related questions contact productsafety@bloomsbury.com

To find out more about our authors and books visit www.bloomsbury.com
and sign up for our newsletters.

To all the at-risk youth and to God for helping me write this.

—Feltus Taylor, Jr.

To the victims and their families:

All of you will never know how truly sorry I am that this ever happened, and that I—nobody else—caused it. Please, I ask of you, try to find it within your hearts to forgive me of my wrong. There is nothing, in word or in deed, I can do to make up for the loss and pain I have both caused and brought upon you for the rest of your lives. I never meant to hurt or harm anyone that day, but I did, and I sincerely am sorry for that.

—Feltus Taylor, Jr.

CONTENTS

ACKNOWLEDGMENTS

Monique Morrison

THANK YOU TO ALINA Mitchell and Chip McGregor, for believing in Feltus' story and representing his memoir with unwavering support and determination. Thank you to Becca Beurer for your advocacy, and Bloomsbury for bringing this story to the world through print.

Thank you to my alma mater, Louisiana State University, for your support with this endeavor all these years, and to Andrew Maas and his team at LSU Office of Innovation & Development who dedicated their time and legal expertise.

This book could not have been completed without the talent and dedication of the staff members at LSU School of Social Work, Office of Social Service Research and Development. Many thanks go to the Head of OSSRD, Cecile Guin, for your dedication and service, and for shepherding your team of students: Betsy Doyle, Ari Ellerbe, Jacob Fusilier, Kevin Hurstell, Christina Little, Dustin Drewes, and Frannie Rodrigue, who typed hundreds of handwritten pages of Feltus' manuscript, and contributed many hours of proofreading; and, editors Ronlyn Domingue and Mary McMyne, who worked with Feltus up until his death in helping him complete his manuscript.

The pursuit to get Feltus' manuscript published has long been my mission, not only for him, but for Cecile and everyone who tirelessly helped Feltus in his journey of growth and positive transformation. There have been so many people along the way who have offered a hand in helping me get to this point. Thank you to all of my loved ones and friends, sponsors, donors, attorneys, and members of Feltus' trust, who believed in me and entrusted me with fulfilling Feltus' dying wish of sharing his story with the world.

A special thank you to Kristen Epland for being a true friend, supporter, and dedicated sounding board all these years. Thank you for believing in the importance of Feltus' story. As a victim of losing a family member to a violent crime, you offer a different and very necessary perspective.

In Feltus' words:

> I want to thank Bonnie Jackson and James E. Boren, my first trial attorneys; Jane Officer and Jan Macdonald, two enduring pen friends; and Sister Helen Prejean, the author of *Dead Man Walking*, who suggested that I write down what I was feeling and thinking.
>
> I would also like to thank Jean Faria, Michele Fournet, Jane Smith, Cecile Guin, and Roger Phillips for all of their help, and for always showing me great care as a human being. I love all of you very much, and thank you for helping me to become the man I am today. I want to thank Charlie deGravelles for helping me to grow spiritually into the person that I've become. One last person is Ronlyn Domingue, who assisted me with all of this writing and putting it together. Without your guidance and help, I wouldn't have been able to get this all done.
>
> All of you never stopped caring for me as a person and showed love and care endlessly. It took me a while to fully understand why all of you just didn't give up on me like I had on myself. But this just goes to show it makes you have a desire to want to become a better person, no matter what you have done in the past.

Thank you to all who have supported this story, including the readers of this book. Thank you to all the advocates, social workers, and volunteers, who devote their time in helping at-risk youth, and raise awareness on the importance of restorative justice and victim perpetrator reconciliation; and, to organizations such as: the Equal Justice Initiative, the Anti Recidivism Coalition, and the Louisiana Capital Assistance Center for the tremendous work you do.

Lastly, to the victims and their families, I hope that you find some peace in hearing Feltus' words and all that he wished he could say to you. I understand that it does not change the outcome, and nothing can take away the pain of your loss and suffering. Please know that I continue to honor you, and all victims of violent crime.

FOREWORD

Sister Helen Prejean, CSJ

LIKED HIM WHEN I met him. I couldn't help but like him. Feltus Taylor, Jr. is soft-spoken and sincere, and there's a little-boy affection in him. I met him at a seminar in a crowded room where, once a year, death row inmates in the Louisiana State Penitentiary are allowed to gather with guests.

His very old grandmother was there. As I talked to him, I learned the two great pains of his life: that he betrayed his grandmother's gentle love and that he'd like to make amends to one of his victims, Keith Clark, a man he shot and almost killed.

And when we first talked, that's what he talked to me about: did I think I could help him meet Mr. Clark so he could apologize and ask for forgiveness? His remorse was raw. He couldn't believe what he had done, and he later told me in a letter, "and to think I did it because I was upset over a GIRL."

He's sorry for what he did, but for a state that executes criminals, being sorry can never be enough. Nor can being spiritually transformed into a loving, caring being ever be enough. The state of Louisiana and its mechanisms of criminal justice have identified Feltus Taylor solely as the man who did the terrible crime—killing one person and almost killing another. He has been freeze-framed in the worst act of his life and now the state freeze-frames itself into having to kill him.

By the time these words make their way into readers' hands, Feltus Taylor will have been killed by the state of Louisiana, and most people will say, *Good riddance.*

But there is this difference. Feltus wanted to do something redemptive for the world. He knew that the human life he took could never be replaced, but he wanted somehow to give life to the world.

And so, he has told the story of his life—how he started out as a child and what happened to him along the way—and his terrible mistakes. Once he said to me, with great earnestness: "Maybe the young people reading my story will learn from my mistakes. Maybe I can help them choose a better way."

At heart, I see the main theme of Feltus's life as a struggle to make connections with people, to belong to the human family. It was, I believe, this sense of disconnectedness from people that triggered the desperate act of violence.

He tells his story well. He doesn't whine or offer excuses. He writes honestly and with a disarming simplicity. His story—his tragic legacy to the world—makes us think of other desperate young people like him who we know and whom we must reach out to before they, too, explode into violence.

NOTE ON THE TEXT

Monique Morrison

EVENTS DESCRIBED ARE BASED on Mr. Taylor's memory of real-life situations. With Mr. Taylor's permission, quotations from interviews and excerpts from court transcripts, reports, letters, and other documents were added after his death. Some names were changed to protect the privacy of certain individuals involved.

Every attempt was made to preserve Mr. Taylor's voice.

INTRODUCTION

Monique Morrison

HOW DOES ONE END up on death row? If you'd asked me that years ago, I might have pointed to one moment—the crime. The truth, though, is more complicated. Hemingway, with his usual clarity, might have said: gradually, then suddenly. We tend to fixate on the sudden part—the flashpoint, the irreversible moment. It's the part that gets headlines, that fills courtrooms, that freezes someone in time. We are trained—by headlines, courtroom drama, and the economy of judgment—to focus on the sudden: and, I understand that. A capital offense is shocking, painful, and often impossible to explain.

But this story is not about that moment alone. Feltus' story begins long before—with small decisions, missed exits, systemic failures, and the silent accumulation of damage. This story is not a cry for redemption. It is a plea for recognition: that even in our most unforgivable acts, there is a human story beneath the surface—one that must be looked at fully if we are ever to understand the violence we condemn.

Feltus wasn't born into safety. Abandoned as an infant by a mother gripped by addiction, the first three years of his life remain lost to time, undocumented and unknowable. But what little we do know from the years that followed reveals clear signs of neglect and abuse. He was severely developmentally disabled, had a speech impediment, lived with major depression, experienced dissociative seizures, and struggled to make sense of a world that often failed to make sense of him. He struggled not only to keep up but to orient himself—to understand what others seemed to grasp instinctively. He moved through childhood with a fragile understanding of security, connection, belonging, and consequence, shaped by instability and absence.

This manuscript did not come to me directly. It was entrusted to me by Cecile Guin, a social worker and researcher who devotes her career to unearthing the human stories buried beneath criminal labels—particularly those sentenced to die. Cecile met Feltus while working on his life history case study during the long, uncertain stretch of his appeals. She was not just a researcher to him; she became a confidante, a witness, and ultimately, a keeper of his promise. Before his execution, Feltus asked her to ensure that his story would not be buried with him. She promised she would.

Three years later, during my final year of college—just as I was beginning to find my own voice in film and storytelling—Cecile introduced me to Feltus' story. When I was first entrusted with Feltus' manuscript, I expected a confession. What I found was something far more complex, more aching, and—perhaps most tragically—more familiar than I anticipated.

While reading his manuscript, I was moved, yet conflicted. I instantly felt an unspeakable bond, both growing up in Baton Rouge, the familiarity of the southern landscape, yet having two very different upbringings.

I was compelled by his honesty and ability to be raw and vulnerable. His longing for an opportunity for forgiveness, connectedness, his commitment to personal redemption, and his dedication to helping at-risk youth, deeply impacted me. His words didn't just stay with me—they altered me. They forever changed and expanded my lens on how I see the world, and widened my understanding of justice, accountability, and grace. In bearing witness to his story, I became a more compassionate, more conscious version of myself.

I never met Feltus, yet I know and feel connected to him in a unique way. It is a rare thing to be asked to shepherd a story like this. I accepted the task because I believe stories like Feltus' must be heard. Not because they justify, but because they illuminate the dark corners most of us would rather not see.

As human beings, we have the opportunity to change and to right wrongs, but not all of us, not in the system that we currently have in play. A question I ask is: *Does the worst thing a person has ever done define who they are?* This is something we all can ponder. Only after one has walked the path that someone else has traveled, and lived their sorrows, doubts, fear, and pain, can one begin to understand. Feltus' memoir allows us to do just that.

His story invites you into a world rarely seen and barely understood. A world—in the heart of South Louisiana, amid the humid swamplands, and the haunting echoes of history—where hope coexists with hopelessness, where faith becomes a lifeline, and where the humanity of a man society had written off rises to confront us with uncomfortable truths.

Feltus' journey to death row is not one of wrongful accusation. Feltus was sentenced to die for a crime that rocked a Louisiana community, but behind the courtroom verdict and prison walls was a person shaped by trauma, shaped by choice, and ultimately reshaped by reflection.

Feltus writes not to excuse, but to understand. And in that understanding, he reaches out in a heartfelt and urgent call to action—not just to the curious reader, but to young readers in particular—to those who may be walking a path like the one he once did. His ultimate purpose in recounting his experience is profoundly selfless and courageous. Feltus' message—a message born out of tragic circumstances, but rooted firmly in the hope of others—is not loud, but it is clear.

Through brutal honesty and vivid storytelling, he seeks to offer his life as a beacon of caution and inspiration. His intent is to deter young readers from paths that lead to ruin and instead guide them toward hope, opportunity, and a future free from regret.

In the pages ahead, you will explore Feltus's narrative structured around pivotal life events, each carefully examined and reflected upon with striking transparency. You will witness moments of youthful optimism and promise, experience the seductive yet dangerous allure of misguided choices, and confront the devastating consequences that followed. This memoir is not merely a recounting of events but an intimate exploration of profound life lessons, the enduring strength of human dignity, and the relentless pursuit of redemption.

While preserving his voice as faithfully as possible, courtroom transcripts, legal filings, historical data, and relevant statistics have been incorporated to provide a deeper, fuller context. These additions are not meant to explain away what he did. Rather, they offer a wider lens: a view of the forces—systemic and personal—that constructed his life, and by extension, the lives of so many others whose names we may never know.

As the steward of Feltus' story for over two decades now, the journey of getting Feltus' memoir published has been long, and, at times arduous, with many winding roads. However, over the years, I could feel Feltus "nudging" me along and serving as the North Star to this journey. This memoir is the result of many hands, many hearts, and one final promise.

I hope you'll read it with the weight it deserves.

PROLOGUE

WELL, AS I SIT here in this cold and ugly cell, I'm trying to think about how my life took such a bad turn for the worse. I get so tired of crying, but I can't help it when I think about all the people who have tried to help me and how I repaid them by getting into this mess. My name is Feltus Taylor, Jr., and I live at Louisiana State Penitentiary on death row. Today, a man named Robert Sawyer is to be executed by lethal injection. He is the first man in three years to be put to death here at Louisiana State Penitentiary, also called Angola.

They say that dying by lethal injection is better than by the electric chair. I would think so, too, considering how bad the electric chair burns you and the smell it creates from the burning flesh. It's enough to make someone watching want to throw up right there on the spot. I'm happy that the state has changed from electrocutions to the lethal injection method, but I pray and hope that I will miss it altogether. No one knows, though, except the Lord, what will happen to me.

They've moved Robert Sawyer from death row to Camp F—the Death House—by now. From my cell, I can see the front gate of the prison and all kinds of news people. They swarm out there like carrion eaters waiting on certain death as they stand with their cameras, waiting for an interview with the warden. I wonder what he will say to them? I suppose I will see it on the TV news tomorrow.

I'm tired but can't sleep as I wait to see what will happen to Robert. It all seems so surreal to me now, but at times, the reality is so tangible that I can feel it in the air I breathe. I'm scared to death, as is everyone here on death row. Everything is ominously quiet, and I wonder what everyone else is thinking. Probably the same things as me. Will they get a chance to do this to me also? My stomach is in knots, and my head hurts just from thinking about this tonight.

At 12:01 a.m., they will begin to put Robert to death. I really didn't know him that good. I had on occasion met him and talked to him once or twice in church, though. He seems to be very sorry for what they say he is to die for. I read in the paper that he was supposed to have killed his girlfriend's babysitter and that he burned her before he killed her. Maybe he used lighter fluid like they say he did and even raped her. But that would indicate that he had serious mental problems, that he was not in control. I don't know what the answer would be in a situation such as his. They let his partner, who was with him during the crime, make a bargain with the state that left Robert in a bad position. I don't think that the courts should make a deal with one of two criminals that allows one to get off lighter when they only have the word of that one against the other. Robert's partner got off with a life sentence. Robert got the death penalty. I don't know the details, since I wasn't there, but I still don't think it's fair.

Earlier today, a guard that I talk to every once in a while, stopped by my cell and told me that he had seen Robert's partner at the main prison, and that he had said that he'll be glad when they kill Robert. The guard said he has a problem with that because the guy seems not to care what happens to Robert, someone that he helped put to death.

The iron door at the front of the tier just closed, and it made me jump. I think everyone's a little jumpy tonight. The guard is making his rounds, to make sure that we are all still here and that no one has killed himself.

All of this is running through my mind now. I can see that everyone outside is leaving, so they must have carried out the execution as planned. I can't help but wonder if they'll be outside like that when my time comes. If it comes.

CHAPTER 1

In my opinion, Mr. Taylor is an individual of limited intellectual ability and education who appears to be suffering from depressive symptoms that probably have been present off and on throughout much of his life. Mr. Taylor clearly knows that his actions at the time of the crime were wrong. He makes no attempt to excuse himself or blame others for his actions, and he does not express a desire for revenge toward others. He continues to verbalize suicidal thoughts and impulses, and he remains depressed in mood. He is remorseful.

—REPORT OF CLINICAL PSYCHOLOGIST THOMAS STIGALL,
NOVEMBER 1991

March 31, 1992

WITHIN A FEW WEEKS of my sentence, I was on my way to Louisiana State Penitentiary in Angola, headed for death row. I had never really thought much about the death penalty or the guys on the row before then . . . well, I sure was thinking now.

A guard took me to the booking area and put me in a holding cell while they cut a check for the twenty dollars I had in my account. They gave the money to me, along with the things I had with me the night of the crime—my wallet and the street clothes that I had worn. Two guards put the handcuffs and leg irons on me and led me to the police car.

The sun was out, and it was a pretty day. The ride to Angola was not that long, and I sat in that backseat looking out of the window, watching the people and cars and everything because I knew I would not see it again. They had the radio on, and we were listening to R&B music. I thought about the time I used to drive my own car wherever I wanted, whenever I wanted. I was mostly thinking about what it was going to be like to be on death row.

I saw the sign that read "Angola—20 miles." They turned off on a road with trees on both sides and hills and big fields with cows all over them. Angola was at the end of the road.

I thought about what my lawyers, Mrs. Jackson and Mr. Boren, had told me before I left for Angola. They said I had a lot of issues with my case to appeal, and they really thought I would get a new trial from the courts. So, in some ways, I was hopeful, and in other ways, I was not.

They parked the car outside the gate by a guard tower. They opened the door for me to get out and got my things out of the trunk of the car and then walked me through the gate to my new home. Right then, I thought to myself, *I will never walk out of these gates again. I will most likely be carried out of them.* It was hard. My mind was running on and on. I wondered what this experience would really be like for me.

I had to go to a brick building to the right of the front gates. There was a big yard surrounded by a tall fence with razor wire on top. There was a guard tower that looked into the yard. Inside the building, a guard looked through my things and took me to the cell they had waiting for me. I was standing at the door looking down the tier, and I heard someone call my name and then wave through the bars at me. It was a voice I knew. It was Lil' Boo, who had just come up to Angola about a month or two before me. He was from Baton Rouge.

They led me to Cell 5. I was right next door to Lil' Boo, who was in Cell 4. The guy in Cell 6, next to me, was Tommy. He asked me my name and after I told him, he said, "Yeah, I seen you on TV. It's not that bad here."

I said to myself, *Yeah, right.*

My cell was nine feet long and seven feet wide. The walls was painted white, and the bunk—my bed—was painted a dark brown. The bars was painted dark brown also. The back wall had one small window with bars that looked out to a yard at the place where people come in and out of the prison. That's the wall where the sink and toilet were. Later on, I would keep a few pictures of friends and family, and my Bible, paper and pens for writing on my table, and my Walkman on my bench.

There was a space between the walls near the front of the cells. If I went to the door and turned my head, I could see the guy next to me so we could talk. There was four TVs for fifteen cells on the tier. If I lay down on my bed, I could look up at a TV or straight ahead at a concrete wall.

There was a shower with a door at the end of the tier. That's about the only privacy we had. (Sometime in 1999, they put a security camera at the entrance to the tier. I think they can see inside. They say they can't, but I'm not sure. And the people downstairs who watch the monitors are all women.)

The tier I was on faced the front gate. That was the best side of death row to be on. You could see everyone coming and going out of the prison, visitors and workers, and different people. I guess in some ways it kept you thinking that you were a part of something, you know. It was the only connection with the outside world.

There was a shed under a big roof. The space on each side of it was big enough for eighteen-wheelers to pass through. People went in on one side and out of the other. One guard checked people into the prison and another checked them out. Another one searched the cars coming in and going out.

In front of death row and next to the prison entrance were about 100 feet of grass. A flagpole stood erect with an American flag atop of a pelican flag—the state flag of Louisiana. There was a neatly edged walkway from the fence inside the prison entrance to the entrance to death row. Within the yard were some ducks and roosters that got the run of the place.

The fence all around the yard had double barbed wiring along the top and bottom, with diagonal lines on the front and left sides of the building. On the other side of the fence was a guard tower, but no one was in it most of the time.

From my window, I could see the prison museum—a tourist attraction for many visitors of the prison—and the small parking lot in front. Across the street was a parking lot for the visitors of the prison. On any given weekend, the parking lots would be full with lines of cars running down both sides of the road.

Whenever there was an execution date for someone, both parking lots would be filled with all kinds of news people waiting at the front gate to find out what happened. They would be lined up trying to be the first to get the story. Like ants running to food left out all night. It is really a trip to see that firsthand. It leaves you wondering if they will be like that if your time comes.

There was one thing that made death row different from parish prison. I was locked alone in a cell twenty-three hours a day. I could have more things with me, like food, clothes, tapes, and tennis shoes, but I could not move around like I wanted to. Being locked up is being locked up. You can't do what you want—only what someone else tells you to do. About the only time I got out of my cell was to shower, walk the yard or the tier for my hour out, have a visit, or go to church.

It was summertime when I started to get settled on death row. I could smell fresh air coming in through the open windows on the tier. I could smell the other guys, a strong musk scent. I smelled cigarette smoke and food, like popcorn guys sent up to the microwave to be popped. Sometimes, I could smell weed. They snuck it in, in little sugar packets, and then they covered that up with cigar smoke or by blowing baby powder in the air.

From my cell, I heard guys talking and the TVs going all of the time. I heard the guards with the keys coming before they got to the doors to open them. People had to talk around the walls unless they were spending their hour outside their cells, walking the tier.

I shared a TV with Tommy. All he liked was sports and the music station, BET (Black Entertainment Television), but we also looked at movies, the news, and wrestling, which I liked a lot. Boo and I would stay up all night talking about the streets and this and that.

Some of the guards on death row would treat you like shit and call you an animal because they had heard of what you did. They have a way of making you feel like less than a person. I remember one incident when I was on the first floor of the C tier. There was eleven of us down there. There was a Black guard that worked the tier. He acted cool and would talk with the guys on the tier, but as soon as the tier was shut down for the night, he and two other guards would sit at his desk talking or playing cards. They would talk about different guys on the tier. This would take place in the early morning when they thought everyone was asleep, of course.

They would say things like, "You see Tommy down there in Cell 6? I'll be glad when they kill his ass because he is smart by the mouth."

Then one of the guards would say, "I'll be glad when they kill all of them motherfuckers. All they're doing is wasting our tax dollars. Yeah, and you see what's-his-name? I'll kill him myself."

They really thought no one heard them. Then that guard would come back on the next night, he would come down the tier, and stop and joke with some of the guys and tell them how he wished all of them well on their cases. He even told me once, "Man, I hope the courts do something for you." But I know he did not mean that because, one night, a guy named J.T. and I heard him out there by his desk talking shit about me.

I have also met some guards who treated me like a person and were nice and kind to death row inmates. They would say they were praying for you and meant it. They were the kind who shared a little food from the outside with you. When those types of people worked, everything ran better, and the guys didn't want to give them any trouble because they treated us like people.

The guys on death row were able to go to church every Friday for one hour, and sometimes I would go and sometimes I would not. Sometimes, I would listen to what the man was saying, and other times I would not. Most of the time, I was only going to get out of the cell.

Being in these cells has a way of playing with your head. I mean, you are waiting to be killed. Most guys don't know how to deal with their confinement. A lot have no family to come see them or write them. Damn, there are some who can't even call home. So, they are mad with themselves and everyone around them. They hate God. Some wish they could die now, and some go crazy within their own minds. It's not hard to go crazy. Life on death row is living like an animal in a cage until they take you away and put you to sleep like a mad dog.

I started looking at girly books and gaming, making homemade wine and smoking weed. The only money I had was what I got back from my income tax check for 1991. I kept $200 and gave my grandmother $100. I guess it took me less than two weeks to lose it all from gaming with other guys on the row. I bet on anything and everything just to fit in.

After losing all of my money and a pair of tennis shoes someone had bought for me, I told myself I would not do that again because I stayed broke a while after that. I was going to have to find a way to get money for what I needed. My grandmother was just getting by, and I didn't want to put any more on her. So, Boo gave me this address for a woman in England who was part of some pen pal program over there. They would find people to write to guys on death row in the United States because a lot of guys did not have help from their families. J.T. had told Boo that people would send money. So, I wanted to write her to see if I could get money.

In late **spring of 1992**, I wrote to the lady in England. Her name was Jane Officer. I told her I had just come to the row, and I asked her to see if she could find a pen pal for me. I got a letter from her about three weeks later. She said she didn't want to write me herself because she had been Andrew Lee Jones's pen pal over the years before they killed him. It had hurt her too much when he was executed in July 1991. But she told me she would put me on the waiting list to get a pen pal, and I was okay with that.

I was still broke, so J.T. told me about a nun that worked with death row inmates and found people to write to them right here in Louisiana. I sat down and wrote to her after I got the address from J.T. I guess it was about a week or two later when I got a letter back from Sister Helen Prejean, saying she would see what she could do. She said I wrote her such a nice letter that she wanted to use it on one of her talks. I wrote her back and said I did not mind if she used it.

Sister Helen read my letter when she went to do a talk for *Life Lines*, the group in England that Jane Officer was in at the time. Two people were really touched by my letter. Jan Macdonald and Carol ____ asked Sister Helen for my address, and they began to write me. Jane ended up writing me herself, too, even though she said no at first. It wasn't long before I found myself looking forward to their letters, just to read them.

I continued to write him for several reasons. He asked me to; I could not let him down if that was what he asked; he was so sad, lonely and lost; Scotty Lloyd next to him, who I also write to, told me in his letters how badly Feltus needed people outside to care for him; I felt he was only a child really . . . I used to say to friends who asked me, that he was 31 going on 12 at the time.

—Jane Officer, pen pal

Feltus was the first death row prisoner, to whom I had written. I was living in England at the time and as a result of watching a BBC documentary, I had joined an organization called "Lifelines." This group provides support to DR prisoners in the United States, through correspondence.

I was attending their bi-annual conference in London where Sister Helen Prejean was the main speaker. At the end of her speech, she held up a piece of paper and waved it, saying "I have three here, three names of men [who] just arrived on Louisiana's death row, please come and take a name if you would like to write." I went up to her and she handed me a piece of paper on which was written, "Feltus Taylor #93130" and the address at Angola.

—Jan Macdonald, pen pal

I never entered into it lightly, and knew that once I started writing I would have to continue. Luckily, Feltus's reply came quickly and I could tell straight away he had a lot of good in him and we would be friends. It was just like when you meet a stranger for the first time and you know you will hit it off. Every letter I sent I enjoyed writing and I loved getting mail from Feltus.

—Carol _____, pen pal

In late **August 1992**, Hurricane Andrew came through Louisiana. It was a bad one for people in Florida. It hit Baton Rouge, too, but it didn't do too much damage there. It left a lot of trash and stuff in my grandmother's yard, though. After the storm, Mama Henrietta got out there and tried to clean it up herself. She had a heart attack. I found out when I called home about a week later and her sister, my Aunt Nig, answered the phone. I talked to her for a while, then asked if I could speak to my grandmother. Aunt Nig told me what happened.

I was so hurt. It was like when my mother died and no one told me what had happened. I felt the same thing happening again. When I got through talking to my aunt, I went back to my cell and started crying because it hurt that no one thought I should know what was going on. I knew they did not care for me anymore because of what I had done, but I always wanted to know if my grandmother was well or not. Maybe Mama Henrietta had told them not to let me know, like my mother had before she died.

I got so mad over not knowing that my grandmother was sick and at myself for getting into such a mess when I should have been there to help her out. I started throwing all of my stuff around in my cell. I picked up my lockers and threw them against the bars and the wall. I even tore the top off one of the lockers.

When they got me out of my cell, they sent me to Camp D lockdown, which was called Tiger. I went to court that Monday and told them why I had trashed my cell. They said I would have to pay forty dollars for the two lockers, but they suspended my sentence for ninety days. That meant I could stay in my cell on the row, as long as I didn't cause any trouble.

Later that evening, some guards came to get me to go back on the row. Boo and J.T. talked to me and told me they understood what I was going through. But they said I would have to be cool or I could end up on all types of pills or shots that would make me not know where the hell I was. At the time, I was already on some pills to help me sleep and some others to keep me calm. I felt Boo and J.T. knew what they were talking about, but I really did not care too much right then what anybody at Angola did to me.

My grandmother came home from the hospital. When I talked to her, I begged her to get someone to call when something like that happened so I could know what was going on, even if I could do nothing to help. She promised me that she would, if there was a next time. She said she got sick from all those days at the court, being there every day and staying late and all the worrying she had been doing.

I knew that was what it was from. I felt like a dog, lower than a dog. What if she had died? It would have been me that killed her. I had enough to live with, without adding my grandmother to that list, too.

Mama Henrietta got better, and she had people that cared for her—good friends and some family who would always stay close to her. I did not care that they did not care about me anymore or would not come see me, as long as they took care of her. That is all that mattered to me. I knew that family and friends were disappointed in me and did not care about me anymore.

When she was just getting over her heart attack, my grandmother told me something that really touched me. One night my mother had come to her and told her not to worry about me, that God would take care of me, and for her to take it easy. Now, when she told me that, I didn't really know how she meant God would take care of me. I was a little scared, but I felt at peace about it. I prayed and prayed for God to let me see and talk with my mother too, but he never did it. I don't know why.

My grandmother finally got well enough and wanted to come up to visit me. I had Ardessa, my friend since childhood, and her aunt, Nancy, on my visiting list, and they brought her up to see me. We had a good visit, and it hurt me to see them leave, knowing I could not go with them. Ardessa came up a few times by herself and with her aunt, too, but then they both faded off. I did not hear from them or nothing. I won't lie. It hurt like hell. My three pen pals in England cared more than they did. My friends and family was right there in Baton Rouge, no more than an hour away.

I began to hate them—and myself. Because I knew I had no one but myself to blame for where I was at. I knew I had trapped myself in this prison on death row. I trapped myself when I put that gun in my hands.

I could not forgive myself for what I had done. And I knew that God had not forgiven me either. So, I would look at the girly books, drink homemade wine, and bet here and there. But it did not stop the way I was feeling inside.

Day to day, hour to hour, my life goes on in pain. I reach for comfort but none is offered. My heart is filled with anguish and sorrow. I feel I am going insane. I want, I need, but what, I don't know. I'm sure that somewhere, sometime, somehow the feelings I have will leave. Until that time I yearn for something that I can't explain. Is it love I need, or something else? Something that requires more thought?
—Feltus Taylor, Essays, "Day to Day"

Sometime in **early 1993**, Ardessa brought my grandmother to visit again. Sister Helen was there visiting someone, but she came over to talk and say a prayer with my grandmother and me. Sister Helen and I talked about how I was feeling over this whole mess.

"Why don't you write your feelings down? It would be a good way to work through your feelings," she said. "Maybe you can write a book about yourself and how you got to death row."

"That sounds good," I told her, "but, I doubt if I could write a book."

"Well, think about it anyway," she said.

At that time, she was in the middle of having her book published. It was about two guys she had been coming up to Angola to see that were put to death. That book was *Dead Man Walking*.

I thought about what she said, but I put it out of my mind because I knew nothing about writing, and I could not spell all that well. Then a guy who was on death row with me got a bad date. His name was Robert Sawyer. What I got from the talks we had sometimes was that he was a bit lost in the head. I do not know how many execution dates he had had, but the one in March 1993 looked to be it for him.

The day of his execution, I was looking out of the window into the parking lot, and all of the news people were running around like ants running to food. I stood at the door of my cell, thinking, *Is this how it will be if my time comes?*

My head was really hurting because Robert's was the first execution I was on death row for, and it was hard on me. I noticed something around me, too. I could feel it in the air. Everyone got quiet, like they got inside themselves.

I stayed up the whole night and looked out of the window. I could tell when it was all over because I saw all of the news people leaving and the other people coming out of the prison. I felt a need to come inside of me to write about my crime and how I was feeling about the whole thing. I thought, *Maybe I could write a book.* I started by just writing my feelings down.

A few days passed, then things got back to normal with everyone talking and playing around. After Robert's execution, I started writing off and on. Just keeping a journal and writing my feelings down. I read a few books on writing. I read different kinds of books and saw the way people wrote. I got some of my ideas about writing from that.

It wasn't long before I just went back to doing what everyone else was doing around the row.

But I always felt I had a story to tell, and maybe it could help someone not to make the same mistakes I made. And the book stayed in the back of my mind.

I was in a lot of mental anguish. Some of my anguish was from being on the row and some of it was from the events that put me here. I was a captive of loneliness. The daily struggle—fighting for my life and keeping my sanity—was an all-out challenge. Being on death row is hard. You are under stress all of the time—waiting to hear from your lawyer, waiting for the courts to let you know something. Sitting in that small cell, thinking, reliving everything that has happened—it's very hard. A lot of people can't take it. A lot of them go crazy in that cell. There was this guy on my tier once who did just that. He sat on his bunk all day looking at the walls, or in the corner of his cell hitting the floor with a piece of paper for hours and hours at a time. He showered like once a week. He was forty-three years old and very skinny. I really don't believe he weighed more than eighty pounds, if that much. No one ever came to see him, and he never called anyone.

I had to get into something to keep my sanity. But as time went on, I became tired of doing what everyone else was doing. I did not know what I really wanted to do.

Every day is the same on death row. I mean, the only thing you looked forward to was getting a visit or going to church or hoping that just maybe the courts would do something good for your case. On the other side of that was the reality that you may very well die. And your loved ones might die or start to fade off and leave you all alone.

PART ONE

ON THE OUTSIDE
19 YEARS

CHAPTER 2

Feltus was born in Manhasset, Nassau County, New York, in 1961, to a drug addicted mother and unknown biological father. There is no record of how he spent the first three years of his life. Feltus was severely developmentally delayed, with no indication that he had ever been taught to play, respond to people, or even maintain bowel and bladder control. He wore diapers until the age of four or five.

Mrs. Rowan [Feltus' grandmother] describes Feltus when her daughter, Willie Mae, and her husband, Feltus Taylor, Sr. received Feltus Taylor: Feltus, Jr. was bowlegged. He could not talk, nor could he stand. He arrived in "very dirty" clothes and had a "filthy" bottle with something "yellow" in it. When he was put to bed the first night, Mrs. Rowan stated he experienced horrible nightmares. Reminiscing about the toddler in bed, she said he was laying down asleep fighting with his hands. She described a flailing of the hands as if pushing someone or something away. While those physical movements were going on, he was screaming "dop, dop, dop." It is a reasonable assumption that this child with the documented articulation problem at this age could have been saying "dop" instead of the word "stop." From the condition that Feltus was in at the time Willie Mae and Feltus, Sr. received him, it is quite reasonable to assume that he had experienced neglect during this early stage of development.

—CONFIDENTIAL MEMO FROM JANE SMITH, BOARD CERTIFIED SOCIAL WORKER TO JEAN FARIA (FELTUS' ATTORNEY), JULY 23, 1997

BONNIE JACKSON (FELTUS' ATTORNEY): I'D LIKE FOR YOU TO TALK TO THE JURY ABOUT FELTUS' ADOPTION.

HENRIETTA ROWAN: YES, MA'AM.

Q: DO YOU KNOW HOW OLD FELTUS WAS WHEN HE WAS BROUGHT HOME BY YOUR DAUGHTER?

A: WHEN HE WAS ADOPTED?

Q: YES.

A: YES, MA'AM. I DON'T KNOW EXACT, BUT AROUND ABOUT TWO YEARS, I THINK, BUT HE COULDN'T WALK.

Q: OKAY. WE'LL TALK ABOUT THAT. WHERE HAD YOUR DAUGHTER GOTTEN FELTUS?

A: IT WAS A LADY SHE KNOWED; WHAT SHE WENT TO SCHOOL WITH. AND SHE KNOWED SHE WANTED A LITTLE BOY BABY. AND SHE HAD BEEN MARRIED SEVEN YEARS AND DIDN'T HAVE NONE. AND SO, SHE TOLD HER ABOUT THIS LADY. AND SHE WENT TO THE LADY HOUSE. AND THIS LADY TOLD HER THAT THE BABY MOTHER LEFT THE BABY THERE WITH HER. HE WAS JUST A LITTLE BABY. AND ASKED HER TO KEEP IT TILL SHE GO THE STORE, AND SAY SHE NEVER COME BACK.

Q: DO YOU KNOW HOW OLD THE BABY WAS WHEN HE WAS LEFT WITH THE LADY AND HIS MOTHER NEVER CAME BACK?

A: NO. NOT TO MY KNOWLEDGE. BUT MY DAUGHTER SAID WHEN SHE LEFT HIM, HE WAS JUST A BABY IN HER ARMS; JUST A LITTLE BABY, AND SHE COULDN'T RAISE HIM.

Q: SO, YOUR DAUGHTER WHO COULDN'T HAVE CHILDREN WANTED TO ADOPT THAT BABY; IS THAT RIGHT?

A: YES, MA'AM.

Q: DID SHE BRING THE BABY HOME TO YOU AND LET YOU SEE THE BABY?

A: YES, MA'AM.

Q: AND WHAT WAS THE BABY LIKE?

A: THE BABY, HE WAS LITTLE, AND HE COULDN'T WALK.

Q: WAS HE OLD ENOUGH TO WALK?

A: HE WAS ROUND NEAR TWO. AND HE WAS JUST SO LITTLE AND POOR.

Q: YOU MEAN SKINNY?

A: YES, MA'AM. AND HE DIDN'T HAVE NO CLOTHES BUT WHAT HE HAD ON. AND SO, I ASKED MY DAUGHTER, I SAID, NOW YOU WANT A BABY. I SAID, YOU AIN'T GOING TO RAISE THIS LITTLE BABY, IS YOU? I SAID, YOU TAKE THIS BABY BACK. I SAID, BECAUSE YOU AIN'T GOING TO RAISE HIM; TEND TO THAT BABY. AND SO, THEY TOOK HIM BACK, AND THEN THEY WENT ON HOME. AND MY SON-IN-LAW CALLED ME AND TOLD ME THAT SHE WAS CRYING AND GOING ON SO BAD. AND THEN I TALKED TO HER. AND SHE WAS CARRYING OUT SO BAD, I TOLD HIM, WELL, CARRY HER BACK AND LET HER GET THAT BABY. I SAID, SHE MUST MEAN SHE'S GOING TO TAKE CARE OF HIM. AND SO, THEY WENT BACK AND GOT HIM.

Q: NOW, WHEN YOUR DAUGHTER FIRST GOT THE BABY TO KEEP, YOU SAID HE DIDN'T HAVE ANY CLOTHES?

A: NO, MA'AM. AND WHEN THEY WENT AND GOT THAT BABY AND BROUGHT IT BACK, ME AND MY HUSBAND WENT TO THEIR HOUSE AND WE WENT OVER THERE ON FOSTER DRIVE TO A STORE, AND WE BOUGHT HIM SOME CLOTHES, AND BLANKETS, AND SHOES, LITTLE SHOES, AND MY HUSBAND BOUGHT HIM A LITTLE RATTLE TO PLAY WITH. AND THEN WE BROUGHT THEM BACK TO HER.

Q: DID THE BABY KNOW HOW TO TALK?

A: NO. HE WAS A LONG TIME AFTER HE GOT TO WALK. HE WAS GOING TO SCHOOL AND HE COULDN'T TALK GOOD WHEN THEY FIRST PUT HIM IN SCHOOL. AND SHE HAD TO GIVE HIM THERAPY. HE COULDN'T TALK GOOD. HE JUST MUMBLED LIKE.

—Penalty Phase, Day 1: 49–50, January 23, 1992

F. A. SILVA: In the case of Feltus, we have a pattern of continuous abandonment and poor attachment to maternal or paternal figures. He was abandoned by his biological mother. He was abandoned by the person who took care of him for some period of time, even his adopted mother sent him back and took him back . . . I think in part that explained his difficulty in school, difficulty having establishing normal peer relationships, etc.

—Penalty Phase, Day 2: 47–9, January 24, 1992

think a lot about when I was younger. I was born in Manhasset, New York, with the name Steven Roy Wiggins. I was found in Louisiana and brought into the Taylor family at the age of two. My parents adopted me when I was three. I know that my adoptive mother, Willie Mae, really wanted me. I don't think my parents could have children of their own. I am named after my adoptive father. My early memories are of my parents fighting. They argued, and sometimes, they hit on each other. It made me scared and upset. I used to try to make them stop, but it didn't work out that well. I guess a lot of their problems had to do with my dad staying out late and sometimes all night. And he drank all the time.

When I was about six years old, my father would take me riding in the car, and he would take me to a woman's house, telling me that it was my aunt's house. We would go there every Sunday, and I would pass the time watching TV while they'd be in the back room. Now that I'm older, I know they were having sex, but I don't think that I ever really suspected it then. When we would return back home, my mother would ask me where we'd been, and I'd tell her, "To my aunt's house." This one day in particular, my mother asked me where my aunt lived, and, not knowing any better, I told her. Little did I know that all hell was about to break loose. My mother didn't say nothing then, but she told me to call the next time we went to her house. I called Mamee, and she caught the bus and came over there.

My mother knocked on the door, and my "Aunt" Mary came to answer it. My mother already knew what my father was doing, but she just didn't know that he had been taking me along with him when he made these trips. When Mary opened the door, she and my mother started yelling at each other. My dad came and tried to get them to quiet down so that no one would call the police. My mother said, "I want my son, and I want him now."

She told my father that he didn't have to worry about coming home because he didn't have a home to come to anymore. She took me with her.

Later, my dad came by to see us. He tried to talk to my mother, but she didn't want to hear it.

He turned to me and asked, "Did you tell her about this?"

"Yes," I said.

He slapped me across the face, and it hurt like hell.

I ran from him, and he called me back, but I went into another room. My mother told him to leave me alone, but he wouldn't listen.

She grabbed a butcher knife off the counter and said, "If you don't leave him alone, and if you hit him again, I'll kill you."

He tried to take the knife from her but got cut, so he turned and started to run. They ran out the back door together, my mother chasing after him, and once they were outside, she threw the knife at his back. I'm glad that she didn't hit him with it, but she came really close.

My dad came back the next day for his clothes. My mother had them waiting for him on the front porch. He told her that he wanted to talk. They tried for a while but ended up fighting again. My mother went outside and cut the tires on his car so that they were flat. She told him to get back to Mary's any way that he could. He left walking and mad. Sometime later, while my mother was at work and I was at school, he came back and got his car.

They got a divorce in July 1971, when I was ten years old. They had been married twenty years, since July 1951. That was something that I was sorry to see, but I guess it was for the best since they couldn't get along. I used to hope that one day they would get back together again, but they never did. I don't know how much they loved each other, because since I was old enough to remember, they were having problems.

After he left my mother, and they got divorced, he married Mary in October 1971. I never did see what he saw in her because she was a really big, fat woman.

As far back as I can remember, I can't ever recall him sitting down and talking to me. There were times when he'd take me to the City Park Lake, not far from the LSU campus, and we'd talk and throw rocks in the water. But he never talked about anything of importance. Many times, when I saw him, he was drunk or almost drunk. If I'd go to visit him, he'd give me five or ten dollars and tell me he'd see me next time. If I stayed at the house at all, I'd cut the yard for him or play in the game room by myself. Sometimes, when I cut school, I'd go by his house before he went to work to ask for money. He'd give me some to get me out of his face. I would take the city bus to Bon Marche Mall and spend the day there.

We never did do the things that a father and son should do together. Sometimes, I wonder why he went along with my mother when they adopted me. I think that if it would have been up to him, he would have left me where they found me. As I sit here in this cell now, thinking about my past, it hurts me inside.

At one time, I hated my father. All he did was drink, and his side of the family never acted like they cared anything for me. Mary didn't like me either, and maybe that's because of her feelings towards my mother. I have to be honest and say that I didn't really like her too much either, because she came into my father's life and messed him and my mother up. At least that's what I thought, anyway.

After I got big, my father never told me that he loved me, and I never said it to him. I wish now that I had. I loved my father, but he just wasn't there for me when I needed him. As I got older, he seemed not to care anymore about himself or anything else. I really wish that he would have spent more time with me.

I don't remember too much about my first years in school. I remember [1967] that my first-grade teacher used to read to us a lot, and all the kids would sit on these mats around her. Then after she read to us, we would lie down on the mats and go to sleep. We played a lot outside, too.

Feltus attended all Black schools, as none of the schools in Baton Rouge were fully integrated until 1977. Even though Baton Rouge was embroiled in the massive federal school desegregation case, Blacks did not enter White public schools for many years.

Fourth grade [1970] was about the time everyone started to make fun of me because I couldn't talk right. Only half of a word would come out when I tried to talk. Other kids would call me names. I hated to go to the board because kids would tease me later. The teachers were nice to me, but the kids would get mean when they weren't around.

I was usually quiet in class, and I didn't talk much to anyone. Every now and then, I would act up, like laugh loudly at times. But I didn't like school because I couldn't seem to learn right and I had those problems with talking.

The developmental tasks [of Feltus Taylor, Jr.] at this stage [in his life] appeared to have been postponed. It is safe to conclude that the child described was developmentally delayed. He could not talk and family members could not understand what he was saying most the time. He was enrolled in speech therapy in July 1967. Feltus entered grade school with numerous deficits. His classroom teacher indicated that he was not very attentive in class, he had difficulty following directions, and he did not always finish assigned tasks. She also noticed that he was always taking things that did not belong to him.
—Report from Caroline Dodson, MSW to Bonnie Jackson, December 26, 1991

I was in the fourth grade twice. In fifth grade, I started taking special ed classes. By the time I got to middle school, I started skipping class. In the morning, I would act like I was going to school. I'd leave and wait, watching until my mother went to work, and then I would get the key she would leave for me in the mailbox so that I'd be able to get into the house after school.

When I got home one day, my mother was waiting for me, and she was really mad. One of her friends had seen me during the day and told her. She didn't whip me right then. No, she let me think that she wasn't going to. But later on, when it was time for my bath, I went into the bathroom and took my clothes off. As soon as I got into the tub, my mother came into the bathroom with the cord off the telephone, and she started whipping me with it. You want to talk about something that hurts, let someone beat you with a telephone cord while you're naked and wet.

I went to visit my father every other weekend. My mother made him let me go over there. I was at Mary's house one day when I heard her tell my father that she didn't like me coming over there. I never did tell them that I had overheard them, and I started doing little things around the place to let her know that I didn't like being there either.

She started telling lies about me to my father, saying I'd done things when I really hadn't. One day, I was there when my father had gone to work. While Mary was in the other room, I took twenty dollars from her purse. She must not have missed it or noticed it, so I kept doing it whenever I needed some money. I would justify this by telling myself that she didn't like me, so why should I be nice to her?

At some point, my father called and told my mother that Mary didn't want me over there anymore because I'd been stealing from her. My mother didn't believe it, though. I guess I did play right into Mary's hands. I gave her a reason to complain about me visiting.

After Mary was saying I stole from her, I didn't care anymore. I was just a kid, and I felt like no one liked me because I couldn't talk right.

The stealing didn't stop, though. One Saturday, in 1972, my grandmother took my mother and me shopping with her. When we got to the supermarket, they told me to stay in the car until they were done, but do you think that I did? No. I got out of the car and went into another store in the shopping center called Shopper's Fair.

I went into the toy department and saw a Batman doll that I wanted real bad. I tried to steal it and ended up getting caught. The man who caught me took me upstairs to an office and sat me down. There were a couple of other people in the office, and they asked me where my parents were. I told them what store my mother and grandmother was in, and they called them. My mother was mad and upset with me, but mostly she was just disappointed that I'd done something like that. The people at the store told her to take me home and have a good talk with me.

The minute that we got outside of the store, my mother said, "Why did you do that? You're doing nothing but letting me down."

I felt really bad inside.

"When we get home," my mother said, "I'm going to whip you for this."

Let me tell you, I was scared when she said that. The only thing that I could think of was that telephone cord.

Luckily, before we headed home, we went to the Burger King to get something to eat, where, once again, I was told to stay in the car. My mother stared at me and said, "Don't you even think about getting out of this car while we go in and order."

I was so scared of that whipping that the second they were inside I was out of that car and running across the parking lot. I told myself that I was going to run away and live on the streets for the rest of my life. I sure didn't want one of those whippings again, not on my bare ass. I just couldn't understand that my mother was trying to do the right thing for me and my future. All I could think about was that telephone cord.

I was only about a mile from my house; and I knew the area fairly well. I didn't like it too much—that part of the neighborhood—so I headed toward my own area. When I got back to my part of the neighborhood, I went back to my school and hung around there and played basketball. Once it got late, I walked down two blocks to a street named Capital Avenue.

It was an avenue for anything and everything. It was an area of town that most people tried to stay away from. It was known for its shootings. There must have been about fifteen bars up and down the street. On the weekends, it would be in full swing. There was people all over the place. You had your pimps and whores out looking for johns. You had other people drinking and smoking dope, talking and feeling on women or being felt on. It wasn't nothing to see a woman getting boned on the side of a club or in a car. A few guys would be outside shooting dice or playing cards for money. You would always see someone fighting or getting cut with something.

Feltus experienced the brunt of racism and a segregated South most of his life. In the 1960s, Baton Rouge was still heavily segregated, slowly transforming into North and South Baton Rouge. North Baton Rouge, where Feltus grew up, had lost its middle-class White status as refineries modernized and employment deteriorated, becoming predominantly Black. "White flight" was significant. South Baton Rouge enjoyed an economic boom, as Whites fled to newly developed suburbs. North Baton Rouge became rampant with crime, and today this area of Baton Rouge has one of the highest crime rates in the parish.

I just don't know why I felt drawn to this kind of life. Maybe it was the people laughing and seeming to have such a good time. Things looked good on the outside, but on the inside, it was a different story altogether.

When night fell, I started wondering where I'd go and what I'd do. I had nowhere to go, and no one to stay with, so I decided to go home even though I was scared to face my mother. At about seven o'clock, I went down the back street to my house and jumped the fence into the backyard.

When I came down the side of the house, where my mother's window was, I saw her talking on the phone. I couldn't hear everything that she was saying, but I know that I heard my father's name. That's how I knew who was on the other end of the line.

She was crying and telling him that she loved and missed me. I heard her ask him if he had me over there with him. He must have said no because she started to cry harder.

I said to myself, *My mother loves me, and I shouldn't be doing this to her.* All I could do was stand there and cry. I really wanted to be a better son to her.

Now, when I think about it, my mother and grandmother must have been very worried about me. I really cared a lot for my mother and grandmother. They showed me nothing but love, but for some reason, I just couldn't seem to do nothing right. I still can't understand why. Why was I like that? I also didn't feel like I was the child my mother was supposed to have. I just always felt like I was letting my mother down. She deserved better. My mother was working so hard to take care of me, and my father wasn't doing nothing. He was supposed to be paying child support, but he neglected to do even that. I felt that it would be so much easier on her without me around to worry about.

I left after I heard her talking to my father and walked back to the Burger King where I'd made my escape. I noticed a police car in the parking lot, so I walked inside and told the officer that I was lost. He asked me if I knew where I lived, and I told him.

I will never forget the look on my mother's face when he brought me home. She was so happy to see me and that nothing had happened to me. But I could still see the anger in her eyes from what I'd done. She asked me why I had run away, and all I could do was stand there with my head hung and cry. Not because I knew what she was going to do to me for running away, but because I knew what I had put her through.

She told me to never do that again and scare her that way. I said that I wouldn't, and she thanked the policeman for bringing me home. When he left, I knew what was coming, but first she called my grandmother and my father and told them that I was all right. Finally, the only thing that was left was for her to deal with me.

I was in the bathtub when my mother came in with an extension cord and whipped my butt. I was wet, and it really stung. I was crying and hollering at the top of my voice like someone was killing me. She gave me a whipping that lasted for a month.

CHAPTER 3

MY MOTHER STARTED DATING again after my father remarried. She met a man named Samuel Woods, Sr. He was from Los Angeles, California. A few times a year, he visited his aunt, Ms. Tea, who lived near my grandmother. I liked him a lot because he was a nice, kind man. He was retired, and he was pretty well-off, too.

My mother had had a nervous breakdown at one time because of everything she had gone through with me and my father. It took a while for her to get better. She had a lot of pressure on her from trying to raise me, working, and trying to pay the bills. Not to mention all the extra problems I used to cause her. My mother was a very strong woman. I wish that I had done more to help her, but I was blind to what I was doing to her and to myself.

This was a time of lots of changes for me. My mother had found a boyfriend, and I would soon lose my grandfather, Clyde Rowan.

I called him Daddy Joe. He liked to smoke a pipe, and sometimes he would drink a beer, never hard liquor. He was a muscular, heavyset man who wore glasses. He worked at the State Capitol as a janitor for many years. He was the man who taught me how to work and enjoy it.

He was more of a father to me than my father was. If there was something he had to do, he would take me with him. He showed me how to fix things around the house when I would visit on weekends.

But when I was twelve, he had a stroke that left him unable to care for himself when he was in his middle sixties. He couldn't walk or talk that well, and he used to forget things that he had just done. He had the mind of a young child. He always liked to sit on the porch in front of the house, but if my grandmother didn't watch him, he would leave the porch and go off down the street. My grandmother was scared that he would get hit by a car, so when she couldn't watch him, I would.

My grandfather really liked me, too. We would sit around and talk all day until he got sleepy and then he would go off to bed. I had to help him into bed, because he couldn't do it by himself. We also had to bathe him every day because he would go to the bathroom on himself. He was a lot of trouble, but we all loved him. He was like that for about a year.

In January 1974, my grandfather was in the hospital because he had gotten sick. I came home from a class field trip, and I'll never forget what happened when I walked into my grandmother's house. My mother had her head down, and she was crying. It was strange that no one was talking.

My grandmother told me that my grandfather had died in the hospital. I cried a lot over him because he was a good man. Before he got sick, he used to do a lot of things and work. Plus, he used to take me with him when he went fishing. Damn, I was really hurt over him dying on me like that.

I remember running out of the house and going into the backyard. I got on my ten-speed and started riding up and down the street. I rode my bike all the way across town. I didn't know what else to do, and I was hurting inside real bad. I spent the night with my grandmother because I didn't want her to be alone. My grandmother was really sick over my grandfather's death. She loved him so much. She never dated or married another man after she lost him.

Within a week, she and my mother had made the funeral plans. The night that we went to the True Light Baptist Church—where my grandfather's body was—I hated seeing him lying in that coffin. My grandmother really took it hard, but she tried to be strong for my mother. When it was time to go up and look at the body, I started crying. I had never touched a dead person before, but I wanted to touch him, and I did. I touched his arm. I had something that was in my pocket—I can't remember what it was now—but I remember that I wanted him to have it. I put it down between his arm and his chest.

I stayed with my grandmother the night after his viewing. Later that night, I was outside with Coffee, my mother's poodle that we had named because of her color. I was looking up into the clear night sky, and the stars were out in full force. I couldn't do nothing but think of my grandfather. I took Coffee back inside and told my grandmother goodnight. I went into my grandfather's room, where I'd be sleeping, and got into bed. I fell asleep in my grandfather's bed with Coffee next to me until around one or two o'clock in the morning, when for some reason I just woke up. It was still dark outside, and in the room. But, when I looked up, I couldn't believe what I was seeing. I saw my grandfather walking with his cane across the room. He opened the door to the kitchen, which was next to his room, turned on the light, and went in, shutting the door behind him.

I couldn't believe it at first. I thought that I was dreaming, but I was wide awake. I finally got out of bed, and I walked over to the door he had just gone through. I was scared for some reason, but I opened the door and went in. I looked around, but I didn't see anyone at all. I was in shock.

I looked everywhere, trying to see if anything had been moved, but everything was in its place. I stayed there for about another five minutes, waiting to see if I was dreaming or not. Finally, I got a glass of water, drank it, and went back to bed.

That was my first time seeing a real dead person, a ghost. After that, I started to believe that the dead could walk on the earth again. Even my grandmother told me later about a time that she had seen my grandfather too, and my grandmother wouldn't lie for nothing. Ghosts weren't strangers to our family. Years later, my mother would see my stepfather, Samuel, after he died. She would tell me that he sat on her bed and said that I was getting into trouble and she should have a talk with me. I told her that I wasn't doing nothing wrong. But I was lying, and I wondered how she could be so right like that.

When I woke up the next morning, I told my grandmother what had happened. She believed me, and she told me that he was just letting me know that he loved me.

Not long after my grandfather died in 1974, I learned that my mother wanted to get married to Samuel. I was happy, but there was one problem—me. They wanted me to go to Los Angeles with them. I really didn't want to go, because I was in school in Baton Rouge. Most importantly, I didn't want to leave my grandmother behind. They really understood, so they came up with a plan. They would let me stay with my grandmother and go to stay with them during the summer. That was fine with me, and I think that my grandmother really wanted me to stay, too. She kept it to herself, though. She wanted me to make the choice for myself. I just couldn't leave her alone. My mother tried to get her to move with them too, but she wouldn't go because Baton Rouge had been her home since the late 1940s.

I was sad when my mother left for Los Angeles. I was happy for her, but I also felt lonely and unloved. Don't get me wrong. I had my grandmother's love, but it wasn't like my mother's. She whipped me a lot when I was bad, but she loved me, and we could talk to each other just about anything.

Before my mother left, I found out something that was a shock to me.

One Sunday, we was at my grandmother's house, and I was in the back, playing with my dolls. Batman and Robin, Superman, G. I. Joe—I had them all. I was in my grandfather's old room, and my mother and grandmother were in the living room talking. I went into my grandmother's room, which was between the living room and my grandfather's room. Their backs was turned to me so they didn't know I was there.

I heard my grandmother say to my mother, "When are you going to tell him about it?"

My mother said something back, but I couldn't make it out.

My grandmother said, "You've got to tell him that you adopted him."

I was wondering who they were talking about. I heard my mother say something about losing a baby, but I didn't know if she meant that she had lost a baby at birth or sometime later. I didn't tell her I had overheard them.

About a week later, my mother sat me down and told me some things that I didn't know about myself. She told me that she and my father had been visiting some of my mother's relatives. She said that a woman lived next door to her relatives, and she had had a baby that she really didn't want. The woman had been saying that she was going to throw the baby out of a window or throw it in the trash and leave it there. The woman had been leaving the baby with a neighbor when she went out somewhere.

One day, the woman told her neighbors to keep the baby until she came back from the store. The neighbors, as always, watched the baby for her. The woman had said that she would be right back, but as the day went on, the lady never came back to get her baby. After about a week, my mother and father brought the baby back with them to Louisiana and had their lawyer prepare the adoption papers. Eventually, they adopted the baby—a little boy—and my mother said that had made them happy.

She asked me, "Do you know who that baby was?"

I already knew, and now the conversation from the week before made sense. I said, "Yes, it was me, right?"

She smiled and said, "Yes, it was you."

I told her that I didn't care where I came from, that she and my daddy were my real parents, and that was all that mattered to me. They were my real family.

BONNIE JACKSON: MS. ROWAN, WHEN FELTUS WAS GROWING UP AND LIVING WITH YOU DID HE HAVE A LOT OF FRIENDS THAT VISITED HIM AT YOUR HOUSE?

HENRIETTA ROWAN: NO. FELTUS WAS A CHILD LIKED TO STAY TO HISSELF.

—*Penalty Phase, Day 1: 60, January 23, 1992*

Mama Henrietta was really protective of me. There were times when she wouldn't let me go anywhere except to school and to church, but I had other ideas about that. Many times, my grandmother would send me to Sunday School at nine o'clock, and she would come later at eleven o'clock for church. She never knew it, but a lot of times, I wouldn't go to Sunday School. I would go over to my friend Joe's house, and we would get high until about 10:30 a.m. Then I'd go to church so that I could be there before she got there.

There was times when I would take a joint to church with me. I would share it with a guy who ended up playing basketball for LSU years later. We would leave out of church and go down the road to smoke the joint. Then we'd go back to church and sing. We both sang in the Junior Choir together, and we were pretty good, too.

I guess that I just wanted my way because I couldn't have it at home. Even after I got big, my grandmother acted like I was a baby, and I guess I didn't like it. I saw all the other kids running around and doing what they wanted, and I wanted to be the same way. She didn't let me go to movies with friends until I was about fourteen. I wanted to hang out with the other guys so bad that when my grandmother would go to sleep on the weekends, I would sneak out of the house and hang out with them on the corner until 2:00 a.m. Then I'd sneak in the back door without my grandmother not even knowing.

One night, I got into a fight with the neighborhood tough guy who used to hang out with us. He had been drinking a bottle of Mad Dog 20/20, and he wanted me to drink too. I wouldn't because I didn't like to drink. I tried weed when I was about thirteen. Sometimes I'd smoke on weekends. But I didn't like alcohol.

He asked me if I thought I was too good to drink with them. "No, I just don't like to drink," I said.

The next thing I knew, he hit me on the side of the head with the bottle. I went down, and he was on me. I couldn't do nothing.

We were about four houses down from where a friend of my family lived. I tried to run there, but I was too dizzy to make it. My head was killing me, and the guy wouldn't stop beating on me. One of the other guys hanging out with us felt sorry for me and stopped him from killing me.

I finally got away, stumbled home, and took a bath. I tried to clean up the best that I could, to keep my grandmother from finding out what had happened. After that night, I kind of cooled it. I still went out at night, just not every night. I was careful to avoid another incident like that one. But even though I became more careful, it didn't last long, because my mother came home from Los Angeles for a visit. She could always catch me doing something, like there wasn't nothing to it.

She had been home for about a week. I went out for a little late-night meeting and to hang out. I came back at 2:00 a.m., as I'd always done before, and I gave Coffee her candy bar as usual. She didn't make a sound. I locked the back door behind me and went to my room. It was dark when I walked in. I never turned my light on. I would throw my coat on the chair across from my bed, take off my clothes, and get into bed. On that night, as I shut my bedroom door behind me, I was in for a big surprise.

I took off my coat and threw it over to the chair, but it seemed to miss and fall on the floor. I went over to pick it up. As I bent over, my mother got up out of the chair and hit me right across the back with a belt. She scared me to death. I thought she was a ghost or something at first. She really whipped me, too. I was crying and screaming like she was killing me.

Now that I think about it, it was funny as hell. I can say this for sure—my mother knew me like a book. She had gotten up to go to the bathroom, then went into my room to look in on me. I wasn't in the bed, of course, so she waited up for me to come back, in that chair. My grandmother was mad at me, too, but after about three days she and my mother laughed about it.

A few weeks later, my mother invited my grandmother and me to visit her in Los Angeles. It was my first time on a plane, and I enjoyed the ride. I was a little scared, though, being that high off the ground.

We took pictures and had a good time on the plane. When we arrived in Los Angeles, my mother and stepfather were waiting for us. Their house was so nice and pretty, and my stepfather had a dog that looked just like Lassie. I was told it was one of Lassie's puppies. His name was King. At first, I was scared of him, and he knew it, too. He was mean as hell, nothing like his mother on TV, but after about two weeks I could go in the backyard and play with him. He started to like me, but every once in a while, he would try to bite me on the leg.

My mother and my stepfather took us around the town, and it was so beautiful there. We saw houses up on the sides of mountains. We went to Disneyland, Magic Mountain, Farmer's Market, and a movie studio. It was so great. I wanted to stay there forever. My mother asked me if I wanted to come out there to live with them, and I did, but I wasn't going to leave my grandmother alone by herself. My grandmother and I went back to Baton Rouge about a month later. We didn't want to leave but I had to go back to school.

BONNIE JACKSON: WHAT WOULD HE DO TO ENTERTAIN HIMSELF? HOW WOULD HE KEEP HIMSELF OCCUPIED?

HENRIETTA ROWAN: WHEN HE'D COME HE'D GO IN HIS ROOM. AND HE HAD HIM SOME TOYS, BATMAN, AND HE HAD A NAME FOR THEM ALL. AND HE'D HAVE ALL THEM TOYS. AND HE'D HOOK THEM UP AND HE'D LET THEM FIGHT TOGETHER AND ALL THAT, WHEN HE PLAYED BY HISSELF.

Q: DID HE PLAY WITH TOYS AFTER HE STARTED TO GO INTO HIGH SCHOOL?

A: YES, MA'AM. WHEN HE WAS GOING TO CAPITAL HIGH, HE'D GET OUT THERE AND I'D TELL HIM, I'D SAY, YOU GOING TO HIGH SCHOOL, AND YOU'RE HERE, COMING IN HERE PLAYING WITH TOYS. I SAID, THAT DON'T LOOK RIGHT, BABY. BUT I NEVER SCOLDED HIM. I JUST TALKED TO HIM. I NEVER WOULD SCOLD HIM AND GOING ON. BECAUSE LOOK LIKE HE JUST DIDN'T UNDERSTAND ME.

—Penalty Phase, Day 1: 60, January 23, 1992

My grandmother rented the house next to a man, his wife, and their one child. Ray, Janet and Ardessa, their daughter, became longtime friends of the family. Janet was a schoolteacher, and I don't really know what kind of work Ray did. Ardessa was a year younger than me. Ardessa and I became real close through the years.

I had another friend, too, a girl named Tammie. We used to pretend that we were cousins. We always used to play together on the weekends. Tammie was a very bright young girl, and so was Ardessa. They always brought home A's and B's, nothing under a B, but I always brought home the F's. They tried to help me with my work and read better, but it just seemed like it never did any good. I would get mad and stop, go outside or into my room, and start playing with my dolls. I would make them fight each other for about an hour until I started to feel better.

I think Tammie was always kind of scared of me because sometimes I would make her cry and talk mean to her. I guess I did it because I was mad that she could do so good, and no matter how hard I tried, I always did bad. But no matter what I did to her, she would never stop caring for me. We always made up and started playing back together. I always looked at her as the sister that I never had.

Other than Tammie and Ardessa, I really didn't have any friends whose houses I could go to or who could come to my grandmother's house. My grandmother always tried to keep me inside the house or in the yard.

Ardessa used to come over to my grandmother's every evening after school, and we'd play in my room. We would laugh and talk for hours. She liked me, and I liked her. Neither of us was seeing anyone at that time, so I guess we were just keeping each other company.

One evening, she came by, and we were in my room, talking. My grandmother was lying down, taking a nap. Ardessa was sitting in a chair, and I was on the floor in between her legs, sitting there while she put grease in my hair. We would watch TV when she came over to visit. I always liked to watch TV, and when I saw a good movie, a love movie, I would always wish that it was me living that type of life. It seemed that people in the movies were living the kind of life I wanted. I always wanted to play the guy that got the girl and went off and got married and had kids. I felt that the good life was on the movies, and that was the life I wanted for myself. Where every day was good and fun. The world that I lived in wasn't like that. Everyone was just making it and was going through pain and stuff like that. The movies was where I wanted to be.

Tammie still came over to my grandmother's house on the weekends while her mother worked, so we still played together like always. Even though I had Tammie for a close friend, I still loved to play with my toys, like my Batman and Robin dolls. In my room, I had a stand for them all. I remember my grandmother told me one day to get rid of them, but I told her that I was keeping them to pass down to my kids when I had some. That wasn't my real reason for keeping them, though. I kept them because I felt free with them. I could take out a lot of my frustrations. My grandmother and other people couldn't understand. I wasn't eight years old and playing in the backyard anymore. I was starting high school, but I didn't care. I really enjoyed them. I wish that I had them to play with now to ease my mind some.

For years, I had trouble with this guy named Kenny. He was taller than I was, and he was skinny. He had a real mean streak. He always wanted people to be scared of him. He couldn't fight at all, but he would shoot you or cut you in a heartbeat. He was known for that. When I was in elementary school, he and his boys beat me up for my lunch money. I figured it would hurt less to give it to them than get beat up. It ended up being an everyday thing. At lunchtime, I couldn't go eat like everyone else, so I would go to a store near the school and wait until a lot of people were in it. I'd go to the back of the store and take a Coke and a bag of chips then head back to school.

In eighth grade, there was a guy called Donnie who used to hang out with Kenny and his boys. I had a comic book that I was looking at in class, and he asked to see it. I waited until our next period to ask to get it back. When I asked him, he wouldn't hand it over. He said it was his now.

It was a Batman comic book—the only kind that I liked—and I got really mad. Before I knew it, I punched him in the mouth, and we started fighting. I won my first real fight. Of course, both of us got into trouble. We got put out of school for two weeks, but I never told my grandmother about it. Every morning, I'd get up and act like I was going to school, and hang out instead. Then one day while I was suspended, I saw Kenny and his boys. He told me he was glad to see I wasn't scared anymore, but he was lying to me. He wanted something. I didn't know what it was, so I just played along.

He told me to come with him, and we went to his house. When I went in, I was shocked to see his sister, who was really nice-looking, shooting dope into her arm. Kenny sat down, got some dope, and started shooting up with her. I couldn't believe it. He told me to sit down and shoot some with him, but I said that I wasn't into it.

He told me that if I left, we would be enemies, but I still didn't do it because I didn't know what was in the needle. He may have wanted to kill me, for all I knew. I told him that I had to go home. He said that he had something he wanted to show me, so I waited to see what it was.

He went into another room and came back with a gun. It was pretty, and there was just something about it that drew me to it. He said that he was going to rob someone, and he wanted me to go in on it with him. I told him I couldn't do that. I left there fast, and I knew that he was serious because he was known for shooting people. I didn't know what to do, but I knew that the next time I saw him, I'd better be ready.

When I started back at school that next week, the first people I saw were Kenny and his boys. When they saw me, I started running to get away from them, but they caught me about two blocks down the street. They beat me like a dog. When they were finally finished, I went to an old, empty house to get myself back together.

When I got home, I told my grandmother that I had gotten out of school early so she wouldn't think anything. I went into the back bedroom while she was watching TV. I went into her room and got her keys out of her pocketbook. My grandmother had a gun that she kept locked up in a drawer. I told her that I was going up to the corner store to buy something, and that I'd be right back. I went out and ran back to school. I waited behind the school, where I knew Kenny and his friends would be coming by.

I stood out in the open where they could see me. I wasn't the only thing they could see. They saw the gun in my hand, and they just looked at me like they couldn't believe it. I raised the gun and started shooting at them. They began to run away. I wasn't going to hurt anyone. I just wanted to scare them like they had been doing to me, and it worked. I told myself that I wouldn't have to worry about them anymore. They ran away real fast, and I was happy about that. I wanted them to feel what I had been feeling every time I saw them. I just wanted to get even with them for once.

I've thought about that day a lot since it happened. I admit it was a very dumb thing to do. What if one of those bullets had hit someone that day? I would have felt really bad about it.

When I got back home, my grandmother was waiting on me. She had gone into her pocket book for something and saw that the keys to the cabinet were gone. It's funny about old people. They can just feel when something isn't right. She knew that I had taken her gun, and she was real worried. As soon as I came in the door, she asked me where the gun was and why I took it. I tried to look like I didn't know what she was talking about, but I didn't do a very good job. I gave her the gun back and she asked me why I took it in the first place. She wanted to know if I had hurt anyone with it.

I told her that I didn't hurt anyone and explained why I took it. She was mad as hell at me over the whole matter, but she didn't beat me for it. She just told me that if it ever happened again, she would call my father and tell him about it.

I said to myself, *Shit, my father doesn't give a damn about me.* He didn't care if I lived or died. I knew that I had hurt my grandmother again, though. She was scared that the police would come and get me, but they never did. I guess it wasn't that big of a deal. Hearing a gunshot in my neighborhood was like hearing music in someone's car as they went down the street.

After that, I didn't have any more problems out of that little gang. They never knew if I was packing or not.

CHAPTER 4

BECAME FRIENDS WITH a guy called Benny when I was in junior high. I thought he was cool. He had a lot of girls who liked him, and I remember that's what I liked most about him. I wanted to be like him. When girls would hang out with him, I would be right there. They would talk to me, too. By then, I didn't have that speech problem anymore. People at school didn't see me as a scared little boy anymore, and that's what I wanted. Nothing ever changed, though. I would always be that scared little boy. I am even now.

I have to admit that my way of thinking wasn't that good because I would always dream that I was someone else. I guess that's because I never liked myself. I felt like I wasn't worth anything.

I felt better being around Benny. I felt needed—or more liked—I guess.

Benny didn't do any drugs, except for every once in a while, he and I would smoke a joint together. We went to the movies and went roller skating, which were popular things to do when I was growing up. Every now and then, we hit the clubs, too. Benny used to bring his girlfriend with us, and she had a friend who would come, too. That girl and I would kiss a lot, but we never had sex.

Many times, we skipped school together and caught the bus to the mall. One time, Benny asked me if I knew how to steal. I told him, "Yeah, a little, but just when I need to." He told me he was going to steal some clothes and that he wanted me to be the lookout for him. We went into J.C. Penney's, to where the suits were hanging.

I had never in my life seen a person steal like him before. He was very good at it. I would look out for him while he took his clothes off in the changing room and put a suit on. Then he would put his clothes back on over it. He asked me if I thought I could do the same thing, and I told him that I'd try.

We went back to the store. I tried the same thing, and I got away with it. That day, we must have taken six or seven dress suits. Very nice ones, too. We kept two suits for ourselves—one for me, one for him—and sold the rest to people around the neighborhood. I had to leave my suit at his house because I couldn't take it home with me. My grandmother would have killed me.

I kind of hated to do it, but I wanted to keep hanging out with him. I really wanted to be like him in a lot of ways.

By then, my grandmother was letting me go out to the movies as long as I was home by ten o'clock. I wouldn't leave home until six or seven to go to the show. When she first started letting me go, I was always home by 9:30 p.m. After a while, she began to trust me.

The nights I would go out with Benny, we would meet at his house. Before I started going over to his place, I used to really wonder what type of family he had. I finally met his mother, and she seemed nice and kind. He also had two sisters and one younger brother. He didn't have a father. Benny was the man of the house. He helped his mother pay the bills. I could tell that his mother worried about the things he was doing, but they were poor and living in the ghetto, so they had to make it any way they could.

He sold what he stole to make money for his family. Whatever was left over he would keep for himself. Eventually, he saved enough money to buy a car. It was old, but it looked pretty good, all things considered.

Benny and I started pulling off jobs regularly, like stealing clothes and selling them for money. One day, he told me he was going to break into a house that had some money in it. He wanted me to help him, but I didn't want to. He kept on me until I finally decided to go along with him. I had a really bad feeling about it.

We were on the side of these people's house, looking around to make sure that no one was looking at us, and making sure no one was home. Benny walked up on the front step and knocked on the door. No one came. We went back around to the bathroom window. He found something round that looked like iron. He broke the glass and then he reached in and unlocked the window. He pushed it up and jumped through it. Then I went in after him. Once we were inside, I found a .38, and Benny found some money.

What I didn't know was that the house we had broken into belonged to a man who knew my grandmother. Someone had seen us leaving and told him. To make matters worse, the man was a policeman. When he reported the break-in, he told them that he knew one of the boys who had done it. He didn't want me to go to jail, but he wanted to teach me a lesson. The police came to my grandmother's house to get me, and she looked so sad. I had a feeling she thought this would be good for me.

I didn't really get in too much trouble. When I went to court, they put me on probation. They didn't know that Benny was the other guy, and I didn't tell them, so he was safe. It worked out good for me to be on probation because it gave me a chance to get myself together. I started going back to school. I was going to fail the eighth grade, so I had to go to summer school to pass.

At the start of tenth grade, my grandmother got sick. She had been feeling really bad one day. When I came home from school, she didn't even know who I was. I got scared and ran next door to let her friend know what was happening. Her friend was my stepfather's aunt. She came back with me and said that she was going to call 911. After she was through, I called my mother in Los Angeles to tell her what had happened. After that, I called my grandmother's sister in Tennessee. I was scared, and I was calling everyone I could think of. I thought I was about to lose her. The next day, my mother was in Baton Rouge. About a day later, my grandmother's sister drove down from Memphis to be with her.

My grandmother stayed in the hospital for about three weeks, and we would go to see her every day at visiting time. She had had a stroke, but thank God, they helped her in time. I can't help but feel that the reason she had it was because of the way I had been acting. When she started doing a little better, her sister Maggie—who everyone called Nig—went back to Memphis. While she was here, she really helped my mother a lot with me. I liked her because she was caring, fun to be around, and didn't take shit from anyone. We had always been close, and I knew that she cared for me a lot. She was always sweet to me and showed me much love as a member of the family. She told a person what was on her mind. She didn't hide nothing. She always said what she felt. She would cuss like a man when she got mad. Her and my grandmother are really close sisters. When something went wrong, you could always count on her to drive down from Memphis to see about us. Everyone loved her a great deal.

After Aunt Nig left, it was just my mother and me at home, like old times. My mother would be so tired when she came home from the hospital that all she could do was try to get some rest. We still had some good times together, because she would talk with me and try to help me with my homework. She told me how much she loved and cared for me. All she wanted me to do was make something out of my life and be somebody.

About two weeks later, something really bad happened to my mother while she was cooking for us. She was wearing a pair of slippers in the kitchen. The can she was opening fell off the table and hit her on her big toe. It hurt her really bad at first, but it wasn't broken. It just swelled up and turned real red. She thought it would get better. It would have, if she would have stayed off it, but she couldn't. She had to see to my grandmother every day and take care of me.

When my grandmother came home from the hospital, my mother looked after her until Mama Henrietta could do things on her own. While all of this was going on, my mother's toe got worse until she had to be put in the hospital herself. Luckily, my grandmother was well enough by then to look after me and my mother.

Now that I look back at it, it seems like my family was going through some kind of test. My grandmother was worried about her. I was worried, too, but I didn't think it was anything that bad. I was still going to school every day, but so much was going on with me at home that my mind wasn't on schoolwork.

I would go to see my mother at the hospital every day. We found out that my mother had let her toe get infected. They were going to have to cut it off. She didn't have any choice, because if it got any worse, they would have to cut off her whole foot. The doctors also discovered that she was a diabetic. Before then, she didn't even know that herself.

The doctors cut off her toe, and about a week later, they still had to come back and cut off her foot. We were really hurting inside for her. My stepdad came to be with her, and it was a sad time for all of us. The doctors thought that that would be the end of it, but it wasn't. They found out that she had waited so long before she had come to get help for her toe that the infection had spread almost all the way up her leg. It was about to become gangrene, so they wanted to do one more operation before it got all the way up her leg.

Once again, she really didn't have that much of a choice. The next time they operated, they cut off everything below her knee. That stopped it for good. The doctors were glad that they had stopped it, and so were we, but it didn't help the way that my mother felt.

My stepfather had to go back to Los Angeles after a while, to check on the house and everything, but he came back to see about her. My grandmother was tired all of the time, but she never stopped going to see my mother every day. When I got home from school, I would stay across the street with Ardessa's aunt Nancy until my grandmother got home.

My mother stayed in the hospital for about a month. After she was able to come home, she stayed with me and my grandmother for about five months. Then she went back to L.A.

Feltus was referred to Baton Rouge Mental Health Center by his school in 1977, when he was in 10th grade, was evaluated, and diagnosed with Disassociate Petit Mal Seizures, in which a person dissociates, or loses touch with reality. He was treated three times, but Feltus' contact with BRMHC was terminated before treatment had been completed.

I had to talk to my grandmother about school. I had stopped going when my mom went back to L.A. I was scared at first of what she might say, but I was tired of lying to her. It was killing me, and I wanted to get out for a while to find a job or something for a year or so. I would go back the next year. I thought that it would do me good, to be able to clear my head and get myself together. I needed to see what I really wanted out of life.

We talked, and I told her how I felt about school. I admitted that I hadn't been doing very well. She thought that I was doing good in school, but I wasn't. That winter I had changed my report card from F's to A's to fool her. I told her that I was failing in a lot of my classes and that I needed a break for a while. I promised her I would go back the next year and that I would get a job and help out around the house.

She didn't want me to leave school, but she said if I did, I would have to work and not just lie around the house. She called my mother and talked to her for a long time about the matter. My mother told me how she was unhappy about what I wanted to do, but she said that as long as I promised to go back to school the next year, I could work and see how things were in the real world.

It was my ballgame then. The next thing I had to do was find a job, something I had never had before. I walked for two days to look for work because I didn't have a car. On the third day, I passed a car lot. The sign in front of it read "Bill Crow's Car City." I went over and asked them if they needed any help doing anything around there.

The owner told me he could use someone to wash cars and start them every morning. He would pay me a hundred dollars a week. I was really happy about that, and I took the job. I started that same day, and I worked really hard to show him that I did good work. The owner, Bill, said he liked the way that I worked. From then on, I was on my way. My grandmother was really glad. After about a month, Bill started to let me drop the cars off at another dealership.

Bill had an old 1969 Grand Prix in the back of the lot that needed a little work done on it. It was a pretty green and white car, and I loved it. Green is my birthstone color. I guess that's why I liked it so much. I asked him if he would sell it to me, but he said that we'd have to work on it some to get it running right. Bill's son worked there also, and he helped me fix it. Bill said I could pay him fifty dollars a week for the car and get paid the other fifty dollars of my paycheck.

I had a car. My first one ever. My grandmother had to teach me how to drive. I was doing really good, and I was looking for another job. A better one than what I had. I knew I was going to have to try to work something out with Bill on the car.

After my mom had been married for about four years, Samuel got sick and had to go to the hospital for something. My mother was going every day to see him with two of his three children. They thought that he was getting better until one night he suddenly got the flu and started to get sicker. Mama Henrietta said he had the eight-day pneumonia.

A few days later, my mother and his son left the hospital after visiting him and went home. When they got to the house, they were getting inside when the phone rang. It was the hospital. They were calling to tell my mother that her husband had just passed away. They had just come from the hospital not more than a half-hour before. I believe that Samuel's death was the most painful thing that had happened to my mother since her own father had died.

Sometimes, I think that bad luck loves my family. My mother went through so much in her life. Her divorce from my father, her father dying, all her trouble with me, losing her leg, and then her second husband dying like that. I don't know how she made it through all of those bad times. I think that God had a lot to do with it. He kept her strong. He helped her when she needed him most.

Samuel had treated my mother well, and she had been crazy about him. Samuel was like a father to me, at least in the summertime. He talked with me, took me to different places, and gave me gifts. He was kind and polite to people.

My grandmother and I were very sad that he died. Mama Henrietta went out there to be with her. She left me across the street with Nancy until she came back. She didn't stay long, just until they had the funeral, and then she came back. My mother didn't want to leave Los Angeles right then. She stayed there a few more months.

CHAPTER 5

Feltus' school records indicate he was [16 years old] reading at a fourth-grade level. And, his grandmother requested that he be placed in special education once again. Review of the records at this point indicate an individual who had much difficulty expressing himself along normal or acceptable channels. An individual who had so much difficulty with basic learning tasks that he did not participate in extra-curricular activities or develop and maintain relationships with peers.

—REPORT FROM CAROLINE DODSON, MSW TO BONNIE JACKSON, DECEMBER 26, 1991

WHEN MY REPORT CARD came in **winter of 1978**, I got mad. I had been going to school and everything, but I had to change the F's to A's again. I thought and thought about it. It wasn't no use in me trying so hard and still failing. I started to think, maybe I just wasn't cut out for school. It upset my mother and grandmother, and I felt bad, but I dropped out. I was seventeen years old.

I asked Bill if he cared if I got another job. He said no, so I got another job at Sizzler Steak House part-time, working nights.

Bill used to write checks out for me to buy parts for the cars at the lot. He had a big book that all the checks were kept in. One time, when he was out of the office, I went in and took a check out of the book, wrote it out, and cashed it for myself. I never heard anything about it, so after that, when I was short of money, I would take another check.

It seemed like I just couldn't stop stealing. I guess it became a habit. The more I did it, the easier it became. Eventually, as will always happen, my luck ran out and I got busted trying to cash a check. I didn't actually get caught right then, I had run out of the store, but the police were looking for me. I never went back to work at the car lot after that. Bill had called the police on me for taking the check, and he had also told them something about my car.

I guess he wanted it back because I still owed on it. Well, as I was turning the corner to come down the street I lived on, I saw a police car turning the corner behind me. I was so scared that I just hit the gas without even thinking. I took off, and they were right behind me. We were running about seventy-five miles per hour down a street where the speed limit was only twenty. I tried to turn a corner at about sixty when I lost control and crashed into a fence. I jumped out of the car and took off running down the street, but the police cut me off and caught me.

They arrested me and took me in, but to my surprise, my manager from the Sizzler came and made my bond so I could get out of there. He really liked me, and I could always talk to him about things. We had a good friendship and understanding with each other. After the Sizzler manager made bond for me, Bill took away my car.

This all happened in the **fall of 1979**. During this time, I had been walking to work, but sometimes the manager would pick me up, or he would send his girlfriend, who also worked with us at Sizzler.

We all had fun at the steak house. When we would get done with work, we would all sit around and talk and laugh with each other. I used to wait for the manager to get done with his work, like counting all of the meat in the walk-in coolers. The last thing that he would do was count all of the money we'd made that day. I would sit in his office with him while he counted it. He would even leave me in the office at times with all of that money sitting right there on his desk.

I never even thought about stealing it, either. I was happy with what I was doing, and I liked my job. He even told me the numbers to the safe. The manager really trusted me, and I didn't want to do nothing to let him down. I liked him too much to do that, and I knew that as long as I kept doing my job as I had been, he'd help me up the ladder all that he could. When I worked at the car lot, Bill just wanted me to get women for him on the weekends and paid me like a bird.

During that time in my life, I had a friend named Butch. He was two years younger than me. I had gone to school with his sister, and I met him through her. I liked her a lot, but we were just friends. I liked to hang out with Butch. We used to go around the neighborhood and check out the scene.

I went through some wild things with him. One day as Butch and I were walking down a side street to his house, a brown van came towards us at about fifteen miles an hour. The van just kept coming, and it drifted across to the side of the street that I was walking on and hit me. It knocked me down hard, and I hit the street headfirst. I bounced up and fell back down out cold. Butch was scared to death. There were two white guys and a woman in the van, and they were in their early twenties.

They were high on weed and something else, and they hadn't seen me walking on the side of the road. They put me into the back of the van and tried to wake me up. My head was killing me when I finally came to, but other than that I was okay. They were scared because they didn't have any insurance on the van. They gave me thirty dollars and a big, big bag of weed and asked me not to say nothing about what had happened. I told them that I wouldn't. I still to this day have trouble with migraine headaches that last all day.

After we'd been hanging out for a while, Butch took me to a punk's house that he knew. We called homosexuals punks. I was scared of guys who dressed and acted like women, but I went with him anyway. He told me that the boy paid him every time he went over there, but he never told me what the boy liked to do. When we got there, Jake was playing music and smoking weed. He gave us both a joint and told us to have a seat. He was playing a record by Michael Jackson, *Off the Wall*.

Butch left to go into the back room with him to have sex while I was in the living room getting high. Later, I went into the back to see what they were doing. Butch was standing on the bed, letting the punk give him a blowjob. I wondered how long this had been going on.

After they were through, the punk asked me if I wanted some of that, too. I said, "No, I'll pass on that this time."

Before we left, the punk gave Butch twenty dollars and a bag of weed, and he gave me ten dollars for nothing. When we left, we were both laughing at the whole thing. I asked Butch if he always went there and got paid like that. He told me that he had been doing it for about four months. He said that the next time that he went back, he wanted me to come, too, and get some. I told him that I'd go as long as I could just chill and wait on him. He said that it was up to me.

Jake told me that he was having a party for New Year's Eve and had asked me if I wanted to come. I made sure to ask for New Year's Eve off, so I could go to the party. I left my grandmother's car at home because paying for gas was killing me. My money was always short because I was giving my grandmother half of my check for bills. Whatever was left after that I spent on clothes. I loved to wear nice clothes, and my grandmother always told me that I had a body for clothes. No matter what I would wear, I always looked good in it. I dressed in slacks and nice-looking shirts all the time. I got that from a soap opera called *The Young and the Restless*. I liked the character, Victor Newton. He always dressed nice, and I used to say, *Damn, that's the way I want to dress myself.*

When I opened the door and walked in, I was shocked. I saw women, beautiful women, Black and White, in long dresses who looked like movie stars. But there was a problem. After I started talking to one of them, I saw that "she" was a man in women's clothes.

I couldn't believe that. I couldn't believe that all of those beautiful "women" were actually men, so I danced with one of them. She was the finest woman that I had ever seen before. While I was dancing with her, I was feeling all over her to see if she was a real woman or not. Much to my surprise, "she" was a man, too. I thought to myself, *Damn, there's nothing here but gay men. How did they get so pretty?*

I tried to enjoy myself while I was there, but something happened. At about ten minutes to midnight, there was a knock on the door. One of the drag queens went to answer it. When he opened it, I saw three men standing in the doorway with guns in their hands. I got scared and thought that they were going to kill all of the punks and me with them.

One of the drag queens came from the back of the room and said, "Hi, honey." Then all three guys came into the living room, and one kissed the drag queen who had come from the back of the room. He looked like a guy that I knew. When I got closer to him and got a better look, I saw it was him. The guy lived across the street from my grandmother. We were shocked to see each other. He pulled me to the side and asked me to please not tell anything about him being there to his wife. I told him I wouldn't say nothing about it, as long as he didn't say nothing about me. He told me not to worry, that he wouldn't, and I believed him. I mean, he was married and had kids, and there he was fooling around on the side with homosexuals. I couldn't understand why this guy would want another man.

At midnight, when it was officially 1980, they all went outside and shot their guns in the air. They went back inside and partied. I mean really partied, and I was right there with them, smoking weed and dancing just like it was a real party with real women.

I went back into Jake's room to get some more weed, and on his bed were all of these punks' purses. I said to myself, *Damn, what have I walked up on here?* I turned around and went back out of the room. My mind was on how I could go through all the purses without anyone knowing it. Then it came to me, a way to do it.

I asked Jake to come back to his bedroom for a minute. I let him give me a blowjob, but I had something else in mind. After he was through, I went into the bathroom to clean up, and he went back to the party. When he left, I went through all of the pocket books on the bed. I must have found about $700 total in them, plus I found Jake's gun and two more.

I put the money and the guns into a bag and put the bag in the bathroom under some towels until I was ready for it. It turned out to be a very good party for me. I also got about ten phone numbers from some of those drag queens who wanted me to call them.

When the guy who lived across the street from my grandmother was about to leave, I asked him to give me a ride home. When I left, I was loaded down with the goods.

I told Butch about the party, but he had been to one before so he knew how they were. The only reason that he didn't go to that one was because he had to go somewhere with his family. With the money I had stolen, we bought some weed, food, tapes, and a new seat cover for my grandmother's car.

Jake was mad as hell about what had happened, but he didn't know who had done it. He didn't think it was me. He thought it had been one of the other guys that had been there. I was glad for that, and Butch and I still went over there every once in a while. I finally decided to stop going over there before things got too hot, but Butch kept wanting to go.

CHAPTER 6

BONNIE JACKSON: DID YOU OBTAIN INFORMATION EITHER FROM THE SOCIAL HISTORY OR FROM FELTUS HIMSELF THAT CAUSED YOU TO BELIEVE THAT HE HAD FORMED PATHOLOGICAL ATTACHMENTS TO WOMEN?

F. A. SILVA: FELTUS SUFFERS FROM, I THINK, A CHRONIC, NOT A MAJOR DEPRESSION BUT A CHRONIC DYSTHYMIC DISORDER, WHICH IS A DEGREE BELOW THAT MAJOR DEPRESSIVE DISORDER. THIS DYSTHYMIC DISORDER I THINK IT BEGAN TO BECOME MORE OBVIOUS IN HIS EARLY CHILDHOOD IN SOME OF HIS BEHAVIOR AT SCHOOL, AND HIS REAL DESPERATE NEED TO BELONG SOME PLACE, BELONG IN THE RELATIONSHIP WITH FRIENDS WHICH GOT HIM IN TROUBLE BECAUSE HE WANTED TO BE PART OF A GROUP, OR BECOME ATTACHED—TO HAVE A GIRLFRIEND.

—Penalty Phase, Day 2: 53, January 24, 1992

AFTER MY MOTHER CAME back from Los Angeles, I met a girl. As a teenager, I had seen other guys at school who had girlfriends and were already living like adults. I envied them. I wanted the happiness and freedom they had. I witnessed my parents in many fights throughout their marriage. I wanted to remove myself from that. I wanted to be as happy as my peers seemed to be. I wanted a loving and caring relationship for myself. I wanted someone that I could share everything with. Who would love me, for me. I thought it would take the right woman to come along for me to have a good relationship. Two people being able to talk with and be open with each other.

One night, when I was coming home from work, I had a joint in my pocket. I was in my grandmother's car. I wanted to smoke the joint before I went into the house, so I parked the car next to the curb in front of the house. I had the radio on, and I looked up and saw three girls passing by the car. They were going to the house next door to my grandmother's where my stepfather's aunt lived. My step-aunt sold Cokes, cupcakes, and candy at her house.

After I smoked the joint, I was feeling pretty good, so I went over to get something, too. I never had to pay. My step-aunt always gave me what I wanted for free. While I was standing there, waiting for my Coke, I started talking to one of the girls. Her name was Lorraine, and the other two girls were her sisters.

I found out that she wasn't seeing anyone and that she lived down the street, four houses from me. I asked her how she knew where I lived. She told me that she had seen me around and had asked one of her friends who I was.

I had to laugh. "You've been checking me out?"

She smiled and said, "Yeah, and I like what I see."

I just didn't think that it would happen to me that way. I thought that just happened in the movies.

When I got my Coke, I walked with her back to the car. I asked her if I could come by her house sometime, and she told me to come by anytime I wanted.

"Well, in that case," I said, "I'll come by tomorrow evening when I get off from work."

She looked at me. "You work?"

"Yeah, I'm a cook for a steak house."

"That's good," she replied.

I laughed when I said, "I know, that means that I'll be able to take care of you." Later, those very words would come to haunt me.

After about two days, I went back to Loraine's house to meet her family. Her oldest sister opened the door and let me in. Her name was Dionne, and she was really good-looking. She told me to have a seat in the living room. When she went into the back room, I heard her say to Lorraine, "That guy is here that you met the other night."

Lorraine came out into the living room, and we talked for a minute. She asked me how I was, and I told her that I was fine. She wanted me to meet her mother in the back bedroom, so I followed her to her mother's room. As I was walking down the hallway behind her, I could smell something, but I couldn't make out the smell. It was very strong, though.

Her mother was sitting on the side of the bed when we walked in. She was about 300 pounds—a big, fat woman. In my mind, I wanted to laugh because she looked like one of those people that you see in cartoons. She asked me my name, and I told her. She asked me where I lived, and I told her that also. She asked if my mother was named Willie Mae. She and my mother had gone to school together. I told her that I hadn't known that and that I'd tell my mother that I'd met her.

While she was talking to me, I was looking around the room. It was half-dark in there, and from the looks of things, it was a mess. There were things lying all over the place, and the room was funky. I felt strange standing there, but I tried not to show it in front of them. For some reason, something was wrong. I felt like I was in one of those *Friday the 13th* movies, where Jason—the killer—may come out at any moment. I had never felt that way before.

I didn't want Lorraine to feel bad, so I tried to act as nice as I could. I know that she felt bad about how the room looked, about how it smelled—like something had died in it. I was glad when she asked me if I was ready to go back to the living room.

When we were walking back through the hallway, I couldn't help but notice that there were roaches running all across the wall and that the wallpaper was peeling off. I thought to myself, *All the other rooms must look the same.* The only room that was fairly decent was the living room.

I had to go to the bathroom, so I asked Lorraine where it was. I went in and shut the door behind me. It was a mess. There were dirty clothes lying all around by a garbage can that I guess was for the dirty laundry. Some of the clothes were in it, some weren't, and some were hanging out of it over the edge. I had to use the bathroom real bad, but I needed some toilet paper. I didn't see any on the roll, so I looked in the top cabinet for some. Nothing. I opened the door to the bottom cabinet under the sink. I saw candles on a stand that looked like some kind of altar to me. I felt really funny being in there, with all those candles burning like that. I closed the cabinet door like it had been and left the bathroom.

I wanted to get out of there as fast as I could. I don't know what kind of feeling it was that I had, but it wasn't a good one. There was something strange about those people, but I couldn't really figure it out. Once we were outside, I had never felt more relieved in my life.

I asked her to go riding with me. We weren't gone long. She said that she had to do something for her mother, and that she would go with me to meet my mother later. We talked for a short time in the car. When I said that I had to go, she kissed me on the side of the face.

"What's that for?" I asked.

"Nothing," she said. "I just felt like doing it."

A few days later, I went over to Lorraine's house and stayed most of the day. I learned a lot about her family. Lorraine's brother, Donnie, looked like a junkie or a wine head to me. He didn't even know me, but he asked me to give him five dollars so that he could buy a bottle of Whiteport wine. I gave it to him, and he said that he'd pay me back later, but I knew better.

Lorraine's youngest sister was Latesha, and she was going to junior high school. She still had one year left before she went to high school. I could tell that she was hot and that she messed around a lot by the way that she acted around me. Dionne, who I already knew, was the oldest girl. She jumped from man to man a lot because she didn't have any other way that I knew of to take care of her child. She was on welfare, but what she did with the money, I don't know. I found out that the man who had gotten her pregnant had left her after he'd found out that she was about to have his child.

Lorraine's mother said that she was some kind of spiritual woman who could see into the future. She also told me that she could take off and put on curses. Lorraine's mother said that she knew voodoo, and that she always had people coming to her house for palm readings and to get spells taken off of them.

I took Lorraine out a few times, and the thing that hit me the most was that she wore the same clothes all the time. I asked her if that was all she had to wear, and she told me it was. I felt bad because I didn't like to see anyone always wear the same things. I told her, after I got paid, I would take her to the mall to buy some nice clothes to wear before she met my mother. She seemed real happy about that, and I was glad I could do that for her. I've always felt sorry for people who didn't have nothing. I wished that I could help them in some way. A lot of my troubles have come from trying to help out others so much that I always came out on the short end of the stick.

On payday, I cashed my check, picked up Lorraine, and bought her all kinds of things. I didn't know what I was going to tell my grandmother about my half of the money for the bills. I still needed money to buy gas. I know that my grandmother knew the week I got paid, and I told myself I was going to have to get that money some way.

Lorraine showed her new clothes to her mother and her sister. They acted like they had never seen new clothes before. They thought that she was a queen or something. I was glad to help her, but I was sorry that I had overdone it a bit. When I went home, I didn't tell my grandmother that I had gotten paid. I just tried to get by, but my grandmother finally said something about a bill that I owed on the TV. I told her that I would take care of it and not to worry.

When I went to work that night, my mind wasn't on work. I was thinking about where I could get the money that I needed. I did have an idea, but I really didn't want to do it. I couldn't see any other way at that time, though. I thought of breaking into a house. When I got off from work that night, I drove down the street behind my grandmother's house to see what I could find.

I had been around the wrong type of people for so long that I started thinking like them. I thought that when I had to, it was all right to take from someone else, but I was dead wrong for that. Up ahead, I saw a good house. I knew the people that lived there. I knew that they had to go to work the next day, and I didn't have to go to work until that night. I decided that that would be the one.

The next morning, I got up early and told my grandmother and mother that I had to help one of my friends move to a new place. It was about 8:00 a.m. when I walked around by the house that I had picked. I could see the people getting ready to go to work. I walked around the corner then back. I walked straight up to the house and knocked on the door like I was looking for someone, to make sure that everyone was gone. When I knew for sure that they'd left for work, I walked to the back door to see how I was going to get into the house. There was a window right next to the back door. I took a rock and hit it against the top of the window. I reached my hand through the broken glass and unlocked the window.

I crawled into the house and searched it to make sure it was empty. I went into the bedroom to check all of the drawers. When I looked under the bed, I found a shoebox with $400 inside. I put the money in my pocket and left. I didn't look for anything else after I found that.

I went back home. My mother and grandmother were there. I told them that I didn't have to go to work until that evening, and that I had gone by a friend's house. Later, when it was time for me to go to work, I drove past the house. I saw a police car there, so I knew they were home and had found out that their money was gone. I really felt bad, because I knew that I had caused someone else pain, but I thought it was the only thing that I could do. I know I should have been talking with a doctor or something. My mind was working so funny. I didn't understand why I was doing those things.

When I got off from work, I gave my grandmother the money for the bills. I told her I was going to get Lorraine and bring her over to meet them. When I got to her house, Lorraine was really glad to see me. I told her to go put on something pretty, that I was going to take her to meet my family. So she put on a dress and combed her hair nice.

She looked really pretty. Lorraine was a little shorter than me, about five feet four inches. She had brown eyes like mine, and she had a shape like an hourglass with a nice, round butt. You know, the things that a guy looks at. Her face was kind of round, with big eyes that I thought were pretty to look at. I said to myself, *Maybe this is it. I've found my lady of love.* To me, she looked real good, but I was in for it when we got to my grandmother's house.

My grandmother opened the door and smiled as we came into the house. My mother was sitting in a chair, and she told us to sit on the sofa. She looked at us kind of strange, like something was wrong, but she didn't say anything. My grandmother and mother talked to Lorraine. Lorraine said her mother knew mine.

"Oh, yes, I remember her," my mother said about Lorraine's mother. "We went to school together."

We all talked for about thirty minutes. I could tell that something was wrong, and I wanted to find out what it was. After I walked Lorraine home, I came right back to find out.

"Don't you ever bring that girl back in this house again," Mamee said.

My mother and grandmother told me that Lorraine's family was always getting into trouble with the police. The police practically stayed at their house, for one reason or another. Plus, Lorraine's brother was in and out of jail. My grandmother told me that I got into enough trouble on my own without being around people who were getting into more. My mother said that she didn't want me over there anymore. I thought about it for a minute and told her that I would stop seeing Lorraine. Inside, I knew better, but I didn't feel like Lorraine was like her brother and sisters.

Lorraine didn't go to school, but I was hoping to change that. I wanted her to have better than what she had, which was nothing. I really felt that if Lorraine had someone to show her love, if she had someone who really cared for her, she would be a better person. I liked that Lorraine was easy to talk to. She was a dreamer, and I liked that, because I was one, too.

I had a friend who had known Lorraine and her family for a long time. He told me that Lorraine wasn't anything but trouble, but I didn't believe him. He also said that she had another guy that she was seeing, even while she was seeing me. I didn't believe that, but shortly after hearing all of this, I started to find out things for myself.

The next day, Lorraine and I talked in her bedroom for a long time. She shared her room with her two sisters. Latesha was reading a book, and Dionne was talking to her mother in the front room. I told Lorraine about what my mother said, but I told her that I couldn't stop seeing her now. She meant too much to me, and I cared about her.

"What are we going to do?" she asked.

"I'll think of something," I said.

I decided to go to the store to buy us something to eat. She said that she'd wait.

As I was about to walk into the living room, I heard Dionne and her mother talking.

I stopped to listen. I heard her mother say, "This is what you need to do to keep your man doing things for you. You take his underwear and put them on a nail somewhere where he won't find them. Then while you are cooking his food, take your Kotex and put it in with the food to cook, and then take it out. Make sure that your pad has been on for at least two days before you use it, and you'll be able to tell him to do anything, and he'll do it."

When I heard this, I said to myself, *Damn, my mother was right*, but I still didn't believe in that voodoo stuff.

Later, Lorraine's mother said that she wanted to talk to me. She asked if I would loan her a hundred dollars to pay her rent. She said that she would pay me back when she got her check next month. I told her that she would have to wait until the end of next week before I could do it.

When I got back home, my mother said, "Come here, I want to talk to you." I went and sat down, to see what she wanted.

She told me that a friend from Los Angeles had called her that day. Somehow, they had started talking about me. The woman told my mother that I was about to get into trouble and that if I didn't stop, something bad was going to happen to me. I lied to my mother and told her that I wasn't doing nothing. I said that her friend had made a mistake. My mother said that her friend had been around a long time and knew her stuff. She was known to be some type of spiritual person that could see into the future.

"If something happens," my mother warned, "don't forget that I tried to tell you and you wouldn't listen to me."

My grandmother told me to listen to my mother. Mama Henrietta said the lady across the street had told her that I was still going over to Lorraine's house. I tried to lie, but my grandmother knew better. The lady across the street had been seeing my car parked in front of Lorraine's. My grandmother asked me to stop going over there.

I told her that I had to go to work, but I didn't. I was off that day. I left and walked around the block and back to Lorraine's house.

When I got there, Lorraine wasn't home, but her sister told me I could wait until she got back. During that time, I walked around the house and did anything I wanted. I went into Donnie's room, and we talked and listened to the radio for a while. I had to go to the bathroom, so I went down the hall.

The door to the bathroom was half-open, and I went on in and shut it behind me. As I turned around, I saw Dionne in the bathtub, and she stood up in front of me, naked. "Lorraine isn't here, but we could have some fun, and no one needs to know about it," she said.

I looked at her standing before me, but I told her that I wasn't like that and left the room. Their whole family was messed up. Not only was Dionne like that, but I had also seen her mother in bed with two men at one time. I couldn't believe it.

When I got paid, I went to pay the hundred dollars for Lorraine's mother's rent. The landlord told me he would take the money, but that Lorraine's mother owed him $350 more. He told me that she never paid on time and that he was getting tired of it. He was thinking about putting them out.

I asked him not to do that because I'd pay for them in about two weeks. He said he'd let me do that because I seemed like a good person.

I told Lorraine's mother what had happened. She said people were late in paying her for her services and that she would pay me back if I just helped her this once. I said that I would do my best for them. I didn't want to see them getting put out of their house. I talked to Lorraine about it.

She said that she wanted to leave her house. I asked her where she would go. She told me that we'd find some place to live. I said, "Wait, I can't do that. Not right now, because I don't have the money for it." She told me to think about it, and I said that I would, but inside of me, something was telling me that these people was using me. I didn't want to believe that then, though.

When I got home, I could tell that something was wrong. My mother said, "Didn't I tell you not to go back around those people?" I asked her what she was talking about. I just stood there and looked at her. I didn't know what to say because she had me right. My grandmother really shocked me when she said, "Well, I can't let you use the car anymore because I can't trust you to do like you say."

I said, "You're right. Don't worry. I won't go around there anymore." But what was I going to do? I was in too deep. I told them that I'd get to work and that I'd be all right. My mother was really hurt. I could see it in her eyes.

When it was time for me to go to work, I had to walk. When I got around the corner, I told myself that I'd better tell Lorraine that I wouldn't be using the car for a while. I saw a yellow car in front of Lorraine's house. As I got closer, I saw that Lorraine was in the car with some guy. I watched her kiss him before she got out. I stood behind a tree so that she couldn't see me. I was so mad that I just turned around and went to work.

The whole time that I was working, I was thinking about what I had seen. I wanted to know who that guy was. I thought about what my friend had said about Lorraine being a street woman and not caring about anyone but herself.

When I got off that night, I went to Lorraine's house. As soon as I got in, I asked her, "Who the hell was that guy in the yellow car that you were kissing?"

"Cool it," she said. "That was my old boyfriend, and I just kissed him because I had told him that we could never have anything anymore because I'm with you and that I cared for you now."

Of course, I believed her. I went for it all. I was telling myself that if she had done that for me then she must really care for me, so I'd better do my best not to let her down. The time was coming close for me to get the money for their rent, and I had no idea where I was going to get it.

They seemed really poor, and I wanted to help them in some way. I felt that Lorraine was different from the rest of her family, but she wasn't, and I would soon find that out. It was all a big mind game. They may have been poor, but they did just about anything to get what they wanted.

I was really getting into trouble at home by still going over to Lorraine's house. My mother knew that I wasn't listening to her. She felt that something was about to happen to me. My grandmother was praying that God would keep his hands wrapped around me. But soon, my world would begin to fall down all around me, and it would be too late to do anything.

As the days went by, I was getting worried about what I was going to do to get the money Lorraine's mother needed. I would get off from work at night and go walking around, all across town, looking for some way to get money. I knew that I could use part of my check, but I still needed more.

I went to a part of town that I used to live in when I was younger. There was a small store on the corner of the block, and I went in and bought a Coke and a honey bun. I always liked that. I left and walked down to the school that I used to go to. I sat on the front steps, thinking about where I was going to get the money, but I could only come up with one idea. I didn't like it, but I didn't see any other way to go about getting the money.

I sat for a little longer before I went to get the gun that Benny and I had found when we had broken into the house together. It was wrapped up in a towel with plastic around it in a bag outside, under his house. When I got it, I didn't even load it. I returned to the corner store and bought another Coke and honey bun.

When I went to the counter to pay, someone was in front of me. A Black lady, around her thirties, was cashing a check, and it looked like a lot of money to me. I said to myself, I have to get this money. I went outside and waited for her to come out. She walked out a second later and started walking down the street with another lady. I followed them, hoping that they would go into a house or a yard or a car so that I couldn't rob the lady with the money. A part of me didn't want to do it—the gun wasn't even loaded—but another part of me did. I needed the money. I could feel my heart pumping fast, and my blood rising up in me.

It seemed like it was real dark to me, and it was hot. I had on a pair of sunglasses and a bandana around my neck, which I put around my face when I walked up to them. The gun was in my pants, but it was where you could see it. I raised my shirt and showed it to the lady with the money but didn't take it out from my waist.

"What do you want?" she asked. Her tone of voice was kinda low and a little shocked. She looked surprised that I was doing such a thing because I was really a small guy.

"Give me the money out of your purse," I said. I said it loud and rough so she wouldn't think that I was playing around with her. I was thinking I needed to get this money and start running away from there before someone saw me.

She went into her purse and gave me the money. I turned around and ran. I looked back as I ran away, and the lady was running after me. I couldn't believe it. Why would she run behind me when she knew that I had a gun? The only thing that I could think of was that she wasn't scared of me because I was small at that time. I was faster, though, and I ran off and left her. I went to the school and sat down to count the money.

It was only seventeen dollars. She had given me some other money and kept the big money. Man, I was mad as hell, and I didn't know what to do. My first successful armed robbery, and all I got was seventeen dollars.

I walked home and watched for the police the whole way. After I went into my room, I sat on my bed and wondered what in the world I had just done. I couldn't understand myself or my actions. Now I was deep into something that I really didn't want to be involved in, and for what? Because I let myself think that I could help everyone in the world. Because I let my big mouth get me into trouble. I tried to go to sleep, but I couldn't. I lay awake all night.

The next day, I was still scared. I went down to a club and sold the gun. I tried to relax until that evening when it was time for me to get ready for work. I was worried because I was still short on the money that I needed. I didn't know if that lady had seen my face or not.

I was going about my work when I noticed the manager in the office counting all the money from that day. He had to go out, so he told me to go into the office and wait for him to come back. I sat down next to his desk. All that money was just sitting there staring at me, and I was staring back. I looked around to make sure that everything was still cool. I counted off $300 and stuck it in my sock. When the manager came back, I told him that I had to finish up and walked out. I don't know if he ever missed the money or not. He never said anything to me about it. After work, he took me home. I told myself that I was lucky because I had gotten away with it that time.

I hated myself for doing it. I knew that I was hurting my friends and family, but I couldn't understand it myself. Every time I tried to do something right, I always messed it up somehow. I felt like I had chains all around me. And they just got tighter and tighter around my body. No matter what I did, I couldn't come out of them.

I called work the next day, to tell them I would be coming in late. One of the girls who worked there told me that the police had been by looking for me, but they didn't say what for. I was scared to death, and I really didn't know what to do. I went and put some of my clothes into a suitcase, took it out the back door, and put it under the house.

I went back in and told my mother that I was going to work. I didn't want to tell her what was going on. I didn't want to see her cry over what I had done. I knew that the police were looking for me and that they would soon be coming to my grandmother's house. I didn't want to be there when they came, so I went to Lorraine's house. I told her what was going on with me, and she said that I could stay with her. I told her I had something to do, and I left. I walked to the rent man's house and paid him off. He was happy that he finally got his money.

A few days later, I went to the corner store to buy a newspaper for my mother. When I was coming out of the store and walking back down the street, I saw a police car going to my grandmother's house. I turned around and walked to a street behind Lorraine's house. I went through someone's backyard and jumped the fence to Lorraine's yard. I could see down the street to my grandmother's house from the front of her house. I told Lorraine what had happened and she said that I could stay with her for a while, and that was what I did.

I went back to my grandmother's house, to get some change of pants and shirts. Mama Henrietta and my mother tried to talk me into turning myself in, but I didn't. I didn't tell them where I was staying. My mother was sitting by the door. As I walked by, she told me that she loved me. I turned and looked at her. Those words cut through me like a knife. I saw a tear fall down her cheek. It really got to me.

For several days, I tried to stay away from the police. One night, when I was coming from Butch's house, he and I were walking down the street and saw Lorraine and the guy I had seen her with before. They were hugging each other in someone's yard. I got so mad at her that I ran up to them, and I slapped Lorraine across her face. I punched the guy in the face. Butch ran up behind me, and we started kicking him in the sides. I told Lorraine that I wanted to know what was going on. She told me that this guy was her man and that she was two months pregnant.

"It can't be mine because we've never made love or anything like that. All we do is kiss all of the time," I said.

Butch said, "Come on, man, let's go."

As we walked off, Lorraine came running after us with a bottle in her hand. She threw it at me, and it missed. I wanted to go back down the street and kick her in the butt, but Butch reached for my arm and told me not to.

When we got to Butch's house, we sat in the backyard and talked about the mess that I was in. We smoked a joint, and I told him that I had to go back and talk to Lorraine to find out why she had been lying to me. I walked back to my neighborhood in the dark. Donnie saw me and asked me where had I been. He told me that Lorraine had been worried. I told him I was on my way there now. He didn't seem to know what had happened earlier.

He asked me to walk up to the store with him, and wanted to borrow five dollars again. He still hadn't paid me back for the first five, but I let him have it anyway. He got a bottle of Mad Dog. We were drinking the bottle as we walked to his house. I knew better than to drink that stuff because I couldn't handle it, but I drank it anyway.

About halfway back to the house, we stopped and Donnie drank the last little bit in the bottle. I wasn't looking at him. I was watching down the street for any police.

Donnie took the bottle and hit me upside my head. I went down, and he started hitting me, saying that Lorraine had told him that I slapped her. Donnie never liked me anyway.

I couldn't get up because I was drunk, and my head was bleeding bad. All I could do was try to keep him from hitting me in the face. After a while, he stopped and walked away, leaving me on the ground. He must have told Lorraine what he had done because she came running down the street to where I was and helped me back to her house.

I went along with Lorraine because I needed a place to sleep. When we got to her house, she gave me a bath and told me that she was sorry for what had happened. She said that she had just lied about the baby part because she was mad at the time. But I knew that she wasn't lying.

Yeah, I said to myself, *my mother sure was right. She knew what she was talking about when she tried to warn me.*

I knew that my mother was at home, worrying herself to death over me. I was on the run and with people who I didn't really want to be with. I knew then that Lorraine wasn't worth what I was going through.

A few nights later, I went to a club to use the phone. When I called Lorraine, she answered and said that she had been waiting for my call. I asked her what had happened.

"The police just left, and they were looking for you," she said.

"How did they know I had been there?"

She told me that the lady across the street had told them that she had been seeing me going in and out of the house. Somehow, she knew that the police was looking for me.

"What should I do?" I asked Lorraine.

"Let me think of something," she said. "I'll tell you tomorrow."

To tell you the truth, at that time, I wanted to call my mother and tell her that I wanted to come home and do whatever she wanted me to do. But I couldn't do that. I had gotten myself into this mess, and I had to get out of it myself.

I'd been on the run about three weeks.

I didn't go by Lorraine's house. I didn't want to see her anymore. I went back to my old part of town, where I had lived with my parents, and went to a friend's house who I used to work with. Alan was at home, and he was selling weed on the side to make extra money. I asked him if he would take me to get a bus ticket. He told me to sit down and smoke a joint with him first.

"Okay," I said, "but after this, let's go get the bus ticket."

"All right," Alan said. "I gotta make a phone call, and I'll be right back. Roll up a joint and smoke it until I get back."

I sat there and rolled up a joint, not thinking about him using the phone. What I found out later really messed my head up.

He came back into the room, and we smoked the joint. "Are you ready to go?"

"Yeah, let's go," I told him. I really wanted to get out of there. We got into his car and left. As we were driving, everything seemed okay. I was high. I didn't see any police around, so I felt I was safe. We got to the bus station, and he waited in the car for me while I went in.

When I came back out, he was sitting in the car listening to the radio and smoking another joint. I got in, laid my ticket on the seat, and took a pull off the joint as we left. On the way back to his house, I noticed that he seemed to be acting kind of strange. I couldn't make out what it was, though, so I started looking around, looking for anything out of place. I saw an unmarked police car go right by us, and I knew then that something was definitely wrong. My mind was telling me to jump out of the car and run, but we were moving too fast for me to jump. I said to myself, *When he stops, I'm out of here and running.*

As soon as he pulled into his driveway, I started to get out. But as I turned around, about five police cars came out of nowhere. They blocked off the driveway. The police jumped out of their cars and had their guns out and pointed right at my head. My high left just like that.

They put me on the ground. One of them put his foot on my neck while they handcuffed me. Then they put me in the back of a police car. While all of this was going on, Alan just stood there, looking like nothing had happened. One of the cops said something to him and then got into the car that I was in. As we pulled off, I was wondering how in the hell they had come down on me so fast.

When we got to the police station, they handcuffed me to the chair. I could hear them in the hallway, and they were saying that Alan had called his uncle, who was a police officer, and told him I was at his house. His uncle had told him to stay with me or keep me there until they got there. It dawned on me that he must have called them again while I was in the bus station getting my ticket.

I just sat there, wondering what was about to happen to me. I was thinking about what was ahead for me in prison. I knew that it was a hard road ahead, and I didn't know how I was going to deal with it.

PART TWO

ON THE INSIDE
10 YEARS, 3 MONTHS,
10 DAYS

CHAPTER 7

Going to prison is something you never get used to. It does not matter who you are. Being locked away, restrained and repressed in every way, utterly controlled, goes against your every instinct and desire. Prison life is different from anything you may see on television. You could not dream of the reality of prison. Prison is a society within a society. A society with its own set of rules, laws, and justice system. From the day of my arrest, I was drawn into it and forced to either adapt or die. Sometimes, I feel like I would rather die than have to live day in and day out like this.

—FELTUS TAYLOR, JR.

AS I WAS SITTING there, handcuffed to my chair, I was thinking about everything that had happened to me. All the things I should have done differently. In a way, I was happy that it was all over with. I knew my mother would be feeling much better. She felt that this was what I needed to get my mind together again.

A policeman returned and sat down at his desk. He began asking me all sorts of questions, which I answered as best I could. Afterward, a policewoman came and escorted me to have my picture and fingerprints taken.

As we were walking down the hallway, she glanced at me and said, "Today's your birthday, huh?"

I had forgotten. It was **March 17, 1980**. I turned nineteen years old. What a way to celebrate your birthday—going to jail.

She wished me a happy birthday and told me she hoped everything worked out all right for me. I looked up at her and tried to smile, but I was not much in the mood for smiling. After taking my picture and fingerprinting me, another officer came and escorted me to a room where I could change into a jail uniform. The uniform was a loud orange, almost fluorescent, and the shower slippers matched. Then I was led along a long hallway with cells on either side. He put me in a cell with five other people and locked me in.

Two of the guys were White, and I was the fourth Black. On each side of the cell were three bunks on the wall like bunk beds. The only one still vacant was, of course, on top. It already had sheets on it; so, I climbed up and lay down to do some serious thinking.

Suddenly, I heard a loud ruckus coming from the twenty-four-man cell directly across the hall. My eyes followed the noise, and I saw two Black guys having a go at one another. None of the guards came to intervene, and no one was calling for help. They just let them fight. One of the guys was much larger than the other, and it soon became one-sided, with the smaller being beaten pretty bad. The bigger guy finally stopped and told the other guy, "You know what time it is, don't you?" The smaller guy just looked at him and said nothing.

I rolled over and lay there wondering if something like that would happen to me. I nodded off to sleep. When I woke up, they were serving lunch. I climbed down from my bunk to get my food. It was cold cuts and grape Kool-Aid. I did not have much of an appetite, so I gave my tray away and lay back down.

Later that night, I spoke to one of the guys in my cell. He told me about some of the people I was in the jail with and about the two guys that had been fighting the night before. He explained that the bigger guy wanted to have sex with the smaller one, and he told me to watch what happened when the lights went out. He warned me not to say anything or to call the guards to help him.

"If you do," he said, "they will be after you, too."

After the lights had gone out, I climbed up in my bunk and watched to see what would happen. A half-hour later, the big guy climbed from his bed, went over to the smaller guy's bunk, and woke him up. The smaller guy climbed out of bed and knelt upon the floor. The big guy pulled out his penis and stuck it into the little guy's mouth. It made me sick to look at them, so I rolled over again and tried to go to sleep. However I tried, I could not doze off. I could not seem to block what I had seen from my mind. I'd seen such things before, but this time, the guy didn't want to do it and did it because he was afraid of what the other man would do to him.

The following morning, the guy I had been talking with the previous day came and asked, "Did you see what happened last night?"

I said, "Yeah, I hope no one tries to do me that way."

He told me I would have to fight back and never let anyone screw me around. He told me I had to do whatever it took to survive.

When the guard came for me, I was handcuffed and marched across the street to the courthouse. The judge was already waiting on me, and I had to stand before him while he read the charges to me. He stated that I had one count of armed robbery and set my bond. He then asked me if I would be able to make bond.

I told him that I could not.

He said that they would appoint an attorney for me. "You can leave now," he said.

Not knowing any better, I asked, "Where? Home?"

"Hell, no," he responded. "You'll be held in the parish prison until your court date arrives." I was then informed that people were held at the jail overnight until they could see the judge. I had no idea that I would spend the next eight months in prison waiting for my court date.

The guard escorted me back to the jail. Around one o'clock in the afternoon, the sheriff's deputies came and told me to pack my stuff. They handcuffed and shackled me so that I could not escape. The shackles had a chain about twelve inches long, which prevented me from taking anything other than short steps. After we made our way downstairs, I was loaded on a large bus with bars welded on all the windows. There were around twenty guys transferring with me.

I sat down and tried to get as comfortable as I could with all the restraints on. There were two people in each seat. After everyone was aboard, the guard locked us in. There was a heavy, metal, mesh gate that prevented one of us from getting to either the guard or the driver to hurt them. The ride lasted about twenty minutes.

As we were pulling up to the East Baton Rouge Parish Prison, it occurred to me that the place looked terrible. It was a beautiful day in March, but the sight of the parish prison ruined any pleasure I may have enjoyed from it. I had the weight of the world upon my shoulders that day. I felt like crying, but the realization that I had brought all of this upon myself prevented me from doing so.

We came to a stop before a large gate. There were double fences spanning the entire structure. The fences were ten feet high, and barbed wire was strung along the top. It appeared to be a place that no one returned from. I was entering a strange world unlike anything I had ever experienced before. I was only nineteen, a kid to the men I was about to meet. Better known as *fresh fish* to the guys in prison.

The bus halted inside the gate, and we all offloaded. The guards recounted us, to make sure we were all there, and then escorted us inside. As we approached the entrance, I noticed a camera was pointed toward anyone entering. I heard a loud click, and the door opened. We proceeded through the door in double file. Once inside, we were all led to a big holding cell until the guards called for us one at a time. As we were called, our handcuffs and shackles were removed. By that time, they had begun to hurt my ankles and wrists, so naturally I was relieved to have them off.

Everyone started walking around and smoking while the guards pulled each of us out to make our one phone call. I called my mother and grandmother when it was my turn to use the phone. I told them that I was all right and for them not to worry about me. They were worried anyhow, and my mother told me to tell the police the truth about whatever they asked. I assured her that I would. She promised me that if she had the money, she would get me out of there. I told her not to worry about it. I knew that if she could I would not be there.

My grandmother told me she could put her house up for the bond, but I told her not to.

"Please don't do that. Things will work out somehow," I said. I let them know that I would call again as soon as I was able, and let both of them know that I loved them. As I hung up, a sort of depression set in. I was feeling terrible about everything. I returned to my cell angry at the world, but mainly with Lorraine for using me the way she had.

BONNIE JACKSON: HAD YOU AND LORRAINE EVER HAD SEXUAL RELATIONS?

FELTUS TAYLOR, JR.: NO. I WANTED TO BUT SHE ALWAYS LIKE PUT ME OFF, YOU KNOW.

Q: SO, YOU AND LORRAINE NEVER HAD SEXUAL RELATIONS?

A: NO.

Q: PRIOR TO GOING INTO PRISON HAD YOU EVER HAD SEX WITH A GIRL?

A: NO, MA'AM.

—*Penalty Phase, Day 3: 18, January 25, 1992*

BONNIE JACKSON: WHILE YOU WERE IN PRISON—WHEN YOU FIRST GOT TO PRISON DID SOMETHING HAPPEN TO YOU? WOULD YOU RATHER NOT TALK ABOUT IT?

FELTUS TAYLOR, JR.: YES, MA'AM.

—*Penalty Phase, Day 3: 18, January 25, 1992*

The client [Feltus] reports that he had no sexual experience before going to prison. Shortly after his incarceration, he was [gang] raped by other inmates. Records show him to have weighed 120 pounds and he was a height of five feet, one inch.
—*Report from Clinical Psychologist Thomas Stigall, November 1991*

Soon after he started his sentence in prison, he was raped by several inmates and became involved in fights with defending himself.
—*Deposition from Dr. Paul Ware, January 1998*

*The psychological ramifications of being gang-raped in prison—especially as a
first sexual experience—are profound and multifaceted. Such trauma can lead
to severe mental health issues, including post-traumatic stress disorder (PTSD),
depression and anxiety, complex PTSD, and identity and sexual confusion.
Victims of prison rape may adopt violence as a survival mechanism, which
can persist outside of prison. Repeated incarceration and lack of mental health
intervention create a feedback loop of violence and trauma. These conditions may,
in some cases, contribute to subsequent violent behaviors, including homicide.*

The guards finally called us into another room to see a man that would
determine where we would be placed within the prison. If you were young, they
tried not to place you with the men that are already serving time. They used to do
that, but the guys that have been doing time most of their lives would abuse the
younger guys really bad. They would beat them and force them to have sex with
them. Not just one or two guys, either. Sometimes, it would be six or seven guys.
Then, everyone that wanted to would stick it to the new guy.

As I walked into the room, the man took one look at me and said, "I'm going
to place you with people your own age. The way you look, they'll give you a very
hard time in any other part of the prison." I think he was probably correct, as I had
long hair and only weighed ninety pounds soaking wet. I also still had sort of a
feminine look because of my age.

Afterward, I was led to another room where I was issued some prison clothes,
two sheets, a towel, and some lye soap. The soap—commonly referred to by
prisoners as *state soap*—makes a person itch all over after using it. Then I was
led down a long corridor with heavy iron doors every ten steps or so. When we
reached the cellblock where I would be staying, the officer told me that if I had
any problems just to let him know and he would take care of it. He seemed to pity
me. He appeared to be sad as he opened the door to my living area. I stopped just
inside the door and turned to ask him where I would be sleeping. He replied, "In
Cell One."

As I turned to face the cellblock once more, I noticed that Cell One was directly
in front of the door. Man, was I happy about that. There were already two guys
in the cell when I entered. They were sitting on their bunks talking, and the
only vacant bunk was the one at top. I placed all of my things on the bunk and
returned to the tier to have a look around.

The tier was a long corridor with ten cells along one wall. Each cell could hold
four people. I walked down the tier to see if I saw anyone that I knew, but I did not
recognize anyone. The dayroom had a television in a corner, and two iron tables
for people to sit at. In the corner, there was also a shower stall to the right of the
entrance. The shower was only large enough for one person at a time, and it was
occupied. There was a dingy gray shower curtain with many holes used to block
the water from spraying all over the room. The room was painted gray, and the

bars were brown. There was a walkway on the other side of the bars, which was commonly referred to as the catwalk. The catwalk extended down the entire length of the tier, but it was only wide enough for one person to pass at a time. The guard on duty would use it to make periodic counts and to make sure that nobody was dead. But in the event that someone was found to be dead, it was unlikely that they would just rush in to try and save them. You only see that on television, not in real life.

The whole prison wasn't like my tier. Some places had tiers of cells that held one person at a time. In another section, there were dorms that had twenty to forty guys in them.

The prison smelled like bleach and lemon floor soap when it was first cleaned in the mornings by the inmates assigned to do that work. Right after the first meal of the day at 6:00 a.m., the guards would let the inmates that they wanted and trusted out to clean up for them. They would try to have the ones that didn't get into trouble or wouldn't be trying to escape. A guy would come down the tier with a mop in a bucket of bleach water with soap and a broom so you could clean your cell out. Most of the guys cleaned their cells, but a few didn't. Later on, during the day, that fresh scent would turn to musk from different guys' bodies and cigarette smoke.

It was always noisy. People talked on the phone or looked at the TV all day. Even when guys were playing cards or checkers, they talked about what they had done on the streets all of the time, things like how many women they had had, what drugs they had done, who they had robbed, and what they would do once they were back out on the streets. They talked about other inmates. They told some of the most fantastic lies, trying to impress one another. Guys in jail seemed to gossip more than women in a bingo hall. They would sit around and talk like this day and night until a person would get sick of hearing it.

I called home that night to assure my mother and grandmother that I was all right. Whenever we needed to use the telephone, we had to notify the guard—the *freeman*—on duty, and he would let one person outside the gate at a time to use the phone. My grandmother offered to send me more money, but I did not need any. I still had the hundred dollars that she had given me earlier.

At that time, we were able to keep as much money as we wanted on us. But, I found out soon enough that having a lot of money was dangerous. If people knew that you had a lot of money, anything could happen to you. They would steal it while you slept or devise some other way of getting it. I had a pair of underwear with a pocket on the inside, and I even went in the shower with them on. I would get in the shower and take twenty dollars out at a time and put it in my pants pocket.

Everyone was checking me out since I was the new guy on the tier. I wasn't too worried because they were all around my same age. I started talking to one of the guys in my cell. He had a radio and would play it at night so everyone could hear it. It made it easier for everyone to drift off to sleep.

There were two guys who ran the tier, a short guy everyone called Black Joe, and his friend Ray Charles. Black Joe, although short, was built like a tank. He did pushups all day long and would body punch with anyone who was willing. Ray Charles was a small, light-complected guy. He would fight anyone, and the two of them made a good team. Because of the way they always did things together, some of the guys thought that Ray was Black Joe's punk [homosexual partner].

Bo Rob was an inmate known throughout the jail as a badass and troublemaker. He was the guy assigned to mopping the catwalk. I approached him one day, to ask him to call my mother for me. I needed him to let her know that I was doing fine and to find out what my attorney was trying to do for me. He assured me that he would and left. Bo Rob was assigned to A-9, which was an area where the jail houses the guys with a lot of time to serve, so I did not see him again until later that day. He also cleaned our tier after we were locked down, so I knew he would return later.

When he returned later that evening, he told me that he made the call for me and said that my mother and grandmother would be there to visit me on Thursday, our regular visiting day. I gave him five dollars for making the call, but he said he did not want my money. I insisted that he take it and told him I may want him to make the call for me again sometime. The real reason I gave him the money was because I did not want him coming back on me later saying I owed him anything. I had already heard enough about him to be careful. He liked the punks, and I wanted to keep him on my side, not after my ass. He had already turned a few other inmates out. I guess I was more afraid of that than anything else in the world. I did not want to be anyone's punk, and I was going to do whatever it took to prevent that from happening to me again.

From the moment I gave Bo Rob the money, he began to talk with me each time he came on the catwalk. He would tell me about prison life and how he had started coming to prison when he was my age. Bo Rob got his nickname because he used to rob dope dealers while he was on the streets. He had shot people before and stabbed people in prison. He told me about all the guys on the tier with me, and who to watch out for, who "wasn't about shit," as he put it. I was happy that I had made a friend that was for real. He told me that I looked scared and that I should not look that way if I expected to survive in jail. He advised me to do as everyone else, or they would give me a hard time.

He began telling everyone that I was his cousin, which sure kept me from getting into some trouble. One day, I was lying in my bunk when one of my cellmates told me what Black Joe had been saying about me. He said Black Joe was planning on seeing what I was about before he found out that I was Bo Rob's cousin. That means they were planning on jumping me to see if I would fight back. If I failed to hold my own, they would try to have sex with me. Now Black Joe would have to wait until Bo Rob either went home or was transferred to Angola.

When we all went into the day room to eat, I noticed Black Joe and Ray in the corner talking in a hushed manner, glancing my way from time to time. I was really uneasy and wondering what they were planning. I could hardly wait until Bo Rob returned the following morning to clean up so I could tell him all about it.

When Bo Rob came, I handed him a note explaining what was going on. After he read it, he returned and called me to the bars. He called Black Joe and Ray to the bars. He told them he did not care if they wanted to fight me, but that it was not going to be two on one. If one of them wanted to fight me, go ahead. The day room was completely full. He warned them that if both of them jumped me at the same time, he would have one of them moved over where he was and that he would handle it from there. Man, you should have seen them two kissing Bo Rob's ass.

When Bo Rob asked me if I was afraid to fight either of them, I lied and said no.

I walked to the center of the room and Bo Rob asked Black Joe and Ray which one of them wanted to fight me first. Black Joe came out, and I felt like running up the corridor, banging on the door, and telling them I could not live back there. Then we started to fight. Or rather he started to fight. For a while, I was only holding onto him and trying to keep from getting hurt too badly, He would just push me off and hit me again. Eventually, I got in a few good ones, but he really kicked my butt.

After that incident, Black Joe would body punch with me each day, for an hour and a half, to toughen me up. When we were finished, all I could think about was a shower and a bed. I would always be sore and achy all over. Black Joe and Ray still did not like me, and they would stab me in the back the first chance they had. They were just afraid of Bo Rob. Bo Rob was my ace in the hole. They knew this and were always searching for a way around it.

CHAPTER 8

THE GUARDS MOVED ME to another section of the jail. I went to F-1. The new tier I was in had ten guys to a cell. All of them were middle-aged, but I did not have any trouble there. F-1 and F-5 would go out for recreation together, so I could always visit with Kent and Mule [two guys I got along with]. Mule was at the parish prison for murder along with Kent, his fall partner. Fall partner is the term prisoners use for an accomplice in the crime. They were always into some type of trouble. Mule and Kent would beat people up, turn people out [have sex with them], take what they wanted from people, and otherwise just do as they pleased. It was said that they had robbed and killed a woman who managed a small neighborhood corner store. Both of them had already been sentenced to life in prison and were only waiting to be transferred to Angola.

Across from F-1 was F-2. It was a tier where the punks (homosexuals) were housed. There were not many men there. There was one punk everyone called Candy. He was in his mid-twenties at the time and about five feet five inches tall. He had a Jheri curl and a round face. From the waist down, he really looked like a woman with wide hips and a big, round butt. He had long fingernails like a woman. Every time I would pass from the day room to the sleeping area, I would notice Candy looking at me. On weekends, everyone had to G. I. That is when everyone would clean the day room and all the sleeping areas of the tier. On these days, Candy would call me to the bars to talk. I spoke to him a few times and told him I did not play the homosexual game. That just was not my style.

Yet, when we would go on the yard, where we went for recreation, Candy would tell Mule he wanted me to be his "old man." That is, he wanted me to be his boyfriend. When Mule told me about it, I let him know that I did not mess around with the homosexuals. He just kept telling me to get Candy anyway, and if I did not want Candy, to give the punk to him.

I was thinking to myself, *Man, this is some crazy shit.* Still, I went along for a number of reasons. The main reason was that I did not want anyone to try to turn me out. I knew if I stayed in good with Mule and Kent, I would not have to worry about that again. Then, too, I knew that if I was to get on their bad side, they would be on me like white on rice. I certainly did not want that to happen.

Bo Rob came over to see me when he could. He told me that Candy used to belong to him. Bo Rob told Candy that he wanted me to be Candy's old man and that Candy had better take good care of me. I did not understand what all that meant at first. Bo Rob explained that he told Candy that he was supposed to get me anything that I needed, and if he did not have it, he was to go get it for me. In jail, a punk can get things when no one else can. There are a lot of guards who like them for some strange reason. Even some of the guards who are married and have families will come to work and have sex with them. It happens quite frequently.

The prison officials do nothing meaningful to prevent these relationships because they are an effective tool for controlling the inmate population. The guards use homosexuals to learn what is happening around the compound. For instance, you can take a guy who everyone thinks is strong, and he will snitch to keep from being transferred away from a particular homosexual. Sometimes, you will even have a guard who will have a punk set another inmate up simply because he does not like him or for some disagreement they may have had. Then the guard can bust the inmate and send him to the cellblock. In some cases, it may take the inmate a year or two to work his way back into the population again.

It is strange how some guys will treat a homosexual in prison. You would be shocked to see them treated like real women. In some cases, guys treat them better than they do their own wives. Especially a guy with a lot of hard time on his hands. I have witnessed them hugging and kissing as a man and a woman would in a relationship. Sometimes, a guy will fall in love with the homosexual. He'll follow the guy around everywhere he goes and buy him all kinds of gifts and things from the store.

Candy and I started hanging out when we would go on the yard. We would talk about many things involving prison life in general. I knew deep down inside that this was wrong, but like I said, prison life is totally different from the outside world. If I did not adjust and go with the flow, it could have been me they were after. I just had to play the game and survive the best way I knew how.

After a while, I began to like Candy as a friend. He was someone I could talk to and pass the time with. He would tell me all about his life on the streets and what he had come to prison for. Candy had been a homosexual since he was a small boy. I asked him what his family thought about that. He said they did not approve but allowed him to live his own life. Candy had a lot of knowledge about living on the streets and the games people play out there.

Candy was serving time for armed robbery. He said he had been turning tricks one night and just decided to rob this guy for drug money. He was eventually caught and sentenced to fifteen years. To me, Candy was a good person inside, but he was caught up in the drug cycle.

Over time, I learned many things from Candy, at least as far as street knowledge is concerned. I found myself longing for the chance to talk with him. Now, I know that it was only loneliness making me feel like that. I just wanted someone around my own age who I could talk to. I did not like to associate with many people in prison because they were not the type of people you could trust or confide in.

Before too long, Candy asked me to move to F-2 with him.

Nobody in that cellblock messed with Candy for one of two reasons. One, he could fight really well. Two, he could get you crossed out—set you up in some way—by the free people or inmates. I was sure happy to move into the area with a bed. It was terrific for a while.

Then Candy began asking me when I was going to have sex with him. I asked him to give me some time to think about it because I was new at this game. He did not ask me again for some time after that. I was over there for about three weeks when I began to see others having sex with one another. It was a crazy place to stay.

BONNIE JACKSON: YOU ALSO MENTIONED THAT PERSONS WITH THAT DIAGNOSIS [BORDERLINE PERSONALITY DISORDER], ALSO HAVE A MARKED AND PERSISTENT IDENTITY DISTURBANCE. EXPLAIN THAT AGAIN FOR ME.

TOMMY STIGALL: MS. JACKSON, I WOULD JUST REPEAT WHAT I SAID TO THE JURY BEFORE. I THINK THAT THIS RELATES TO THE PERSON'S UNCERTAINTY ABOUT THEIR ORIGINS, ABOUT THEIR IDENTITY; ABOUT THEIR LIFE GOALS, ABOUT VOCATIONAL CHOICE, SOCIAL RELATIONSHIPS, SEXUAL PREFERENCE, FOR EXAMPLE. AND SO, THEY ARE ALWAYS SELF-DOUBTING, AND THEY FEEL VERY NEEDY WITH REGARD TO REASSURANCE FROM OTHER PERSONS, OR SOMEONE ELSE TO KIND OF HELP THEM FIND THEMSELVES OR GIVE THEM SOME SENSE OF BELONGING OR SOME SENSE OF RELATIONSHIP, SOME SENSE OF CONNECTEDNESS.

—Penalty Phase, Day 3: 143–4, January 25, 1992

My mother and grandmother were the only ones to ever visit me while I was in prison. My other relatives did not even care enough to write. My father thought only of his booze and women. Perhaps this was the reason I was searching for someone to love me as an adolescent. I had love from my mother and grandmother, but I wanted someone aside from them. What I wanted most was a true friend. Most people are just friends with someone if they see that person doing well or have something that the others want. It's like being in a pot with crawfish. If one sees the other trying to get over the top of the pot, what will they do? Pull his ass back in. A real friend doesn't do that. He will help you to get over because he knows that once you're over you will come back for him. And even if you don't come back for him, that person just wants to see you out.

After I'd been in the parish prison a few weeks, it was time to go to court. My mother and grandmother were at the hearing, waiting for me to arrive. I was permitted to speak to my family while I was there, and I took every minute I could with them.

My attorney, which the court had appointed, was a young White guy. He assured me that he could get me five years in prison and maybe even have that suspended. He said that since I had no prior adult record, I had a good chance at some probation. He had already spoken to my mother and grandmother and told them the same thing he told me. That was good news to both me and my family, as the charge carried ninety-nine years. We did not know then that it was all a big lie. He explained that I would have to plead guilty, and I agreed that I was willing to do that. Then he told me that the hearing was to determine what type of evidence they had against me and to see if I was willing to deal.

Everything lasted about an hour, and I did not have to say a thing. I did not understand what was going on. All that legal jargon was new to me.

Later, he came to the jail to tell me that he had spoken to the district attorney. He told me that the five years was a done deal, that the D. A. had already agreed to it. As it would turn out, he had not spoken to anyone.

I never gave much thought to my case. I trusted in my attorney to do as he had said. I really thought the worst I would get was the five years he had promised my family and me. I was in for a rude awakening. The attorneys appointed by the state to defend poor offenders are usually fresh out of law school, and they do not really have more than a basic knowledge of how that particular court functions. Maybe they have never actually tried a criminal case in their lives. They do try, but they do not have the experience needed. Often, their efforts are not enough.

My attorney did not seem to care about what happened to me. I represented just another case for him. Some lawyers try really hard for you, but others want to get you out of the way as quickly as possible. I had one like the latter. He just wanted to get on to his next case. I think about it now, and I am convinced that he knew absolutely nothing about my case, only my charge. Each time I saw him, he would tell me not to worry and that he already had everything taken care of. I do not believe he ever spoke to either the district attorney or to the judge.

A woman attorney named Bonnie Jackson came to see me about a week after I moved to Candy's tier. She explained that the other attorney had been removed from my case and that she would now be representing me. She informed me that I would be going to court the following day. I gave her the information that my previous attorney had told me, but she did not have the time to really check into my case before I went to court. She did not have any way of verifying anything I had told her. I was hurt and mad, and I had no idea what to do about that.

I called home to tell my mother and grandmother that I would be going to court the next morning. They told me that someone had already called to tell them, and they assured me they would be there for me.

My court appearance was entirely different from the last one. The judge asked me many questions and if anyone had promised me any deals. I told him that my first attorney had promised I would only get five years on probation. He acknowledged speaking with my original attorney about that. The judge said that because of the seriousness of the crime of armed robbery, and because I was so young, he felt I needed to learn a lesson. He told me to approach the bench.

When I reached him, he told me that because of what had happened he would not feel right unless he sentenced me to fifteen years at hard labor. Boy, was I shocked. I just knew that I would not get more than five years. I trusted what my original attorney had told me, and I stood there with a fifteen-year prison sentence before me. My family began to cry, and I did, too.

I asked Mrs. Jackson what was happening and why I was not sentenced to five years like I was promised. I did not understand everything the judge was saying, and I wanted some answers. She told me that I was not sentenced to five years because the deal was not in writing. I told her that he had told my mother and grandmother the same thing. She told me that if I didn't have it in writing, I didn't have anything. She looked at me and said she had done all she could for me.

When I arrived back at the jail, all I had on my mind was that I had fifteen years to serve some kind of way, and I had no idea where to begin. I was only nineteen years old. I tried to add all that time up in my head, but all I could come up with was that I would be dead before I finished the sentence.

I called home later that night to talk with my mother and grandmother. I tried to be strong for them on the phone, but they were worried nevertheless. We all cried even though we tried not to. I told them not to worry about me and that I would be all right.

I wanted a way out of this mess I was in. When I returned to the cell, I told Candy I wanted him to give me head. I know that I should not have done that, but at the time, I was lonely and confused. I thought that might help in some way. When he finished, we spent the rest of the night talking.

The next day, I felt terrible about what had happened, but I did not let him know that. I told myself that I would never do anything like that again because it was not my style. I kept remembering what happened to me when I first arrived at parish prison, and I was frightened of becoming like those guys.

I could not go outside or watch television without Candy being right there beside me. I did not like that, but I had to play the role or be marked by other guys there. I could not allow myself to appear soft or weak in any way. I had to just keep on playing the game. Candy would bring me all kinds of things to eat. He even persuaded one of the guards to bring him some weed. After about a month, I was to the point where I could barely stand it anymore, but I did not know how to get away from all those punks. Eventually, something happened to me that helped me be moved from them.

One night, while everyone was in the day room, Candy and I got into a fight with the old man of another homosexual there. The guards came to break it up and take everyone to the hole. Afterwards, me, and the guy we had been fighting, were moved to another cell. We were still on the same tier but further down the hall.

The following week, Candy was transferred to another prison. People just stayed at EBR Parish Prison until they were eventually transferred to a state facility like Angola, Hunt, or Dixon. I was glad to see him gone because I would no longer have to worry about being around him. But I missed him, too. I had no one else I could talk to. I still spoke with Mule on the yard, but we never really talked about anything important. I was lonely—again.

In **December of 1980**—after I'd been in the parish prison about nine months, a guard told me that I would be leaving for another prison. I asked if he knew where I would be going, but he did not. I already knew I would go to Hunt Correctional Center first to be evaluated. They would decide where I would be sent to serve the rest of my sentence.

When that morning came, I was nervous as hell. I had no idea what I was facing. They loaded all of us on the bus in handcuffs and shackles. The trip from EBR Parish Prison to Hunt lasted about thirty minutes. Along the way, I watched the people going about their daily activities outside my window, and I hoped I would one day be able to return to that world. I had heard many stories of guys going in with only a few years and winding up with life sentences for killing someone for messing with them. I was terrified that it would happen to me.

When we finally arrived at Hunt, I was astonished at all the razor wire surrounding the compound. It looked like a German camp scene from an old Second World War movie. There were double ten-foot-high, chain-link fences with a ten-foot span between them. The span was filled with roll upon roll of razor wire, and another roll had been strung along the top of each fence.

Once inside, there were about six big holding cells—three on each side, with a booth in the middle where the guards were. They told us to walk into these two big holding cells directly in front of us.

About an hour later, one of the guards came back to tell us that they would be calling our names to get a haircut and shave. When they called me, I walked up to the front of the cell, and the guard opened the door with his keys. I remember thinking about how much I hated the sound of those big keys clinging together and making that irritating noise. You never get used to that noise, like a set of regular keys six times bigger banging together. It just goes right through you, that ringing sound lingering in the soundwaves for a minute or two. It was just a really weird feeling, and you just know you're in prison.

He led me down the hallway past the cell where guys were talking loud and looking at me. Who knows what they were thinking as they watched me passing them. I was scared because I never liked to be around a lot of people anyway. When we got to the end of the hallway, there was a chair to sit in and a Black guy there to cut our hair. No style or anything like that, he just cut it down really low, and if we had hair on our face, he shaved that off also. I hadn't even started to grow hair on my face at that time. My face was as smooth as a baby's butt.

After everyone got their hair cut, they told us that we would be going to take a shower after they sprayed us with some kind of stuff to kill bugs and lice and other types of germs we may have been carrying. We went to the shower area where five guys went at a time. This was a humiliating thing to go through, but most of the younger guys didn't seem to think much of it. The guard made us spin around when we were naked to put the stuff on us. It smelled bad as hell, like Decon Roach Spray. Even after I took my shower, I could still smell the lingering scent of the spray. It stayed on me for a day or two.

They gave us prison blues to put on—a blue shirt, a pair of state blue jeans, and a pair of flat tennis shoes, no arch just rubber and canvas.

We were lined up to go to some rooms to be classified, which would decide what prisons we would be going to in the next few weeks. Once we got to the classrooms, we took a number of tests. We had to take an IQ test and some other ones. I did some of them, and some I just didn't do. I left them blank.

On Sunday nights, the guard would come to the front of the dorm and tell us to turn the TV down so we could hear him talk. He would have a list of the people who would be leaving the next morning to different prisons throughout the state. Everyone was a little jumpy on those nights. Sometimes, the guard would tell us what prison we would be going to and sometimes he would make the guys sweat. I was worried about where they would put me.

No one wanted to go to Louisiana State Penitentiary in Angola, because of everything they had heard about the place. Like about guards killing inmates and guards having sex with inmates. Guys killing over their homosexual partners. Guys having sex with real women when they were not supposed to. How they liked to kill people on executions. I was hoping like hell that I would never go there.

CHAPTER 9

I N **FEBRUARY 1981**—about eight weeks after I was sent to Hunt—my name was on the list of those leaving Monday morning to go to another prison. I had written a letter to the warden asking if I could stay at Hunt so my mother and grandmother could visit me. Wade was too far for them to go. But they didn't let me stay.

I would be leaving at 6:00 a.m. for Wade Correctional Center near Homer, Louisiana.

That morning, the guards let us go to the bathroom. Then, we were all cuffed, put in leg irons, and walked to the waiting bus. It was like a school bus, but painted white, with bars on the outside of the windows all the way around. The words "Prison Bus" were written on both sides of it. There was two armed guards in the bus to make sure no one tried to escape. It was still dark out, and you could see a half-moon up in the sky. It was pretty to look at. I knew it looked better from the other side of the fence in the free world.

It's funny how I was thinking of everything my mother and grandmother used to try to tell me, but I would never listen to them. Like if I didn't stop cutting school or stealing that I would get myself into trouble or something. Lying to them about the things that I had been doing. Stealing from work. All of that and more came to mind. Now I could see how right they were in what they were saying to me.

Even when they were saying those things to me, to tell the truth, I knew they were right, but I didn't want to listen to them. In my mind, they were old, and I felt I knew more than they did.

But I really didn't. I wanted to do things my way and show them that they didn't know what they were talking about. But they were still at home doing what they wanted, and I was on my way to prison for being a fool. That wasn't on my mother or my grandmother, but on me. I had to deal with that on my own. I always wanted to make something out of myself, not only for my mother, but for myself. I wanted my mother to be proud of me. But I always messed up somehow. On the bus ride to Wade, I was thinking about everything that had happened to me the past year.

I could see in my mind Lorraine and her family sitting around in their living room laughing at how big of a fool I was. I know that they must have seen me coming from a mile away. That's how green I was at the time. I really wanted to help her and her family out, but I went about it in all of the wrong ways.

Our bus stopped at a red light. There were a lot of cars going here and there. People were going to work, school, maybe shopping, and who knows where else. There was a lady sitting in a car next to the prison bus. She turned and looked at the prison bus and then kind of frowned when she saw me looking at her. I was wondering what she was thinking. Was she calling us animals in her mind, or was she saying to herself, *Well, there goes some more Black guys who have messed up their lives*. I was hurting inside and wishing that I was dead. I was wishing that my birth mother wouldn't have let me come into this world.

I had no idea that the trip would take most of the day. I had never seen so much woods and swamps before in my life. The countryside was really beautiful to me. It was a nice day out—the sun shining bright, the trees looking pretty with the moss on them, and a swamp here and there. There were fields of cows and rows and rows of plants in some places. When we passed water, it looked beautiful with the sun shining over it. I couldn't smell anything because the windows of the bus were all rolled up. I wished I could have seen it from a car instead of a prison bus.

It was about 5:00 p.m. when we got to the prison. Wade Correctional Center didn't look at all like a prison. From the outside, it looked like a school to me.

The dorm I was assigned to had two sides and a booth in the front where guards were stationed. There was a small bathroom in front of the control table. The control table had the buttons that opened the sliding glass door that led into the dorm. While we were at the door, I could see a few guys walking around and others talking. A couple of guys in the front of the dorm looked at us waiting to come in.

All of the dorm walls were painted white. To the left of the desk was the TV area with chairs and sofas to sit on. Behind the desk where the guard sat was a coffee pot, a water pot for hot water, and an ice chest. The dorm was big and open where the guard could see everything that went on. There were five rows of beds, fifteen beds to a row. Two rows along the side of both walls and three rows in the middle of the room. Each bed had two lockers at the foot where a person could put his things. Near the back door of the dorm were two big picture windows where you could look outside and see the guard tower about fifty feet away. Beyond the tower, you could see part of the road that led to the prison.

The dorm I was in was where kitchen workers slept. There were about thirty-five people inside. I was in the first dorm along the walkway. The other guys who came with me went on down to the next dorm.

Everyone was checking me out, and I was checking them out, too. I was scared, but I tried not to show it. I would guess that they knew anyway. The bed that they assigned me to was in the middle aisle, close to the front, about four beds from the freeman's desk where he could see me good. I was glad of that, even though I kept this to myself. The bed to my left had no one in it. The one to my right had a big guy who worked in the kitchen.

He was lying down listening to his radio, which had an eight-track tape player on the side of it. While I was making my bed, he asked where I was from and my name. After I told him, he said that he lived in Baton Rouge for a while before moving to Texas. As we talked, I learned that we both knew some of the same people. He asked if was it my first time being locked up, and I said it was. His nickname was Baton Rouge. He was a tall guy with a stocky build with short hair and a scar under his left eye. He was doing time for armed robbery, but he was short to go home—maybe six months left.

He said they would put me in the kitchen to work because they needed more people. I found out that the prison hadn't been open longer than two weeks and that he had come to the prison on the first load. I had come in on the second load. He said that this was good because there were all types of jobs an inmate could get before the prison became full with inmates.

Most of the people who were there by the time I arrived were from Monroe, Shreveport, and other areas in North Louisiana. He said that there were only a few guys from Baton Rouge. One of them was a young man who everyone called Shot Book because he liked sex magazines. He often stashed one somewhere in one of the bathrooms. Then throughout the days he worked, he would make his way to the bathroom to get with his date in a book. He was a pretty cool young guy, but he had a get-over attitude.

Shot Book was doing time for stealing cars and had about ten years to serve. Later, Shot Book, Baton Rouge, and I starting kicking it—hanging out together—when we were off. We would work out with the weights and play ball in the gym. We were even on the prison football team together.

My mother and grandmother told me that they would mail me some money that week so I could get the things I needed. Even in prison, you need money to make it. If you can't get your own things with financial help from friends or relatives, then you will begin looking for ways to get them, like exchange something for sex. At least Wade had a plasma center where you could give blood twice a week and get paid nine dollars and fifty cents each time. That helped some.

The next day, I was told that I would be put in the kitchen to work. After leaving the office, I was able to walk around the place and look around.

The gym was across from the kitchen. There were four pool tables in the gym and a ping-pong table. A boxing ring was set up in there also. The gym was nice. There was a large room where they would put the weights during the winter months. I spent a lot of time learning how to work out the right way. The gym had two hobby shops in it where inmates could make things. They made all kinds of stuff—like belts, clocks, chairs, tables, purses, wallets, little ships that you put on a table or shelf. They painted pictures, too.

Next to the kitchen was the inmate library and school. Across the walkway was the classification office. Behind the gym was a big field to play football and baseball, and there were basketball courts on each side.

We always had to stay ten feet away from the fence, or the guards would think someone was trying to escape. There was a tower at both ends of the fence and a road that went all the way around the place in a circle.

After a few weeks, I noticed that the guy in bed fifteen was looking at me all the time. His name was Larry—he had said a few words to me here and there. He worked in the kitchen, too. He was from a small town called Farmville in Louisiana.

Every time I went to the shower, Larry would sit on the first toilet that faced the shower at an angle where he could see me. I acted like I didn't know what was going on, but he was looking at my butt. I didn't say anything because I was scared. He would leave before I got out of the shower. This went on for about a week. It really was getting to me. I knew something was going to have to be done. I knew sooner or later he would try to do more because it always turned out that way.

One Saturday afternoon, I played basketball outside with a few other guys. When the game was over, I went to my bunk to get my shower things out. As I looked around the dorm, there were a few guys in the TV room and a few sitting on their bunks reading books. Well, I looked in the TV room again, and I saw Larry. When he saw me looking at him, he turned his head like he didn't see me. When he saw me go into the shower area, he went and got his things, too. I put my things on the rack and got into the shower. He came in behind me. While I was taking my shower, he was across from me showering also. He put soap on himself and started masturbating a little to get an erection. I acted as if I didn't see him. I finished showering and left.

I knew I had to do something to put an end to this or it would go on. I put on my pants and a T-shirt. I didn't put on any tennis shoes because he would have known I was coming for him. When you put on tennis shoes at a time you wouldn't normally wear them, everyone knew something was up.

Instead, I kept my shower shoes on. I took the two locks off my lockers and put them in a sock. This was something I learned during my incarceration in parish prison. I stuffed the sock in my pocket, grabbed my toothpaste, and went back into the bathroom. On my way in, I met him coming out. Larry went to his bed to get dressed. I went to the first sink and mirror. From there, I could see his bed through the glass booth where the guard was. The guard who was stationed in the dorm went inside the booth where the other freeman was so he could use the bathroom. Larry had his back to the bathroom while looking in his locker. I stepped out of my shower shoes. I took the sock out of my pocket. I walked up behind him and hit him hard as I could on side of his face. When he turned around, I kept on hitting him.

Everyone watched us. He tried to grab me, and I kept hitting him. I don't know how I did it, but somehow, I threw him across the bed. He was almost a foot taller than me. By the time the two freemen and lieutenant ran in to stop us, we were wrestling. After they pulled us apart, I started laughing at him. They handcuffed us both and took us to the cellblock one at a time. We stayed in the block the whole weekend until Monday morning. On Monday, we both went to the prison's Discipline Board court. The guard wrote us up for aggravated fighting.

That was my first time going to D.B. court, but it would not be my last. There were three people in small rooms behind a desk, reading my write-up on a pink sheet of paper. Whenever an inmate got into trouble, the guard would write him up and lock him in the cellblock until there was a D.B. court board to hear what had happened.

The board could take away different things from you, like visits, store privileges, yard, or good time. Good time meant you would do weeks or months less than the sentence you got if you behaved yourself in prison.

One of the men asked me how I pleaded and asked what happened. I told him that Larry came into the bathroom every time I went to take a shower and that he would look at my butt. I made it clear to the man that I wasn't a punk. After that, I told him what happened in the shower that past Saturday night. They gave us ten days in the cellblock. I would have gotten out of those ten days if I hadn't used the locks. The only thing about doing the ten days in the cellblock was that you couldn't have anything in there with you. During the summer, it was okay because it would be hot. During the winter, you only had two sheets and one thin blanket. You had to wear a white jumpsuit. Most of the time, you slept your time away for ten days and did a lot of thinking. My thoughts were about if Larry would try to get me back for what I had done to him.

I didn't lose my job because of that fight with Larry. I was glad because I worked two days on and two days off. I liked both the off-days and working in the kitchen because I could eat like I wanted to. One of the men who worked in the kitchen was a pretty cool guy. At that time, there were no prison guards in there to watch us work. It was almost like going to work on the streets.

When I got out of the cellblock, Baton Rouge was the first person I saw. He started laughing when he saw me coming.

"Damn, what's so funny?" I asked and began laughing also.

"You can really swing those locks, huh?" he said. He asked me what it was all about, and I ran it down to him.

Baton Rouge said, "Damn, that's fucked up, because Larry had never tried that before."

When Larry got to the kitchen, Baton Rouge put him in check and told him that if he ever did that again, he would get on his ass.

I was glad he did this, but I didn't say it to anyone because I didn't want Baton Rouge or the others to think I was weak. In reality, I was. The only reason I did what I did was because I was scared and didn't want the other guys to think I was funny or something. But, really, that didn't matter because, to some guys, half the fun is making another guy out to be a punk.

I had to do what I did to Larry so people wouldn't get at me. If I wanted to look rough and tough, that's what I had to do. Not just anyone would mess with that type of stuff. If you didn't find some way to look or act rough, then you would be easy pickings for someone to jump on you all the time, beat your ass, and take whatever you had that they wanted—your money for the store, jeans, shoes, tapes, your body. I was thinking that I didn't want these guys to be fucking with me in no form, so I would fuck with others to keep them away from me. I didn't want what happened to me in parish prison to happen again.

CHAPTER 10

HAD TWO MORE homeboys who came to Wade. One of them I knew from the parish jail. They used to call him Coco. He was from South Baton Rouge from a neighborhood called The Bottoms. That was a pretty wild side of town where all type of things go on. Coco was a street-smart person who had been out there for a while. He had a friend named Giles who became a good friend of mine. He and Coco met in the parish jail also. When they came, they were classified in the same dorm I was in.

In 1983, a dude in my dorm named Frog got a letter from a friend he knew at Hunt. The guy told Frog that someone he'd been messing with was being sent to Wade. Herman was his name.

As it turns out, someone else knew him, too. Bread knew Herman from the streets. Bread had done time before, and he was into the punk game.

One evening, after the work lines had come in, we all were on the yard. Coco, Giles, Bread, and me were talking while looking at some guys playing a baseball game on the big field. We sat on a picnic table in front of our dorm.

"Felt, there is this boy that I know from the streets," Bread said. "He just came last night. He's cool, and he's like that."

I laughed and said, "Like what, bro?"

"You know, he's gay, and he wants someone to be up under. He's in the dorm now. I'm going to tell him to come out here with us," Bread said. "You can talk with him if you want to. But he got game and knows how to make money for his man."

Coco said, "Well, if Felt don't want to hook up with him, I will because I need someone to make me some money."

We all laughed at what he said.

Bread left to go get Herman out of the dorm. When they came out, Herman had long hair and had it corn-rolled with little white rubbers in it, just as a real girl would have her hair done. He was about my height and weight, maybe an inch or two taller but not much. He had some blue short pants on that were too tight for him and a T-shirt that was tied in a knot in the front so half of his stomach was showing.

Bread told him all of our names, and he came and stood by me and started talking about how far all of us was from home. Herman was down for breaking into someone's house while they were home. He had thirteen flat years to do, which meant he had to serve every day of it. We talked about prison life and what it had been like for the both of us.

Frog was playing baseball and kept looking our way while he was playing. At first, I thought nothing about it at all. Bread said we should all go for a walk around the compound, and we did. We talked about all kinds of things and laughed along the way. Bread decided he and Coco were going to hang around the gym for a while, and Giles went back to our dorm for something. That left Herman and me still walking the yard.

I guess about this time the baseball game was coming to an end. They were getting everything together to take back to the gym before the yard closed down for the evening. The dorms on the right side were on a little hill and behind it was a picnic table.

We both sat down and were talking when Frog walked up. "What's happening?" I said. "Did J.C. need me for something?"

"No, everything's cool on that end," Frog said. "But I see you have met Herman."

"Yes, I met him."

"Herman, you know my homeboy at Hunt wrote me and told me that you were coming up here, and that I should get you," Frog said. "But I see you are trying to get cool with Lil' Felt. He's my friend, and I don't want us to fall out or nothing over you."

From that point on, it was understood that Herman was mine.

I only wanted to see how he would make money for me and himself. But Herman was different. He had been in and out of LTI [a facility for juvenile offenders] and was doing the punk thing there also. All by choice, from what I had heard from the guys who had done time with him before.

For the first few months, Herman was playing by the rules of the game. I wasn't having any kind of trouble out of him. But Frog had told me that, at Hunt, Herman liked to mess around with young White guys because he could turn them out. Frog said that he was known for doing that and to be careful that he never tried anything out of that way with me.

One night, I asked Herman to tell me about this. Herman said that, for some reason, White guys in prison liked to mess around with Black punks. And most

Black guys liked White punks. I found that kind of funny, as a lot of guys do that on the streets. Herman added that White guys paid him better.

I said, "Well, that's cool, but what about the sex part?"

Herman said, "Well, Feltus, it's like this. If I see a young White guy that wants to mess around with me, I may let him have his fun for a while then I tell him that I want to have some fun also. Some won't go that far and some will. And if that happens you will just have two hos, and I will be able to get my rocks off also."

Herman was a big fan of basketball and played for the dorm team and the prison team that played outside guests. There was this Black guy named Alan, and Alan was the captain of the team and had pull with the other guys to get whoever on the team that he wanted to. Alan was an older guy but looked pretty young. He hung out with a few guys from his hometown and a young guy named Charlie. Charlie was about twenty-one years old. And looked really good. Herman really liked this young guy and tried to get next to him. Because he felt that he could turn Charlie out for himself. This was going on in early 1985.

So, he had sex with Alan to get on Charlie's team. From time to time, Alan would buy Herman stuff from the store. Herman felt that I would never find out about this. But I found out. I went off and was mad as hell over it. I went to the hobby shop one evening to steal a screwdriver. I made a point on the end of it that was sharp. I went to Alan's dorm and had someone call for him to come to the door. Once he came to the door, I asked him to come take a walk with me, that I had something for him. He told me to wait for a minute while he went and put on a shirt.

I had the screwdriver in the waist of my pants and had my shirt over it. We walked behind his dorm, and I started asking him what was the deal with him and Herman and Charlie.

"Look, man, don't be mad with me because Herman wanted to do that," Alan said. "He came to me with that deal to get on the team."

Then I said for him to tell me the rest, and I pulled out the screwdriver and pointed it at him. I wanted to scare him and let him know that I wasn't to be crossed or fucked with.

He backed up and was leaning next to the wall. "Man, don't do nothing crazy. We can work this all out. You need to be talking to Herman and working it out with him."

"Man, I don't disrespect anyone, and I'm not going to have anyone doing it to me," I said. I left him standing up there. At that time, I wasn't worried and didn't care if he had tried something when my back was to him. From that point on, I watched him just in case so he wouldn't catch me on the blind side. I didn't go straight to Herman, because I had something else in mind that would scare him to death.

Later that night, which was a Saturday, we were in the room looking at the TV. "Herman, I want to get my rocks off tonight. What's up?" I asked.

"Hold up. Let me go get it set up," he said.

Herman went to my bunk, which was against a wall. He pulled the blanket and sheet down so it would hang down to the floor where you couldn't see under the bed. Then he asked the guy who slept in the bunk next to me if he would be the lookout later once the lights went out.

"Yeah, sure," the guy said.

The lights went off at 10:30 p.m., but we could stay up as long as we wanted to on Friday and Saturday nights. So, after the lights went out and the freeman made his rounds, and went back to his desk, Mark went up there to talk with him, and Herman went and got under my bunk. Then I came out of the TV room and got under the bed also.

"What do you want me to do?" Herman asked.

I told him to turn around with his back to me. I had the screwdriver with me, and I put the screwdriver to his throat.

"Baby, what're you doing?" he said. He was shocked and scared.

"Shut the hell up," I said. "You've been lying to me and messing around behind my back. Now, don't lie to me because I know all about it. Now, I want the truth from you or you won't be able to get up from under this bed."

He started crying and told me what he had been doing. He admitted that he had sex with Alan behind my back.

"Well, why you couldn't tell me this from the start?" I asked. "If you ever do this again, I will kill you dead. Don't play with me or my feelings."

Then I made him tell me about Charlie and his plans, but I felt that he was still leaving something out. I pushed the screwdriver into his skin a little hard, and he really thought that I was going to kill him. He was begging and pleading with me. I felt in control of things at that point. Then I moved the screwdriver from his neck and told him to get from under the bed. I don't know if I really would have hurt him with the screwdriver. Maybe if he tried to fight me back. He moved, and then I rolled from under it and went back into the TV room.

Herman sat on my bed for a while just looking around the dorm. Some guys were sitting on their beds talking, and some were in the front playing cards and looking at the TV. I sat in the last row of seats in the back next to the wall. Herman came to where I was sitting and sat next to me. I kept looking at the TV for about an hour, then I got up and went to bed and still didn't say a word to him. After I got in my bunk about ten minutes later, he went to bed also.

I had gotten a write-up for cussing out one of the guards the night before when he told me I was talking too loud. After I got through cleaning the bathroom and shower, I had to be at the little prison court for 9:00 a.m.

The only problem was that J.C. had left for the gym early that morning and for some reason I thought that the screwdriver would be safe under my blanket. I didn't give it to him to put in the hobby shop. Boy, that was crazy to do. But I didn't feel that they would do much about the write-up. I plead guilty on the write-up, and the major gave me ten days in the hole. Damn, I was shocked because I didn't think I would get that. Then I thought about when they called the dorm to tell them to pack my stuff up and put it in storage. The guard would be there with the orderly that would be packing my stuff up. Then they would take the blankets and sheets off of the bed to put them into my lockers. The screwdriver would be sure to fall out.

About an hour later, I was given another write-up for the screwdriver. I went to court that next week for it, and they say that I would be staying in the cellblock for a while and would be sent to Angola. I believe they told me that to scare me, but I stayed in the cellblock for a while. And in that time, Herman was very much free to do whatever he wanted to do. He moved out of my dorm and into H-2-B—the dorm that Charlie was in. David [a White guy with a life sentence in love with Herman] had friends who could get me stuff on the cellblock. Herman would use them to get me stamps and other things. A guy who cleaned the cellblock and protective custody would usually do it.

I was sent to H-1-A dorm when I got out. There was six homosexuals in there. I thought, *Why put me there? I'm tired of being around that shit*. But I was glad to get out of the cellblock. Everyone was at work the day I went to the new dorm. One of the dorm orderlies called Big Cat saw me and got Herman out of the kitchen to let him know I was out. I went outside with Herman to walk the yard.

The next morning, Big Cat woke me up at 5:30 am so I could wash up and eat before I went to [my new work assignment in] the field. I got my work gloves from my locker and put on an old sweatshirt, faded jeans, and a baseball cap.

Herman was outside when the guards opened the door for chow. He was off that day, so we ate breakfast together. I got my work stuff from my dorm. Then Herman and I sat on a picnic table where I could see the sally port gate where I'd go to leave for the field.

Herman gave me three joints. I said, "Well, where did you get this from?"

"Don't worry about that, as long as I take care of my man," he told me.

"Well, I like that," I said.

He told me that one of his brothers had been shot by a so-called friend over some money. Man, I knew it was hell on him. I hugged him and told him to hang in there for me. I said he could call my grandmother and mother if he wanted to. I never told them that he was gay. But they liked him as a person and would talk to him when he called. Really, I felt sorry for him and wondered why his family was dying off that way. But it's like that for a lot of Black families living in the ghetto.

After I saw all the other inmates gathering at the gate, we walked over there so I could hear my name when the guard at the gate called it. I was in the last group to go out.

It was a nice day out, a few clouds in the sky and a cool morning. Just a little wind blowing. There were four guards on horseback, one on each side and one on each end with shotguns in hand. They led us around to the front of the prison through the parking lot right out into the street.

When we came into the street, we turned to the left to walk down the long road. We walked every bit of five miles before we got to the work site. We went over hills and dirt roads and little water holes that I know the animals used to drink from. It really looked so beautiful out there.

Once we made it to the work site, the tools and water coolers were already there.

Two trustees brought it on a big truck that a guard drove. The trustees would go into town with a freeman whenever the prison needed feed for the horses or something else.

I was thinking to myself how good it would be to make trustee. To leave all the chaos behind for a while and get a tease of the real world again. I made up my mind that I wanted to work toward that. I chose a sling blade to work with and got right in the middle where the freeman running the line could see me work. I worked my butt off until they called break time. I was having fun. Work never made me mad. I always liked to work.

By the time they called the second break, this other guy and me had a very big part of the job done. The guard was so impressed with what we had done that he came over to talk with us.

He said, "Damn, you two guys are damn good workers. If you keep that up, well, you two will make trustees in no time. Because they are always looking for good work men."

I liked that. I made up my mind that every day would be just the same.

We worked until they called "head line," which meant work was over for that morning. Everyone had to line up in twos so the guard running the line could count us before we started back towards the prison. For some reason, the walk back always seemed to be longer than the one going to the site.

CHAPTER 11

A TURNING POINT FOR me came early in the **summer of 1985**. I went through something that was a reality check for me. It made me stop dead in my tracks.

It was on a Saturday night when I called home to talk with my grandmother and my mother. I dialed the number, and it rang about three or four times before anyone answered it. I heard the phone pick up, but no one said anything.

"Hello, Mama Henrietta?" I said.

"I'm here," my grandmother said.

"Let me talk to my mother."

She didn't say nothing.

"Is she there?" I asked.

"No." Then she said, "Look, I have something to tell you."

I was thinking that maybe she was in the hospital again having trouble with her leg. But, was I ever wrong.

"Willie Mae died last week," she said.

Boy, I remember those words cutting through me like a knife. It seems that everything within me and out went numb. I dropped the phone and started screaming, "No! No! No!" I remember crying, and I guess everyone in the dorm must have turned around to see what was going on.

Herman ran over to where I was and asked me what was wrong. I pointed at the phone, and I ran outside. I started walking the yard, crying and trying to understand what was happening to me. As soon as I turned the corner, I saw a guy named J.C. having a meeting with the guys on his baseball team. J.C. was like a father to me, and I trusted him. I ran up to him and hugged him. He asked me what was wrong.

I told him my mother had just died. He hugged me back and told the guys that was the end of the meeting. We sat right there on the ground and talked, and I cried until I couldn't cry anymore. I took the news really hard. Nothing would have ever prepared me for the death of my mother. All that I could think of was that I was locked up, not able to be there for my grandmother when she needed me the most. Then Herman came where J.C. and I were talking. He just looked at me. I knew that he knew what I was feeling inside. He told me that my grandmother said for me to call her back. J.C. told me to go and do it. So, I did. I left him and Herman behind the dorm talking.

When I got back to the dorm, everyone was just looking at me. Some knew and some didn't. They were just looking on. I couldn't stop crying over it. When I called my grandmother back, she was crying. We both were letting it out when I asked what happened. She told me everything—plus something else that I couldn't understand at all.

Mama Henrietta told the story with a slow and shaking voice. The week before, Mamee had been doing okay, it seemed. That weekend I called, she had been sitting out in the yard with my grandmother and another friend. It was a pretty summer evening. I imagined that there was a little wind blowing, that the evenings are always a little cooler. They were sitting there talking, and my mother said something out of the normal.

"This may be my last time out here with you all like this," Mamee said.

My grandmother told her not to talk like that. Then on Sunday, my mother got up and fixed their meal. Mamee said that she wanted to fix my grandmother's meal for the last time.

Mama Henrietta said, "Stop talking like that. You're not going anywhere."

"I'm getting ready to go and see God," Mamee told her.

My grandmother didn't know what to think, so she didn't say anything else about it. Monday morning, when my grandmother got up, she went to check on my mother. Mamee was lying in the bed. She told my grandmother that she wanted a little cold drink in her glass. My grandmother got it for her and sat down next to her on the bed and talked.

Mamee said to her, "I love you, and I love Junior, too. But when I'm gone, I don't want you to tell him until everything is over with. I love him, and I don't want those people to bring him home with all of those chains on him."

"That was her last wish, so I honored it," Mama Henrietta said. "If you hadn't called when you did, I was getting ready to call up there so they could let you know."

Then my grandmother told me that Mamee said that she hoped I did right once I was home. Mamee said how much she loved Mama Henrietta again and died in her arms.

After hearing all of this, I told my grandmother that I couldn't talk anymore about it. Before I hung up, my grandmother said that when I called, they were just coming back from laying her body to rest in the ground. It was **June 3, 1985**. My mother had died on May 28.

I just couldn't believe that all of this was happening and that my mother was dead. It was so unreal to me. My mind and heart just couldn't process everything. I walked out of the dorm again and walked the yard crying and looking up into the sky asking God, *Why? Why does everything have to happen to me?* It was late in the evening, and they would be blowing the yard soon. I didn't know what I wanted to do. But I knew that I didn't want to stay in that dorm that night.

Herman saw me and came to walk with me. He asked if I wanted to talk about it. I said, "It's hard to deal with right now, and I don't want to stay in the dorm tonight. I'm going to go to the security office and ask the lieutenant to lock me up for a few days so I won't do nothing crazy like trying to run away or nothing. Or fighting because someone said the wrong thing to me." I mean, I was in prison, and my mother was gone and laid to rest, and I had just found out about it.

It was too much to deal with at one time, plus knowing my grandmother was at home going through her own hell by losing her only daughter. I really couldn't understand why God had to take her away from me. I loved her so much, and I did want a chance to show her that I could live a much better life once I got home.

The lieutenant at the security office wrote a note for the major letting him know what was going on and left it on his desk for him. He walked me to the cellblock and left word with the guards that I could use the phone when need be. He said if I needed anything to just let him know. A guard walked me on to my cell. Later, they brought me sheets, pillowcases, and a blanket. I fixed my bed and just lay there looking up at the ceiling.

The ceiling was painted white. It was like I was looking at a movie on the big screen about my life. I could see and replay different events from my past that took place with my mother and myself.

I remembered a time when she wanted me to part her hair and put grease in it for her. We were laughing and talking to each other. She said, "You can come to me for anything and tell me anything. I will listen to you. I love you, and I just want you to make me proud of you."

I couldn't help but replay all the times that she worked her butt off trying to take care of us while going through all kinds of hell with my daddy. She was a strong Black lady. And I knew that she got that from Mama Henrietta.

When I talked to my grandmother, she said, "I never would have thought that I would outlive your mother. I always thought that I would leave her here."

But I guess God had his reasons for letting it happen the way that it did. I may never understand it really until I see God and ask him about that myself.

I got down and prayed and asked God to let me see my mother in a vision or just let her come to me so I can say my goodbye to her. But for whatever reason, He didn't let it happen. I got back into my bunk and cried myself to sleep.

The next morning, after they fed us, one of the sergeants let me call my grandmother. She told me how nice the funeral was with a lot of flowers and singing. I was still mad, and I told her that I should have been there.

"If anything ever happens to you," I said, "don't tell anyone that you don't want me to be there, because I have a right to come."

She said that she wouldn't.

All I could do was think about my mother and what I had lost from her not being in my life anymore. I even wished that I was dead so I could be with her because I missed her just that much. I felt that I had let her down as her son by getting into things that kept her worried about me. At the time, I felt that I didn't have any self-worth and that I was better off dead. My Mamee died knowing I was in prison and that so far, I had made a mess of my life. What was I going to do about it now?

It came to me clear as day. Every time we'd talk, she'd say she loved me and wanted me to make something of my life, for me to finish school and make her proud. I said to myself, *That's what I'm going to do. Make you proud of me and proud that you adopted me, Mamee. I love you, and I'm going to finish school and get myself together. I know that you loved me and always wanted what was best for me. Most of the time, I let you down, but I'm going to change all of that.*

I had about five years left to serve, and I was going to make the most of it.

It was around this time I [began] working as a trustee [out in the field]. J.C. had a talk with me about doing better than I was. He always told me that I needed to read more and that I should get back in school. J.C. wanted me to make it on the streets because he said I was like a son to him. I wasn't trying to hear that, because me and school just didn't cut it. I was too slow, and I couldn't stay focused on what was going on long enough to learn it. "Man, I been down five years now," I said. "And I got five more to go."

"Those next five will go just as fast as the first five went. You got to start getting yourself ready in some way," he said.

"Well, why are you still coming to prison? You're in your forties, and you're not getting any younger yourself."

J.C. told me that he liked the fast money. When he was coming up during the 1960s and 1970s, a lot of young, inner-city Black males didn't have the right mindset after going through the Civil Rights Era and the Black Panthers Movement. There was a lot of bitterness toward Whites, and there weren't that many jobs for Blacks. So, if you had a family or bills, you had to do something to make it.

"It's not like that today, though," J.C. said. "Young people have everything laid out for them, and they and you still don't want to do the right thing."

Standing there listening to J.C., I knew he was right.

J.C. was good to talk with. He always got me to think about the real deal of life.

I thought, since my first few years at Wade, I had seen a lot of guys go and come back. I wondered why that was. At first, I couldn't understand it. But as time went on, it came to me, They weren't ready, and they weren't equipped to face life outside of prison.

CHAPTER 12

A FEW MONTHS AFTER my mother died, Herman was shipped to Dixon Correctional Center in Jackson, LA. That's where Giles and Coco were. After he left, I slowed down a lot.

Herman wrote off and on, but it was a blessing for Herman to be gone. I had more time to get myself together and try to get a plan of action about what I really wanted to do while I was in prison, and once I was out.

When I finally got back in school, it took me much longer than the nine months of classes to finish. In fact, it took me a while to finally get that diploma—almost six years.

I couldn't get back into school until sometime in 1988. It was hard for me because I was slow, and it seemed that I would never get math right. I was faced with the same things that I was faced with on the streets. I found it hard to hold on to whatever I learned. Other people around me weren't slow like that, and I would be mad with myself. I thought that I was dumb or something.

The first time I took a ninety-days test I did well in everything but math. It was hard for me to get past fractions at first. Once I left fractions, I was lost, but I liked English and did well there. That was my best class. It was hard, too, but I liked it.

I found out that I had not passed and that I would have to take it over again in ninety days. I really did not think that I would ever pass that test. I started getting help from a guy in the dorm, and my math teacher was a very nice, old White lady that really tried to help me because she saw that I was trying. She had not seen that from me before.

The last time I took the test, it was a little late coming back. I looked at the board every day to see if the grades were up yet. To my surprise, one evening, I stopped in the school to look at the board, and there was my name where the people were that had graduated. Man, I felt so damn good inside.

I felt that I had finally done something right for a change. It was a damn good feeling on the inside of myself, and I wanted it to stay there.

When I was two months short, time seemed to be moving so slow for me. It just was so hard to believe that I would be going home soon. June 27, 1990 was my date to go back into the free world. I could not wait to put all of this bullshit behind me.

The last month that I had left to serve, they had this program for short-timers. You only went twice. They would tell you that you could go to the unemployment office and get a check and some food stamps, and they could maybe find you a job. They showed you how to fill out the papers to get a job, but that was it.

As for teaching you to deal with the change from prison life to the real world, they did nothing. Living on the inside is one thing, but living on the outside is another. With life inside prison, you pretty much do what you're told to do. You don't have to pay bills or buy food or pay rent. Plus, in prison you are used to dealing with males all of the time. It's hard relating to people other than the guys that you hang out with all of the time.

They don't help you to deal with being around people again. That was my problem. I wasn't prepared to deal with relationships or nothing like that.

They did not help you to readjust, and I did not think that was right. I had been down more than ten years. They were about to throw me back out there with nothing. It is not easy for anyone, as I would soon find out.

I think that the last week of my stay at Wade was the longest ever. It was like a dream—I could not believe that I was about to go home after all of that time. I got my jeans pressed, and I had a nice shirt to wear and a new pair of tennis shoes that I had bought from a guy at the prison because they were the wrong size for him.

During that same week, I was talking with a guy, and we were talking about women. He said after ten years [on the inside], I would fall in love with the first woman that came along.

I said, "Man, I am not that bad off!" Then I told him, "Don't worry. I'm not coming back to prison ever. The only way that I will come back is if I have to kill someone that was messing with me and my grandmother."

"Well, in that case," he said, "I don't see you coming back because you are a good dude."

Grandma Henrietta Rowan and Feltus, around age 3

Feltus Taylor, Sr., Willie Mae Taylor, and Young Feltus

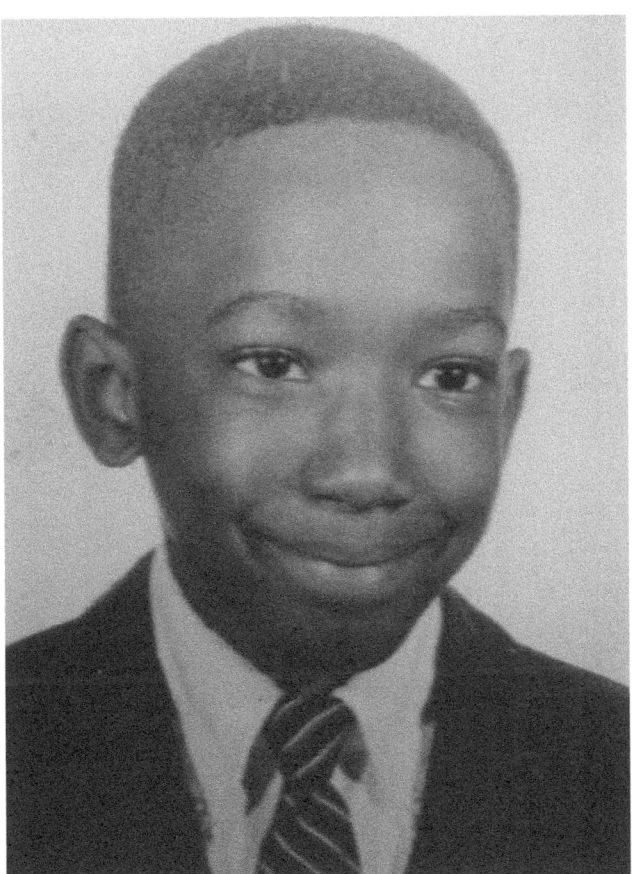

Feltus Elementary School Photo

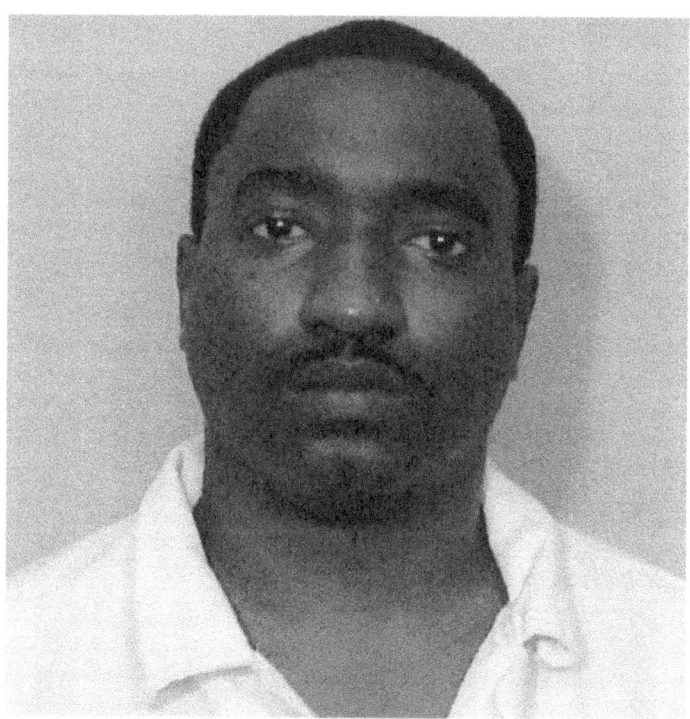

Feltus Police Booking Photo, 1991

"Mr. Smiles" Feltus on Death Row 1999

PART THREE

ON THE OUTSIDE
9 MONTHS

CHAPTER 13

"Things I need to do when I get out of here."

1 *Go see my mama's grave*
2 *Driver's licensing = Class D 22.00*
3 *Job*
4 *Help out at home with the bills*
5 *Get the car fix up like I want it until I get another one*
6 *Go to unemployment office and fill out the 1-9 card, Take <u>birth certificate</u>, <u>adoption papers</u>, <u>driver's license</u>.*
7 *Find out more about the TJTC or OJT Targeted Jobs Tax Credit 40% on the first $6000, 2400*
8 *Go to the Social Security office and try to get the S.S.I. benefits. Take I.D. card and discharge papers. Than go to the food stamp office and try to get food stamps and check.*
9 *The main thing is to take my time and do things slow and right. Know matter how hard things get just be cool and it will work out for you.*
10 *Go to Gym and workout hard to get in top shape and go win something. Pump that Iron hard and work hard and things will happen for me.*
11 *Help Mama Henrietta around the house. Take care of her to the end. Make something out of myself for them and me.*
12 *Help the old people and lil children. Do some good for other people.*

—*List handwritten one week before Feltus Taylor, Jr. left Wade Correctional Center*

JIM BOREN: NOW, I UNDERSTAND THAT CERTAIN SENTENCES PROVIDE FOR PAROLE. WHEN FELTUS WAS RELEASED FROM PRISON WAS HE ON A SYSTEM OF SUPERVISION AND SUPPORT PROVIDED BY THE DEPARTMENT OF CORRECTIONS?

C. PAUL PHELPS: NO. ARMED ROBBERY WAS NOT ELIGIBLE FOR PAROLE.

Q: AND SO, WHEN HE WAS RELEASED, HE WAS RELEASED WITHOUT ANY SUPERVISION, AUTHORITY, HELP, OR SUPPORT PROVIDED BY THE STATE?

A: BASICALLY, WHEN THE LEGISLATURE IN ITS INFINITE WISDOM MADE ARMED ROBBERY NOT ELIGIBLE FOR PAROLE, THEN YOU TOOK PEOPLE WHO COMMITTED ARMED ROBBERY, WHICH IS A VERY SERIOUS OFFENSE, AND JUST TURNED THEM LOOSE.

—Penalty Phase, Day 3: 112, January 25, 1992

C. PAUL PHELPS: THERE IS NO PARTICULAR PROGRAM THAT PREPARES YOU TO MOVE FROM, AT LEAST THERE CERTAINLY WASN'T IN 1988 WHEN I RETIRED FROM THE DEPARTMENT, TO ALLOW YOU TO MAKE ANY SORT OF TRANSITION FROM PRISON LIFE TO CIVILIAN LIFE WITH THE EXCEPTION OF WORK RELEASE. AND HE WAS, AS I READ THE RECORD, WAS NOT IN THE WORK RELEASE PROGRAM, THAT HE DISCHARGED DIRECTLY FROM WADE. HIS FIRST EXPERIENCE WITH CIVILIAN LIFE WAS AT THE BUS STATION.

—Penalty Phase, Day 3: 106–7, January 25, 1992

June 27, 1990

WHEN THE GUARD WOKE me up, I could not believe that the day for me going free was finally here. I showered, got dressed, and got my few little things ready to go. I signed out, and they gave me my bus ticket and my account money in cash. Boy, it felt good to feel money again.

Once we got to the bus station in Shreveport, the guard let me out and said, "Good luck, Feltus."

Man, I just stood in the city and looked around me. I had a big-ass smile on my face. I did not know a thing about Shreveport, but I guess that I was downtown because of all the tall buildings around the bus station. It was very pretty on that warm June morning. The sun was bright already, and it looked like it would be a very wonderful day for me. I think, even if it had been raining, it would still have been wonderful because I was going home.

I went inside, and everything seemed small because I was used to being in that big dorm for so long. When the guy came over the loudspeaker to say that the bus was there and what gate to go to, I went to the bathroom and then on to the gate. After getting on the bus, I went to a window seat so I could look out at the world. This young White lady asked me if the other seat was taken. She was pretty, sort of tall, and had brown hair to her shoulders and pretty green eyes. I guess she was about twenty-four or twenty-five years old. After I told her no, she sat next to me.

I did not say much to her. I just kept looking out of the window because I did not know what to say. I was used to talking with guys and not women. She started talking to me instead, asking me about myself and where I was going. I really did not know what to say at first, so I told her that I had just gotten out of prison and that I was going home. I thought that she would stop talking to me, but, to my surprise, she did not. She wanted to know what it was like and how long I was there for. I said to myself, *She must be crazy or something*, but she was just a cool person that did not judge me for my mistake that had landed me behind bars.

The bus must have stopped in every town between Shreveport and Baton Rouge because it was taking a long time to get home. I had to change buses twice. When I got on that last one, I knew that it would not stop anymore until it hit Baton Rouge. The trip was nice, and the view was wonderful. The land was so pretty. God really knew what he was doing when he made trees, swamps, and everything else in Louisiana. The day just seemed like a day for new beginnings to me. When we came to the Mississippi River Bridge that led over into Baton Rouge, I started to get excited.

Once the bus pulled up to the station, I saw my grandmother's car in the parking lot. I would know that car anywhere. I did not have to go into the bus station because as soon as I got off of the bus, the first person I saw was my sweet grandmother standing there with a big smile on her face. We hugged, and I kissed her, and we walked to the car. She was so happy to see me. She kept saying how good I looked and how much she missed me. She took the same route home that she always did when we were coming from downtown. Nothing had changed that much.

I still could not get over how everything seemed to be so much smaller than I had remembered it. When we came down North Street and turned onto North 37th Street, it looked the same as I had remembered it. There were a few houses missing that had been torn down, and the lots were empty with a little overgrown grass in them. It was a nice evening; a few people were walking on the street. I looked to see if it was anyone I knew.

Grandma Henrietta's house looked the same as always. We walked through the door of the little screened porch where my grandfather used to sit. We went on inside, and everything was just as I remembered it—even the smell of the house. It seemed smaller, like everything else. It was decorated the very same way it was when I left—pictures of family on the walls and pictures of me and different knickknacks out all over the place. She had put my diploma and my graduation picture up, too. There was the fresh scent of whatever perfume she would wear.

I could smell some food, of course. She gave me another big hug and a kiss and told me how good it felt to have me home again.

I felt the joy that she felt. I was glad to be home. No more listening to the guards hollering "work call" or "chow call" or "clear the yards." I could stay outside all night if I wanted to.

I wasn't that hungry, but I went on and ate a little. She made me fried chicken— breast and wings—and red beans and rice. Then she gave me some of her famous poundcake with lemon icing on it, which I loved.

After that, I told her that I was going outside to look around, that I would not be gone long. I went for a short walk down the street. It felt so good to be able to do that. I could not believe it. I walked around the block and then walked back to the house. I saw a lot of kids out and about but not many grownups. I was feeling good, to be able to walk outside at night and go and come as I pleased. Seeing cars coming and going made me feel good also. I was just glad to be home.

Once I was back home, my grandmother and I sat down to talk. Then she took me into my old room, which had been my grandfather's room, and everything was just as I had left it ten years before. There were men's clothes lying on the bed. She had gotten a few things for me. They were all nice dress pants and shirts, just as I liked, and they looked to have cost a lot. Some of it came from a lady next door who worked for a White family and had a son about my size. I could fit in everything, and they all looked good on me. All I needed were shoes, and I was ready to go.

Early July, 1990

My grandmother wanted to give me my mother's old car. I said I'd use it until I could buy my own.

By the end of my first week home, I went to get my license. The lady who gave me the written test asked where I had been because I had not renewed my license in so long. I told her where I'd been. She said she had a brother in prison. I did not know him. Then she gave me the driving test.

Normally, I would have had to wait a week before I got my license in the mail, but she took my picture and gave it to me the same day. She gave me her phone number and address and said if I needed anything to call her if I needed someone to talk to. She said she would try to help me out because she just felt something good about me. I found it strange, myself. But I was grateful just the same. She even wanted me to go to church with her. She seemed to be a very nice woman.

After getting my license, my grandmother wanted me to take her to the store to pick up a few things, which I was happy to do. Driving was cool, and it felt great to be doing things for myself. It felt funny, too, because it had been longer than ten years since I had driven a car. It was a good feeling, one of excitement and nerves to be out around other cars again.

I went job hunting. I wanted a job cooking because that is what I liked to do. I had learned how from Mama Henrietta and from when I was at Wade. I went to three places and filled out job forms. They said that they would give me a call if something came open. I did not feel they would, because on the job form where they said, *Have you ever been arrested?* I put *yes*, because I did not want to lie. I wanted to be open about it.

After leaving the last restaurant, I drove downtown to the riverfront to look around and see the sights. I parked next to the old train station, which is a museum, and walked up the levee to check out the great Mississippi River. The sun was out, and it was hot, but it was such a pretty sight. I just stood there and thanked God for blessing me to see this again because I did not know if I would ever make it out of prison. He helped me to make it through that time in my life, and I thanked him for the blessings so far.

Once I was back at home, I saw a car pull up to my grandmother's house—a nice four-door. I did not know what kind it was. I had been gone a while and didn't know cars like I used to. It was Ardessa, going to see my grandmother. She had gotten somewhat bigger than I remembered her being, but she still had that sexy face that I would not miss anywhere.

We hugged, and I kissed her on the side of her face. Then she said that I looked good, but one thing she did not like about me was that I had a goatee. She did not like men that had hair on their faces. I found that funny because her father had a full beard as long as I could remember.

We went out on the porch to talk for a while.

Mid-July 1990

The next morning, something told me to go by McDonald's where I used to eat a lot when I was small. After I filled out the form, the manager, Ray, came out to talk with me.

I told him I had just gotten out of prison and what for.

He said, "Well, I respect you for telling me this on your own and not trying to lie about it."

He gave me the address to the headquarters where I would have to go to get my uniform and take a class for two days. My grandmother was happy for me and said that God was blessing me, and I had to thank him for it. She wanted me to get back in church, and I said I would soon.

Three weeks after being out, I had a day job, but that was not enough for me. I wanted a night job, too, because I wanted to save up some money so I could get a car of my own. That night, I took out that list I had made at Wade and checked off the things that I had done so far, which were clothes and a job. Next was the car, and I was working on that.

That next week, I went to Popeye's Fried Chicken to get something to eat. It was on Government Street, about two blocks behind the McDonald's where I worked. I told the manager that I was a cook, and I was looking for a night job. I also said I had just gotten out of prison about a month ago. She was really cool and told me not to worry about it. She said I did not look like I was planning on going back, and I said I was not. She wanted me to start that night at 5:00 p.m. That was good, because my shift at McDonald's was from 4:30 a.m. to 2:00 p.m. I could rest a while, then go to work there. She gave me the address where I had to pick up my uniform and fill out some more papers.

So, now I had two jobs. McDonald's paid every two weeks and Popeye's every week. I would have money coming in steady. The only bill I had was to help my grandmother, and that was like a hundred dollars a month. She wouldn't have to get much food for me because most of the time I brought food home from work at night, what they would have thrown away after we closed up.

Ray put me down at McDonald's for the days the trucks would come in to bring supplies in also. It was an all-day job. I would help them unload, write down everything that came in, and stock it in the right place. I would always try to show off for the girls. Most of the young ladies that worked there were going to Southern University and working part-time. I would wear a pair of jeans and a tank top under my T-shirt and a pair of army boots. Once the trucks would start to come in, I would take off the T-shirt and help them unload all of the meats and food products first. I was buffed up because I was working out—I had signed up at the YMCA. When I would get kinda tired, I would walk in to get a Coke or something, and the girls would check me out. I knew it, but I acted like I did not.

CHAPTER 14

F. A. SILVA: BECAUSE OF HIS LACK OF MATERNAL NURTURING, HE HAS DEVELOPED PATHOLOGICAL RELATIONSHIPS WITH WOMEN, IDEALIZED WOMEN . . . I THINK THAT YOU CAN TRACE WHAT HAS HAPPENED TO FELTUS FROM THE BEGINNING, THE ABANDONMENT, THE FEAR OF ABANDONMENT, HIS CLINGING TO HIS IDEALIZED RELATIONSHIPS WERE QUITE DISTORTED.

—*Penalty Phase, Day 2: 52, January 24, 1992*

August 1990

WAS SITTING IN the break room, eating one day, and a nice, fine sister named Marcia came in for her break. I had met Marcia like three weeks after I started working at McDonald's. Her eyes were brown, and her jet-black hair was a little past her shoulders. Her shape was like a Coke bottle with a nice rounded ass, but she was slim and sorta tall. Her lips were small and juicy-looking. Her ears were small and rounded-like. I did not say anything when she came in because I didn't talk a lot at work. I was shy. I knew she was going to Southern University to study nursing.

"Feltus, I heard that you were in prison for ten years," she said.

"Where did you hear that at?"

"It got around. Is it true?"

"Yeah, it's true," I said. "Why?"

"Well, what did you do all of that time without a woman?"

I laughed. "That's what they make *Playboy* for, you know."

She laughed at that. She seemed to be cool and did not mind talking to me, and it felt good to laugh and talk with a woman. When my break was over, I said maybe I'd talk with her again sometime.

As I was working, I saw her come out of the break room and hit the clock back in. Then she walked over to another woman, and they started talking. I could not hear what they were saying, but I felt that it was about me. I looked at Marcia when she was heading back to the front counter where she worked at taking orders. One of the guys that I worked with, Deryck, told me that every guy that worked there tried to hit on her, but she did not go out with the people she worked with. I said to myself, *Well, there is a first time for everything.* I really liked her and thought maybe I had a chance—who knows? Later, during the day, she went in the back to get more cups, but she could not reach them. She left to go get a chair. By the time she came back, I had them down for her. She smiled and thanked me and went back to work.

When I got off at 2:00 p.m., I drove down the street to Popeye's to see what the work schedule looked like for that week. They had a truck coming in but nobody to unload it. I told the manager that I would help if she put me on the clock, and she did. I helped unload the truck, stocked up everything inside, and took the papers in to her with everything checked off.

"You seem to know what you're doing," the lady manager said.

"I do the same thing at McDonald's all the time."

"If you ever leave there, you can come here, and I'll give you a good spot making more money," she said.

I said I liked it the way it was for now.

"Since you have done this, you don't have to come in until seven tonight."

It was already about 4:00 p.m. when I was done. I said, "Okay, I will see you later."

I was stopped at a red light in front of Popeye's, and I heard someone blowing a horn. I turned to see Marcia in a little rust-colored car. She was waving for me to pull over in the parking lot across the street in front of a Subway sandwich shop. She pulled over next to me, and we both got out of our cars.

She came over to me while I was leaning against the car and said, "Where have you been?"

"I was at my other job, helping out a little."

"You have another job?"

"Yeah, I work at Popeye's at night," I said.

"Why are you working so hard?"

"Well, I'm trying to have something in life."

"Do you have a pen in your car?"

I said I thought so, and I looked and found one in it. I gave it to her, and she wrote down her phone number and address and told me to call her sometime. I said that I would do just that on one of my off-days. She said that was cool and turned around and headed back to her car. I was looking at her butt the whole time. *Damn, I like that,* I thought and started smiling.

On my days off from McDonald's, I would work the day shift at Popeye's.

When I got off, I would stop by McDonald's because I knew Marcia was working. If they were short-handed, like they were most of the time, the manager would tell me I could get on the clock if I wanted to, and I would because I needed that extra money. I worked these crazy hours a lot.

September 1990

One night I got off from Popeye's, and I did not have a ride home, so I decided to walk down to McDonald's to see if I could get one there. Ray was still there, and they were short-handed. He asked if I wanted to make some overtime. I said I had just got off from my other job, but I wanted my check to look good. The pants did not matter, but I had to change shirts. There was one in the back that I put on. I called my grandmother and told her where I was if she needed anything. Much to my surprise, they had called Marcia in to come work that night, and we were busy the whole damn night. It was a Friday night, and they did not close until one in the morning on Friday and Saturday nights.

When we closed, I helped clean up, and Ray told me and Marcia that we could go because we both had to be back at 4:30 a.m.—three and a half hours later. I asked her if she would mind dropping me off at home, and she said she would not. Once we got in her car, we just sat there for a minute. I was wondering what was up with that, but I did not say anything. The car was parked in the middle of the parking lot between two cars.

She turned on the radio and said, "I bet you want to have sex bad, huh?"

"Not too bad, but it will be good when it happens," I said. I was horny as hell.

"I like you, Feltus, and I want you now."

"You do?"

She asked if I had ever done it in a car before, and I said I hadn't. "This will be your first," she said and leaned over and kissed me. We kissed for a while, and then I was ready. She pulled the front seat back to let it out to the back seat. Then she opened up her shirt and pulled her pants down. I could not believe it. We were about to do it right there in the car. I got on top of her and looked at her body from the night-light, and it turned me on. We started kissing again, and then we had sex. Knowing that someone could come out to their car and see us made it all the more exciting for us both.

When we were done, she said, "Boy, that was good. I did not know you were that good," and that went to my head because I started smiling and laughing to myself. Then she took me home. Man, I was so damn tired; I did not think I would make it through the next day.

At work, later, we looked at each other and smiled. I said to myself, *If Deryck only knew that I have done something the rest of them could not—and that was to hit that.* I wasn't telling, though, because I wanted her again but better the next time.

I called Popeye's and told the manager that I would not be in because I needed some rest. When I got off at 2:00 p.m., I went straight home to bed. My grandmother woke me up to tell me that she was going to a church meeting, and I went back to sleep. About 8:00 or 8:30 p.m., I woke up because the phone was ringing.

When I answered, it was Marcia. She was crying and asked me if she could come over, and I said yes. I took a bath and put on some shorts and a T-shirt. I walked into the back to get something to eat when I heard a knock on the door. I went to let her in, and right off I could see that her face was red like someone had hit her or something. She said that her boyfriend had jumped on her, and her mother did not do a thing about it, and she was scared of him. She went on to tell me that he went to school with her at Southern University. He sold drugs for a living, and she was tired of it. Her mother liked him because he was always buying stuff for the house and giving her money for this and that. Marcia said she was tired of him always putting his hands on her. She started crying again while we were talking.

It kinda got to me, to see Marcia like that, so I put my arms around her and just held her for a while. I told her that everything would be okay.

My grandmother came home, and I told her who Marcia was. They said their hellos. I told her that I would be going out for a while, but I would call to check on her. We left in Marcia's car and went riding around and talking. We went to a Daiquiri Cafe across the street from the Southern campus. We ordered and talked a while longer.

After seeing that she was much better, I said that she should go home and get some rest. I said I would call her the next day, and if the guy came back over there that night to call me, and I would come over there.

Once we were back in front of my grandmother's house, we kissed and said goodnight to each other. Something was building inside of me for her. I watched her leave before going inside. My grandmother said she seemed nice, and I said she was.

The next day, I called her before she went to school, and she was okay. She asked me if I would see her that day. I said I would try to stop by before I went to my night job. I called the manager at Popeye's and said I would be an hour late. She said she would stay at McDonald's until I got there.

Marcia was standing outside, talking to a guy that looked to be about six feet tall, and there was a green Good Time van parked right behind her car. I remember her saying that Frank drove his daddy's van a lot, so I thought that had to be the guy. Once I parked and got out of the car, I saw him try to grab her arm. I ran over to them, and I told him not to touch her again. He asked her who I was, and she said I was her new boyfriend. I looked at her, then at him, because she caught me by surprise when she said that.

Frank told me not to leave, and I told him I wouldn't. He walked to the van like he was going to get a gun. I walked to my car and opened the trunk: I pulled out a tire jack and wrapped it up in a towel. From afar, it looked to be some type of gun. He just stood there and looked, then he said something to Marcia and jumped in the van and left. She ran over to where I was and hugged me and said thank you. I asked her what that new boyfriend stuff was about.

She said, "It's true. I want to be with you now because I care for you."

Well, that was all I needed to hear—I was down with that.

When Thursday came around, I got up that morning and went to the paint store to buy supplies because my grandmother's house needed painting really bad. I told her I would do it so she would not have to pay someone. I started about lunchtime, and Marcia came by.

When she came around, she said, "Can I help?"

"Sure, but you don't have the clothes for painting in," I said.

So, we went inside, and I gave her an old pair of jeans and an old T-shirt to put on. We had fun. We laughed and talked and stopped every now and then to kiss and play around with each other. Man, I remember thinking to myself, *Could this be my future wife right here?* I was hoping that it got that far for us. I was starting to fall in love with her, and it was so easy to do. At that time, she was everything that I wanted in a woman and more. I wanted to be with her for the rest of my life, and I was hoping she felt the same way. She didn't seem to mind helping me out or getting her hands dirty. I liked the way she carried herself. I liked her smile. We had things in common, like going for long walks, talking to each other about all kinds of things. She could dance really well. She was a sweet person in a lot of ways. She was a good listener. She used her beauty as her strength.

I did not know how Marcia's parents felt about me because I had not met them yet. I had already met her godmother. She was a sweet, old lady everyone called Mae-Mae. Mae-Mae liked me right away. She knew I had been to prison, but she said, "Everyone makes mistakes, and God will forgive anyone, so I will, too." After we met, I would go over there a lot by myself just to sit and talk with her. She was cool, and she cared for Marcia a lot and had helped raise her and her brother.

I took a bath and got ready and put my work clothes in the car because I would have to go to work later, after our date. I kissed my grandmother goodbye, and I called Marcia and told her I was on my way.

When I got to Marcia's house, her sister Karen let me in. Karen was a little shorter than me, with short, black hair. Their mother came into the living room to say hello and talked with me. She seemed okay, but we really did not hit it off right away and I knew why.

She was mad that Marcia had left Frank, and she would not be getting all of the stuff he used to give her. When Marcia was ready with her overnight bag in her hand, she told her mother she would be gone for the night. I said I would take good care of her, and we left. Karen was just looking on with her baby in her hands.

Marcia said Karen had two kids and would jump from man to man to help take care of them. I really could not understand why she was like that. I just guess she could not find the right guy to help her take care of them—some men are like that. They just want one thing, and that is sex. Then they are gone. I felt that once she got the right man to care for her and her kids, she would be okay.

Marcia and I planned to see a movie, get something to eat, and find a good motel for the night. We saw *Lionheart* starring Jean-Claude Van Damme, which was pretty good. We went to a nice restaurant and had a little dinner wine. I was feeling good. It did not take much because I was not a big drinker. Then, we went to a little store in Cortana Mall that sold all types of body lotions. She picked out some that got really warm when you rubbed it on your skin. I had never used that before, but I wanted to try it with Marcia. We went to a nice motel in Port Allen, across the Mississippi River.

Once we got to the room, we walked up to it hugging and kissing. She was looking outstanding to me that night. She had on a cute little black dress—it came to her hips, and her legs looked so good to me. I could kiss on them all night long. It was like we could not get into it soon enough. After I closed the door, she put her overnight bag on the table, found a good station on the radio, and told me to sit on the bed, which I gladly did. She started dancing for me while she undressed. Man, I felt so damn good; I did not know what to do. The lights were off, and the only light was coming from the window that was shining right on the spot where she was standing. She looked so sexy and exotic in that light. When she got to her G-string, I walked over to her and started kissing her all over. She got the body lotion and poured some in my hands, and I started to rub it all over her body. Then I picked her up and carried her to the bed. After she undressed me, we made love for most of the night, and it was the best I had ever experienced in my life. To me, that night proved that we should be together.

After we were done, we just lay there in each other's arms with her head to my chest and talked. I wanted it to always be that way for us. She was saying that we had a lot in common, and we did.

We both were looking for love that we could hold onto. She wanted to settle down, get married to the right guy, and raise a family. She wanted to finish college, and I had been thinking about trying to get into college. We both wanted more from life to make it better for ourselves. We talked a while longer, then fell asleep in each other's arms.

I worked my butt off at those two jobs. One day, Ray called me into the office. "Feltus, you are the best worker that I have here in the store, and you just started. I am going to give you a raise, but don't tell the others because I never give one this soon. If you keep on like this, you may be a manager before the year is over with."

I laughed and said I could use the money. I was getting the same type of talk at Popeye's. Everyone was pleased with the way I worked, and I always tried to do my best wherever I worked. I was always trying to help everyone else with their jobs also. Ray used to tell me to slow down because I was not in prison anymore. I told him I just liked to work, and I was trying to make my mark.

Ray and I became very good friends. I would always go into his office, even when he had all of the money out to put into the safe. Not even once did it cross my mind to try to steal it or do anything wrong, because I was happy with how everything was going for me. The first time he left the money out with me there, I felt that Ray was testing to see if he could trust me. Every time he or one of the assistant managers would be in counting the money at lunchtime, the door would be closed or locked.

Ray had called me into the office to tell me that he was giving me another raise because I was doing so well. One of the girls knocked on the door because they were having problems with a customer, and he had to take care of it. He told me to stay in the office with all the money on his desk and the safe open. I sat there and started laughing to myself because I know some guys that I had been locked up with who would have loved for that to happen to them. Ray was gone for ten or fifteen minutes. I could have taken some, but that was not in me to do. I did not want him to ever lose his trust in me.

I was off the next day. I slept a long time. My grandmother did not wake me up until noon. Then I ate and went back to sleep again. The next time I woke up, Ardessa was in my room kissing me on the side of my face. She had come to see my grandmother and me. She asked me why I had not been by or called. I told her in one word—work.

Then she said, "Yeah, your grandmother told me that you are really putting in the hours and that you have some woman named Marcia coming to see you, too."

"What are you all doing?" I asked. "Talking about my life story in there?" She just smiled and said, "When can I meet her?"

"I don't know. Maybe I'll bring her over one night."

"Yeah, do that," Ardessa said.

I told her that I was going to go back to sleep, and she left my room.

Later, someone else woke me up, and it was Marcia. She came over because I had not called her, and she brought me some seafood because she knew I liked it. I got up and looked into her eyes and kissed her.

I told her, "Why don't you go talk to my grandmother while I take a bath and get cleaned up some?"

"Okay, but don't take too long because I miss you," she said.

I took a hot bath, and it felt so good. I just sat there in that tub and thought about how God blessed me to be back home with my grandmother and to have a good woman and two jobs. Damn, you could not beat that.

It was too hard working so late at Popeye's, so I decided to get another job in the **fall of 1990**. I ended up going down Florida Boulevard and checked out this restaurant called Cajun's Fabulous Fried Chicken. I was hired as a head night cook and had to be there at 5:00 p.m., like at Popeye's, but by 11:00 or 11:30 p.m., I would be on my way home. The manager, Keith, was great, and we worked well together. He liked the way I worked and how fast I was at getting things done.

I got along well with everyone there. I worked my ass off, as usual, to show that I wanted and liked my job. And everyone thought that I was great at doing my job and that I was a great guy. I really liked working for him, and it was a nice store.

CHAPTER 15

Early November 1990

ONE DAY, ON MY break, I went to look at a few good used cars. I had saved up enough to buy one, and I wanted a nice one. I did not tell Marcia or my grandmother because I wanted to surprise them both. I did not use my grandmother's car that day, and I walked to work.

I went on Airline Highway to a few good used car lots. This 1982 Grand Prix caught my eye. It was green with a green inside, and it looked really good, and ran good too. Me and the salesman talked about the price of it, and worked out a deal that I could live with. I told him to do the paperwork, and I would be back to pick it up once I got off that evening.

I got money out of the bank for the down payment, and I had Ray drop me off at the car lot. The guy was waiting for me with all of the paperwork done. It was $500 down and $120 a month for about three years, which was not bad at all—with the two checks coming in, I could handle that.

I felt that God was looking out for me, and I thanked him for that. I just knew that I would make it out on the streets in the right way. I was off that night at Popeye's, so I was ready to hang out with my baby. I saw Marcia's car in the parking lot. I parked two cars from her and waited by her car. I saw her coming before she saw me. When she saw me, she ran over and gave me a big wet kiss on the mouth and asked me what I was doing there.

"I just wanted to show you something," I said.

"How did you get here? I don't see the car," she said.

I said, "That's the surprise. Close your eyes and give me your hand." I took the lead, and she followed. I said, "You can open them now. Here's our new car."

She smiled and laughed and hugged me tight. We went for a quick ride down the street. When I was driving back around the other side of the school, she said, "Well, let's break it in right now."

"What are you talking about?"

She told me to park in the back of the school by the field. She took off her pants, jumped in the backseat, and opened her shirt. I jumped back there, too, and we had sex two times. After we were done, she said she had to go back to work. She was getting off at 10:00 p.m., and we could go to a motel or something for a while. We kissed and she got herself together and left for work.

I went back home and checked the car out because I did not want it to be messed up in any way. I got a towel and cleaned the backseat off just to make sure.

Later, I went to the back office at McDonald's and talked with the night manager for a while. I was waiting for Marcia to get off.

He asked me, "When are you and Marcia getting married?"

"I don't know. Why do you say that?"

"Whenever I see her, I see you, and when you are here, she will pop up," he said.

I laughed and said, "I don't know, but I hope it's soon because I want her for my wife."

Then he said, "I don't know what you did to her, because I have seen guys hit on her a lot, and she never went out with them or nothing before."

One of the girls that worked that night was named Kendra. She pulled me to the side and said, "Feltus, you're a good man. Marcia isn't the right woman for you."

"Now, look. Why would you say something like that?"

"I'm just telling the truth," she said, "and you'll find out for yourself soon enough."

That is when I learned another piece of news from Kendra—the women had made a bet with each other after they found out I had been to prison. The bet was which one of them would have sex with me first. Now, why they did that I do not know, but they did.

Guys have been known to do the very same thing from time to time, but it hurt when she told me that. If that was true, I had no idea why Marcia had kept dating me. I guess she really liked me or saw something more that she wanted.

"Okay, then I will find out for myself," I said, and I walked off.

Now, I was kinda messed up with that one, but I did not let it show. When Marcia hit the clock, she came into the office to tell me she was ready to go. I was telling the manager that I got a new used car, and it was nice.

Marcia said, "Yes, we have a new car."

I just laughed and told him that I would see him later. Then I got up, and we left. I saw Kendra standing at the counter looking at me. I acted like I did not see her. I did not know whether to believe her or not, but I was wondering why she told me that. I told Marcia to leave her car and we would come back for it later.

We went to a Motel 6 on Airline Hwy. We got a room and had sex a few times before just lying there, talking with each other. She told me that she loved me and wanted to be with me forever. I told her I wanted the same thing she did—to have my own family—and she was okay with that. I knew that she had been on the pill, but she said she was going to get off because she wanted to have my child. Boy, I got so happy when she said that. I leaned over and kissed her.

Then I said, "Are you sure? Because bringing a child into this world is a big deal, and I would not want to do that unless both parents are going to be there together to raise that child."

She said that she was sure about it.

That was all I needed to hear from her.

A few days passed, and I went by her mother's house while she was at school and talked with her mom. I said, "I want to marry your daughter, and I am going to do right by her."

Her mother acted like she was happy and asked me when I planned on doing this. I told her by the end of next year. She said, "Okay, but you and her need to find an apartment because you been coming by so late at night, and I know what you all be doing in her room. If you have your own place, it would be okay, and you all could do whatever you want."

December 1990

In early December, my grandmother told me she got a paper from the welfare office telling her that if I kept staying there, they would cut her food stamps. I was saving for my own place anyway, and she knew it. I wanted my own place for Marcia and myself.

Then, my grandmother got another letter in the mail, but this time it was from the social security office, saying they knew that I was living with her, and if I kept living there, they would cut her check. Now I could not let that happen because she was not getting that much from them at all. It was only enough for her to pay her bills. I told her not to worry because I would be gone by the end of the week. I lied and said I had found an apartment, Marcia was going to move in with me, and we were going to share the bills. So, Mama Henrietta thought that was good, and she said once I was gone, she would call the people and have them come by to talk with her and see that I was not living there anymore. She didn't want me to leave, but she couldn't have them cut her check.

I decided I was going to find another job that I could do on my two days off a week—that would help out some. I did not want anything to happen to my grandmother because of me. I loved her too much for that. I had to look out for her always, and I was a big boy, and I would be fine on my own. The only thing that might help me was that tax time was coming up soon, and I might get enough in refund money to get an apartment. I told Marcia to start checking around for a nice apartment for us to live in.

In the **winter of 1990**, Marcia came to me and said that her grant for school had fallen through. Some paperwork got messed up, and she needed $400 for that coming semester or she would be out. I missed my car payment for that month, so I could give her the money. Then it was like she needed money for books, food, gas—all kinds of things—and I would be the one to give it to her.

Because I had been so good at paying my car note, it was not a big problem that I missed that month. I had been paying my bill a month or two ahead of time anyway. I found myself working a lot of overtime because I wanted to save up for the apartment and the baby I was hoping we could have, but she had been using more money than I was saving at the time.

I was also thinking about going to college myself. Marcia had put in an application for me so I could start at Southern University in the **fall of 1991**. The lady my grandmother worked for, for about twenty-five years, Mrs. Daggett, found out I wanted to go back to school. Our families had known each other for a long time, and she'd known me since I was little child. Sometimes, she helped out my grandmother with bills and food. So, when she learned I wanted to go to college, she said she'd help me. She told me I could quit one of my jobs, and she would help me with rent and spending money. And if the grants I wanted to get didn't come through, she would help me with tuition. I didn't know how I would pay her back. But Mrs. Daggett told me, "If you graduate, you've paid me back."

Early January 1991

I do not know how it really went down, but Frank—Marcia's ex-boyfriend—was getting into her head some kind of way. At school, he was trying to start talking to her again. Somehow, he found out Marcia was going to move in with me. I think Karen, Marcia's sister, told him that. She was hot as hell that Marcia was doing so well.

Karen wanted nothing more than to break me and Marcia up. One night when I was at work, she called me to tell me Frank had just come by the house and taken Marcia somewhere.

I said, "Karen, how did you get this number? I know Marcia did not go anywhere with Frank. Why are you lying, girl?"

"If you don't believe me," she said, "just come by later. I will call you when they come back."

She did call back later, but I did not leave work to go check it out. I just felt she was lying, and I told her not to call me at work anymore. I did not want to hear that bullshit. I hung up the phone and went back to work. I won't lie, I thought about it some and wondered if it was true, but I knew that was what Karen wanted me to do. I was not going to let her fuck up a good thing. I was crazy about Marcia, and I did not want anything to stop us from being together.

One night, Marcia and I went to a fair across the river, and it was kinda late so we stayed over in a motel. We made what I thought was love. This time after we were done, we just laid up talking like always, and she asked me a question.

Then she said, "Just say I was seeing someone else while I was with you—what would you do?"

I looked at her for a second because I wanted to make sure that I heard her right. I jumped out of the bed and grabbed her by the arm and pushed her on the floor. She landed next to the wall right under the air conditioner unit. I pulled the cord out of the wall plug and put it around her neck and told her that if I ever found that out, I would kill her. Then I let her up; and I walked to the window to look out.

I was in love and didn't want her to hurt me in that way.

Sometimes things can happen so fast that by the time we are able to regain control it is too late, you know. I didn't plan to do what I did to Marcia that night. I wasn't thinking right. I was just acting out of hurt that she would even say that. If I had things to do all over again, I would have dropped her ass and waited for someone else to come along. But I didn't.

Marcia came to where I was standing and said, "I didn't mean it. I was just playing with you. You know that I wouldn't do that to you." Then she said, "I am going to take a shower. Do you want to come?"

I said, "No, I'll wait until you're done."

Then she went on in. She had forgotten to get her deodorant in her purse and asked me to get it for her. While I was looking for it, I ran across a pack of birth control pills that was half-gone. She had told me she had stopped taking those things. I knew that as much as we had been having sex, she should have been pregnant by now.

I remembered what Kendra, the girl at work, had said about Marcia going out with me on a bet. I was thinking about all of this while I looked down at these pills in her purse. I felt like I was on a sinking ship heading down fast. I loved this woman so much. Why would she do this to me? I could not understand it at all. My head was all messed up. All I wanted was to share my life with her and have a child with her. What was I doing wrong? I tried to give her what she wanted and needed. We were great lovers together, what more did I need? I wanted a person to care for me for more than just sex—for the person I am on the inside. I thought we really had something.

After she came out, I showered, and then we left.

I did not say anything to her in the car. She started asking me how long I was going to act that way.

"Why, does it really matter to you?" I asked.

"Yeah, you know it does," she said. "You're my baby."

"If I'm your baby, well, why you have been lying to me?"

"What? I haven't lied about anything."

"Well, if that's true, what's with the birth control pills in your purse?" I asked.

"What pills? I don't have any in there."

I grabbed her purse and pulled them out and threw them at her.

"Oh, I forgot about them," she said. "I stopped using them things."

"Well, if so, why aren't you pregnant yet, then? All of the sex we been having, something should be up by now, right?"

She just looked out of the car window. She did not say a word.

"Well, say something, bitch," I said. "If I drive this car off the road, I bet you'll say something then, won't you?" I saw a truck coming our way in the other lane. I stepped on the gas and turned the steering wheel to the left. I wanted to scare her to tell me the truth. That had worked in prison. I guess I thought it would work on the outside, too.

Marcia started saying, "Please don't kill us, Feltus."

When I was about twenty feet away from the truck, I cut to the right and got back in my lane. Then I slowed back down to the right speed and drove her home.

I let her out in front of her house. Once she got out, she stood like she was waiting for me to say something, but I drove off and left her standing there. I was so damn hurt; I did not know what to do.

I got to work before Marcia did the next morning. I saw her come in. I still did not say anything to her, but I saw her looking at me every now and then. When it was time for her break, she was in the break room laughing and talking with some guy. He was standing at the door. When she came out, I saw her rub up against him, and he just smiled at her. She went to punch the clock back in, then she went back to the drive-thru window. I went into the breakroom, walked up to the guy, and grabbed him around his neck and pushed him.

I pushed him against the wall and I told him if I ever saw him all up on my old lady again, I would mess him up. He did not say a word, he just looked at me. Then I let him go and went back to work. The whole time I was there I was mad as hell, but I did not say nothing to her, and she did not say anything to me.

The next day, I still wasn't talking to her. It really hurt me not to. When I took my break in the area for the workers, she came in and stood at the door. I looked up at her.

"You know that I miss you, and you not talking to me is not right," Marcia said. "I heard about what you did the other day with that guy. You know that you were wrong for that."

"No, you were wrong because you know how I feel about you. I would die for you, Marcia, if I had to. And you should know that by now."

"Well, I want to talk with you later, okay?" she said. "So, try to come by or call me tonight."

"Cool, I'll do that," I said.

Then she turned and walked out. Before I could get out the door, Kendra came in.

"I told you that Marcia will hurt you. She's doing that right now, and everyone can see it," Kendra said.

I looked at her because she knew what she was talking about, but I did not say anything.

She said, "Before you leave today, I want to give you my phone number and I want you to call me if you need to talk, okay?"

"All right, I'll do that," I said.

Then, before I could get back to work, Ray called me into his office to talk with me. He said, "I can tell that something is wrong, and it is showing in your work right now." He asked me if I needed a few days off, and I said I did and that would help a lot.

"After today, take three days off and come by to see me when you come back," Ray said.

"I'll want to make these days up as you know I have bills now, and they have to be paid," I said.

"You can make them up. I just want you back to your old self again," he said.

I said, "Thanks, man, this really means a lot to me for you to do this."

Then I looked on the board to see when Marcia was off. I went back to work.

When it was time to go, I punched the clock out, and I walked around to the front. I did not say anything to Marcia. As I was leaving, Kendra called me back and gave me a piece of paper. Her number and address were on it.

I went to my grandmother's house and told her I was going to find another night job with better hours so I could get my rest and spend more time with her.

She said, "Yeah, you really need to do that because I don't want you to get sick or anything."

But I was already sick in the mind, and I did not want her to know about it. When I left there, I knew I needed to share more of my time with her, but I had to get my life worked out first.

I drove over to Marcia's godmother's house to talk with her for a while. Mae-Mae was easy to talk with, and she knew how I felt about Marcia.

Marcia and I were sorta back together again. I was trying to give her space and hang out with different people. But, one day I went to her house and Karen was there. She said, "Feltus, do not be fooled by Marcia. She and Frank are fooling around again."

A few days later, Karen called me at work. "If you still don't believe me," Karen said, "all you have to do is come by. They're out in the van talking now."

I said, "Okay, I might do that," and hung up the phone.

I asked the guy that was working with me to cover for me for a while. I told him if anyone asked where I was, to just tell them I was on break. I punched the clock out and left. I got in my car and took the fastest way to Marcia's house. I drove past the house—and sure enough, there they were, sitting in the van. I went down a block and turned off on the street behind her house. I parked my car and walked around to the corner behind them and just stood there looking. They talked for what seemed like an hour and once Marcia got out of the van, she leaned back in. I guess they kissed, and she went back inside the house. Man, I was standing there crying, and I just could not believe what I was seeing. I walked back to my car and left to go back to work.

January/February 1991

Things were a little hard, but I was dealing with it okay at the time. I remember the evening I came home and put most of my things in the car and lied to my grandmother like I had an apartment waiting. I told her I would give her the number when I got settled. That night, after I got off of work, I drove over by Raymond's house—a guy I grew up with—and asked him if I could stay until 4:30 a.m. I crashed on the sofa, and he woke me at 4:00 a.m. I told him I had been out late and did not want to wake up my grandmother. He was cool with that, but he was married at the time, and I did not want them to think nothing. They were having problems of their own, and I would not have been helping by staying with them. So, I did not tell him or Marcia what was really going on.

The next day, when I got off at 2:00 p.m., I went to my grandmother's house like I always did. I took a bath and got something to eat and talked with her a while. She said that she had called those people to come by, but they had not yet. So, I told her I would get a few more of my things and pack them in the car. That night, I slept in my car in the McDonald's parking lot. Marcia was wondering what was going on, but I was fooling her for the time being.

CHAPTER 16

Mid-February 1991

DID NOT KNOW what I was going to do about this whole mess I was in.

[On Valentine's Day,] Marcia said that she liked me and she cared about me. She said she wanted to stop having a relationship with me and she just wanted us to be friends. She said she wanted me to still take her out, and we'll go to the movies or go out to eat, but we'll just keep it on that level there.

She got up and left me sitting there. I watched her leave and go back to school. I was hurt, sad, and confused. I drove downtown to the levee and walked up and down, trying to think where I went wrong. I asked God how I let myself get into all of this, but I did not get an answer back. I pulled a joint out and smoked it there, then I drove home.

I drove to Marcia's house one night. She was at her car like she was just about to leave. She turned and walked over to where I was parked. I got out of the car, and I said, "Let's take a walk, if you have the time."

We walked around the block and talked. I poured out my heart to her and even cried some. We stopped and hugged and kissed each other. I told her I really cared for her and loved her with my whole heart. How I just wanted to be with her for the rest of my life. I had never felt this way about anyone before. She just took it all in and didn't say too much, other than that she would think about it all.

We walked back to my car and went downtown to walk the levee. I did not bring up seeing her and Frank in the van because, to me, it was not important anymore. I wanted her heart, and I felt if I had that everything else would be okay for us.

I wanted her right then. There was a motel not far from where we were on Government Street, so we went there. We got there and made love over and over again. I really thought that we were back on track.

But I was just fooling myself.

While I was waiting for my refund to come back from the taxes, I took one of my checks and went and put a deposit on an apartment. It was okay. It was a one-bedroom; but it was plenty big enough for two people. I told the lady I would have the rent part of it as soon as I got paid, about two weeks from that time. I knew the tax refund check should be in then because I went to H&R Block for the Rapid Refund™ deal. I was very surprised. I still had close to a thousand dollars coming to me. I thought I could take care of everything with that.

Man, let me tell you something, $1,000 is not shit these days. I got the utilities turned on and paid the lady the other money I owed her. I paid some of the other bills I had. There was still some left for me to get furniture later.

Late February 1991

Things went well for about two weeks, then I started having trouble in my life again. I was working at Cajun's one Friday night in the middle of the night rush hours, when I got a phone call from Karen. She told me Marcia had just left with Frank. They went somewhere, and she did not know when they would be back. I said, "Okay, be outside in about an hour. I will be there."

I worked through the rush, and when things started to slow down, I told Keith that I needed to leave, and I would be back in an hour. Something had come up that I needed to take care of, and it was a family matter.

He seemed to believe it and said, "Okay, one hour."

I thanked him and hit the clock out.

When I got to Marcia's area of town, I made the block and I did not see anything but Marcia's car sitting outside and Karen out in the yard. I parked on the back street and walked around to where Karen was standing. We started talking, and I said, "I hope that this is not any of your bullshit, or you will have hell to pay for this."

Then she said, "All you have to do is wait until they come back and see for yourself."

I said, "Well, you better go on inside, and I will wait to see what is up."

There was a graveyard right across the street from Marcia's house. I drove back around the block. I parked my car one block away and just sat there for a while. Now, I knew Keith was wondering where the hell I was, but I did not care.

I listened to the radio and just sat there. [Eventually,] I stood up and leaned on the headstone of some guy. I said to him, "Man, I wonder if you went through this kind of shit when you were living up here." I looked at my watch. It was ten to 4:00 a.m. Then a van pulled up right behind Marcia's car.

On taking a closer look, I could see that it was Frank and Marcia. I got a little closer up to where I had a very good view of them both in that van. If I had had a gun, I would have killed them both that night. I was very much hurt by what I saw.

I saw with my own eyes Marcia kissing him in the van. Then she got out and went to the door and turned around and waved at him, then he pulled off. She got to her front door and turned to wave at him. I saw the light in her room come on, and I felt like getting a rock and throwing it through her window. I started crying and wondering what the hell was going on.

From that point on, everything started going downhill for me.

BONNIE JACKSON: WAS THERE A PERIOD OF TIME WHEN YOU STARTED USING DRUGS?

FELTUS TAYLOR, JR.: RIGHT AFTER VALENTINE'S DAY.

—Penalty Phase, Day 3: 39, January 25, 1992

I did not go to work that morning. I did not care about anything else right then. Instead, I went on over to my cousin's apartment to get high. When I got there, he was sleeping, but I woke him up and said that I needed something for my head. We had a little coke and weed rolled up together called preemos.

It was damn good, and it kept you high longer. The weed by itself seemed not to be as powerful anymore for me. We rode around for a while and talked and listened to music. I got high most of the day. I did not sleep or do nothing but get high.

That afternoon, I went to talk with Keith, who was pissed off at me, that's for sure. I told him what had happened, and he offered to give me a few days off. But I told him no, that I wanted to work. That was a mistake on my part. I should have taken the days off to clear my head and think things through, but I didn't. I told him that I wouldn't blame him if he fired me for the way I handled things the past night, but he made me promise him that it would not happen again. He said if it did, he would have to let me go.

"Yeah, I know that," I said.

So, he told me to be there for 5:00 p.m., and I said I would. I did not even go by McDonald's because I knew Ray was pissed, because I was to open the store that day and I did not show. He probably had to come in and do it, and that would have made them late opening up everything.

BONNIE JACKSON: LET'S TALK ABOUT THAT LAST TWO-WEEK PERIOD BEFORE HE LEFT. YOU SAID UP UNTIL THAT POINT HE'D BEEN A MODEL EMPLOYEE. DID THINGS CHANGE IN THAT LAST TWO WEEKS OF EMPLOYMENT?

RAY ROME: HE WAS A LOT MORE QUIET, A LOT MORE TO HIMSELF. HE STILL DID GOOD WORK. LIKE I SAID, HE WAS REAL QUIET. HE DIDN'T TALK TO ME AS MUCH AS HE DID BEFORE.

Q: HE SEEMED TO BE MORE WITHDRAWN AND MORE RESERVED?

A: YES.

—Penalty Phase, Day 2: 92–3, January 24, 1992

BONNIE JACKSON: WHEN DO YOU THINK THAT YOU FIRST NOTICED CHANGES IN HIM THAT CAUSED YOU TO BELIEVE THAT HE WAS ON DRUGS?

CAROLINE JOHNSON [coworker at McDonald's]: WELL, THE TIME HE CUSSED US OUT AND I ASKED HIM WHY. LATER ON, AFTER HE COME DOWN, HE SAID THAT HE WAS UNDER A LOT OF PRESSURE AND HE COULDN'T HANDLE WHAT SHE WAS DOING TO HIM. AND HE SAID THAT HE HAD SNIFFED A LITTLE COKE THAT DAY.

Q: SO, HIS ATTITUDE AT WORK CHANGED?

A: YES. TREMENDOUS.

Q: IN WHAT WAY?

A: HE DIDN'T CARE ABOUT DOING ANYTHING. HE DIDN'T CARE ABOUT BEING AROUND US IN A FACTOR THAT HE FIGURED ALL WOMEN MISTREATED MEN.

—Penalty Phase, Day 2: 114–15, January 24, 1992

I smoked a joint at home and went on to work. Ray came in and asked Keith if he could speak to me. He was very hot with me over what happened. He said, "I know what the problem is. It's you and Marcia. I could move her to another store, if that would make things better for you, because I hate to see you this way. I know that you can do better than this."

He told me to come to work in the morning, and I told him I would be there. I really did not know if I would go or not. I got on with work, and it was a pretty good night. When I got off, I went on home and got high and laid around the apartment until I went to sleep.

I went to work the next morning. I had not talked with Marcia for something like two days. I made up my mind that I had to get Marcia away from Frank and whoever else was trying to keep us apart.

I did not go right home. I drove by the drop house where my cousin and I had picked up those bags of weed. He had a lot of people buying from him at that time. He even had guys out on the corner selling for him. Day and night, they would have the whole block running around. I sat in my car and smoked, and I was feeling pretty good when I drove off.

I drove past Marcia's house, but I did not see her car. I ended up downtown on the levee, looking over the river and thinking where would be a good place for Marcia and me to go. I wanted to leave the state with her and start all over again. I really did not care where we would go, as long as she was with me. I just could not see her and Frank back together. I was not going to let that happen, no matter what I had to do. I loved her, she was going to be with me, and that was that. I was going to do anything to make that happen.

Early March 1991

I woke up at 4:30 a.m., got dressed, and fixed myself something to eat. Then I turned on the radio and smoked a preemo. When I left my apartment, I went past Marcia's house, and she had not left for work yet, so I drove on to McDonald's and parked my car in the same space like always. I waited for something like half an hour. I saw Marcia's car turn into the parking lot. She saw my car, and I ducked down where she could not see me. She parked right in front of my car. When I heard her car stop running, I jumped out of my car and ran over to hers. I said, "We need to talk right now."

She said, "Go ahead. I am listening."

I said, "I saw you and Frank the other night. You did not come home until four in the morning. Where were you and him at all that time? And why could you not let me know that you wanted him back?"

She did not say a word to me. She just looked on.

I grabbed her by the hand and told her to get in my car, that we were leaving so we could talk. I was going to take her out of state so we could be together. She started pulling away from me. Some guy was coming out of McDonald's. He saw us, and he ran over to help. Marcia got free and ran into the store. I jumped into my car and left. I went back to my apartment and called McDonald's and asked to talk to Marcia.

She said she had called the police, and they were now looking for me.

I was looking for some work during the day. One day, I stopped at Ralph & Kacoo's to get a to-go order for myself. I saw them fire some guy while I was standing there, so I asked to talk with the manager. I told him that I was looking for a day job. He told me to come back the next morning, and that he would leave word with the manager who worked days. I went back over there the next day and got hired as a dishwasher that same day. I didn't mind doing that as long as I was working. I was halfway through paying on my car and would have been done with it by the end of the year. I felt as long as I kept a job, I would be able to pay it off on time.

Mid-March 1991

When I was off, all I did was run behind Marcia, trying to get things right between the both of us, but it was not working out.

While I was at work one day, I had a phone call, and I thought it was Marcia, but it was Officer Downing. He said, "When you get off from work, I would like to see you, so come by the office."

I said, "Okay," and hung up. When I got off at 2:00 p.m., I went by my grandmother's house for a while, then on home to take a bath and change clothes. I did not go by to see what Downing wanted, and I was not planning on it, either. I went on to my other job, and I got a call there from him again. He asked me why I did not show up. I told him I was late, and when I had the time, I would come.

"Well, you better make it before you find yourself back in prison," he said.

All that week he called for me, but I came up with a different lie why I had not come by.

Then, one night, when I was going to my car after work, someone grabbed me and threw me up against it. It was Downing and Finch.

Downing said, "See what happens when you do not come see what we want. You should have come to see us, but this is the deal. We want you to work for us, and we will pay you more than you can make at your jobs right now. There is this guy over by where your grandmother lives. We want you to go work for him and let us know where he gets his dope from."

"Man, them people don't know me, and they wouldn't just trust me like that anyway," I said.

"You have a week to decide, or we'll come and pick you up on those other charges from your girlfriend," he said. "We know that you've been around her anyway."

"Man, this is harassment," I said.

"Who will believe you?" Finch asked. "You're an ex-con. What we say will stick, and don't you forget that, okay?"

I stood there and thought about what had just happened. Then I went home and got high. I tried to call Marcia, but Karen answered the phone. I asked her to let me talk with Marcia, and she said Marcia was gone with Frank again.

"I know that you're lying," I said, but I just felt like shit all over again.

I smoked a few preemos that night, and I did not go in to work the next day. I picked Karen up and asked her to show me where Frank lived. She did, but every time I went there, he was not there. I did not know what I would do if he had been there—maybe try to kill him, I guess.

A week passed, and I went in on my own to see Downing and Finch, because I did not want them to come get me again. Then they showed up with a few pictures of some guys that had been robbing people around my way.

"What do you want me to do?" I asked.

"Find him, then call us and tell us where he is at," one of them told me. They gave me some papers to fill out and then they took my picture. "What is all this for?" I asked.

"You're a crime stopper now. This is for our records," Finch said. "Here is thirty dollars for gas money."

I put the money in my pocket and left. They had given me a card with their number on it to call when I had something. I threw the card into the street out of my car window and went by the dope man's house and got me five more sticks.

I was doing okay until Downing and Finch started calling for me at Cajun's. Keith asked me what they wanted, and I told him I had gotten a ticket and that was all. They kept calling until I had to go talk with them. They wanted me to go with some guy who was robbing banks and find out his next hit.

"Man, you want to get me killed or something?"

"You better do something, or your ass is going to jail."

"Okay, just stop calling my job," I told them. "You make it look bad on me doing that."

"Well, we'll think about it."

"Can I go now?"

They said they'd be watching me. Downing and Finch did not stop calling for me at work. They called at least once a week, and it was driving me crazy.

BONNIE JACKSON: DID YOU EVER PROVIDE ANY INFORMATION FOR THEM?

FELTUS TAYLOR, JR.: YES.

Q: WHAT INFORMATION DID YOU PROVIDE?

A: I TOLD THEM ABOUT A COUPLE OF PEOPLE THAT USED TO SELL DRUGS AND STUFF. AND AFTER I DID THAT, THEY DECIDED THEY WANTED ME TO—THEY TOLD ME, WELL, YOU COULD BE A CRIME STOPPER AND YOU COULD MAKE UP TO A THOUSAND DOLLARS A MONTH, AND YOU COULD LET ONE OF YOUR JOBS GO AND JUST WORK FOR US, AND STILL BE ABLE TO GET THE THINGS YOU NEED.

Q: SO, DID YOU TAKE THEM UP ON THEIR OFFER?

A: AFTER A WHILE, YEAH, I DID. WELL, ESPECIALLY AFTER I HAD LOST MY JOB AT CAJUN'S, I TOOK THEM UP ON IT, BUT EVERY TIME I

DECIDED THAT I WAS OR I WOULDN'T CALL THEM AND LET THEM KNOW ANYTHING, THEY'LL CALL ME AT CAJUN'S OR THEY'LL CALL ME AT MACDONALD'S AND SAY, WELL, IF YOU DON'T HELP US, WE'RE GOING TO HAVE TO PICK YOU UP AND HOLD YOU ON THE CHARGE WHAT MARCIA WANTED TO PUT AGAINST YOU. SO, I HAD TO GO BACK AND TRY TO FIND SOMETHING ELSE FOR THEM.

—*Penalty Phase, Day 3: 46-7, January 25, 1992*

I went to see *Ghost* by myself. That movie made me sad. It made me think about Marcia and the love that I had within myself for her. That I would die for her and come back to protect her from any harm. The way that those two people in the movie were connected—that was the same way I wanted to be to the person that I loved with all of my heart. I wish that we had seen it together. Then she would have understood how I felt about her.

CHAPTER 17

BONNIE JACKSON: SO, INDIVIDUALS WHO HAVE A BORDERLINE PERSONALITY DISORDER WOULD BE PERSONS THAT YOU WOULD EXPECT TO SHOW IN THEIR PERSONAL LIFE MOOD SWINGS FROM BEING ANGRY TO SAD OR ANGRY TO DEPRESSED WITHOUT MUCH CONTROL ON THEIR PART; IS THAT CORRECT?

TOMMY STIGALL: YES. I THINK WHAT WE WOULD EXPECT TO SEE IS THAT THOSE KINDS OF ABRUPT MOOD CHANGES WOULD OCCUR SOMETIMES WITHOUT ADEQUATE PROVOCATION FROM THE STANDPOINT OF JUST ANOTHER OBSERVER. YOU WOULD NOT NECESSARILY SEE WHY THE PERSON WOULD REACT IN JUST A DRAMATIC WAY OR SO VIOLENTLY OR SO—BECOME SO DEPRESSED OVER THAT KIND OF EVENT.

—Penalty Phase, Day 3: 143-44, January 25, 1992

Sunday, March 25, 1991

WENT TO VISIT with my grandmother, and I stayed most of the day. I was just trying to be a good grandson to her without letting her know what was going on in my life. When I left from there, I went to my mother's grave to talk with her. I would do that from time to time. I didn't really get to talk to her while I was in prison, so I would go to her grave to spend time talking with her and thinking about how much I missed her. I wished she was still in my life. I knew in my heart that I was letting her down. I didn't know how to deal with that pain, either. Then I leaned down and told her goodbye.

ARDESSA SMITH: BUT I RECALL LIKE THE WEEKEND BEFORE THE INCIDENT ON FLORIDA BOULEVARD, I RECALL HIM COMING TO MY HOUSE.

Q: WHAT WAS IT ABOUT HIM THAT MADE YOU KNOW IF SOMETHING WAS BOTHERING HIM OR NOT?

A: BASICALLY, WHEN SOMETHING IS BOTHERING HIM—USUALLY WHEN HE TALKS TO ME, HE LOOKS ME DEAD IN MY FACE. HE'S RIGHT THERE CLOSE UPON ME. HE CAN TOUCH ME WHEN HE'S TALKING, OR PLAYING OR TEASING ME, OR WHATEVER. BUT WHEN SOMETHING IS WORRYING HIM, HE DOESN'T LOOK AT ME. HE KIND OF WANDERS AROUND THE ROOM, HE PACES THE FLOOR, AND HE'S VERY, VERY, QUIET. HE'S NOT HIS HAPPY SELF. HE'S NOT JOKING; HE'S NOT PLAYING WITH ME.

Q: AND WHEN YOU SAW HIM THAT SUNDAY WHAT KIND OF MOOD WAS HE IN?

A: THAT SUNDAY HE WAS A NERVOUS WRECK. HE WOULDN'T STAY STILL. HE PACED FROM ONE END OF MY COUNTER TO THE OTHER. I WAS IN THE PROCESS OF COOKING AND I CUT THE FIRES OFF AND I STOPPED. AND HE JUST STEADILY PACED BACK AND FORTH AROUND ME . . . BUT HE NEVER SAID ANYTHING.

—Penalty Phase, Day 1: 112-13, January 23, 1992

BONNIE JACKSON: FELTUS, WHEN WAS THE LAST TIME YOU RECALL SEEING MARCIA PRIOR TO THE SHOOTING AT CAJUN'S?

FELTUS TAYLOR, JR.: A COUPLE OF DAYS.

Q: WHERE DID YOU SEE HER?

A: AT MS. BROWN'S HOUSE.

Q: WHAT HAPPENED IN THAT MEETING?

A: WE HAD AN ARGUMENT.

Q: WHAT KIND OF ARGUMENT?

A: SHE TOLD ME SHE WANTED ME TO STOP CALLING HER AND LEAVING NOTES ON HER CAR.

Q: AND WHAT ELSE DID SHE TELL YOU?

A: CALLED ME STUPID.

Q: HOW DID YOU FEEL ABOUT THAT?

A: DIDN'T LIKE IT TOO MUCH.

—Penalty Phase, Day 3:48-9, January 25, 1992

Monday, March 26, 1991

With nothing else to do, I decided to go see a movie at the mall. I went to see *New Jack City*. The movie was good, and everyone in the place was saying "Wow!" and "Yeah!" They seemed to really get off on that. After the movie, I came out of there saying, *Fuck everything! I will do what I've got to do to get mine.*

When I left the movie, I stopped to grab something to eat. Then I decided to drive past Marcia's house. I had been doing it for a while—driving by to see if I could see her or her car in the yard before I went home. I didn't see her car so I kept going. I got on the interstate and just drove and smoked. If the police had pulled me over, I would have surely gone to jail that night. In a lot of ways, I wish I had been arrested. I finally drove on home, and it was almost morning. I went inside and stayed up until day came, looking out of my bedroom window and listening to the radio, getting my smoke on. At that point in time, I don't know where my mind was.

BONNIE JACKSON: I'M TALKING ABOUT A CONVERSATION WHERE SHE SPOKE TO HIM ON THE PHONE AND HE REACTED TO THAT PHONE CALL?

WILLIE MAE BROWN: THIS WAS THE DAY BEFORE THE SHOOTING, OR NIGHT BEFORE THE SHOOTING.

Q: OKAY. TELL ME WHAT HAPPENED THAT DAY BEFORE THE SHOOTING.

A: WELL, SHE WAS SAYING SOME PRETTY NASTY THINGS TO HIM, AND HE WAS HOLDING HIS HEAD, AND ALL OF A SUDDEN HE JUST FELL ON THE FLOOR AND STARTED CRYING.

Q: THIS WAS THE DAY BEFORE THE SHOOTING?

A: YES.

Q: THAT PHONE CALL TOOK PLACE AT YOUR HOUSE?

A: YES.

Q: HOW DO YOU KNOW IT WAS MARCIA?

A: BECAUSE WHEN HE FELL DOWN ON THE FLOOR, I PICKED UP MY PHONE AND SAID, HELLO, AND SHE THOUGHT I WAS HIM AND SHE CALLED ME A NAME. AND SHE SAY, OH, IT'S YOU, MAE-MAE. I SAID, YEAH.

Q: AND YOU SAID FELTUS FELL ON THE FLOOR AND STARTED CRYING?

A: YEAH. HE WAS HOLDING HIS HEAD, OH, LORD, I CAN'T TAKE THIS. HE SAID, I FEEL LIKE KILLING MYSELF. AND I SAID, BABY, YOU

DON'T NEED—THEY GOT PLENTY WOMEN OUT THERE. HE SAID, I DON'T WANT NOBODY BUT HER, OH JESUS. HE WAS ABOUT TO DIE. AND I HAD TO BABY HIM AND SHAKE HIM. I COULDN'T DO THAT. HE JUST WOULDN'T RESPOND TO NOTHING. HE WANTED HER, I DON'T KNOW WHAT SHE DONE TO HIM, BUT I'VE NEVER SEEN A YOUNG BOY THAT CRAZY OVER ONE GIRL.

—Penalty Phase, Day 2: 165–6, January 24, 1992

By this time, it was good and dark. I didn't go to work again, so I knew that I was fired. But the night before, one of the girls told me that Keith had said he was just getting me back until he could find someone to take my place. He had not told me this, but I knew she had no reason to lie to me about it. I decided I would quit before he could fire me. I don't really know why I was thinking this way. I just had one thing on my mind, and nothing else mattered except me and Marcia.

I went back to the car and sat there looking at a picture of Marcia and me that I kept on the dashboard of my car. I looked at it and tried to think how I had gotten to this point. We started out so good with each other. She was my heart. I didn't want to hurt her or myself or anyone else for that matter, but I didn't know what to do at that point.

All kinds of things were running across my mind. I thought about how I was going to pay my bills and my car note. What about Marcia? I couldn't see my way out, and I wasn't used to the kind of stress that I was under right then. It was too much for me.

Tuesday, March 27, 1991—2:00 a.m.

I sat in the living room in the dark listening to the radio, thinking and wondering what I would have to do to get Marcia back. At that point, I was willing to do any- and everything. I loved her that much, but maybe it was just the sex. I don't know—I really couldn't tell the difference between the two. But what about the way I was living right then? I didn't want to keep living that way, with the police on my ass, always messing with me. I had thoughts about taking my life or Marcia's, or both.

I didn't like wondering if Marcia wanted me or not. I had always said that I would rather be dead than live that way. A few times, I told Marcia that I would kill myself and her if I couldn't be with her. There were times when I really wanted to do it, too. I don't know what stopped me. I guess I was scared to kill myself, but there really were times when I wanted to just say my goodbyes and do it.

Finally, around three in the morning, I fell asleep.

Tuesday, March 27, 1991 — ~6:00 a.m.

(Exactly nine months after release from Wade Correctional Center).

BONNIE JACKSON: WHEN YOU WOKE UP THAT MORNING WHAT WAS ON YOUR MIND?

FELTUS TAYLOR, JR.: A WHOLE LOT OF DIFFERENT THINGS. I WAS MOSTLY FRUSTRATED ABOUT HOW EVERYTHING HAD TURNED OUT, AND WHAT I WAS TRYING TO DO AS FAR AS GETTING MY LIFE TOGETHER. AND IT LOOKED LIKE EVERYTHING WAS GOING DOWNHILL. RIGHT THEN AT THE MOMENT I WANTED TO COMMIT SUICIDE.

Q: YOU WERE THAT UPSET?

A: YES, MA'AM.

Q: HOW LONG DID YOU SIT THERE IN YOUR APARTMENT?

A: MAYBE ABOUT—LET'S SEE, ABOUT SIX O'CLOCK WHEN I WOKE UP, MAYBE THIRTY MINUTES; FORTY MINUTES AT THE MOST.

Q: WHAT WERE YOU DOING DURING THAT PERIOD OF TIME?

A: TRYING TO THINK WHERE I WAS GOING TO GET ANOTHER JOB AT.

Q: WHAT ELSE WERE YOU THINKING?

A: ABOUT MARCIA.

—Penalty Phase, Day 3: 52, January 25, 1992

I got into my car and left. I wasn't but about five blocks away from the guy that I was buying weed from. I went over there to get my fix.

When I got there, I had to park across the street because some other people was parked in front of the dope house.

Tuesday, March 27, 1991 — 7:30 a.m.

FELTUS TAYLOR, JR.: WHEN I FIRST LEFT, I WENT ON THE CORNER OF JEFFERSON AND NORTH 30TH TO THIS HOUSE THAT—A LITTLE DRUG HOUSE WHERE THEY SELL DRUGS AND STUFF AT. AND I WENT AND AT FIRST I BOUGHT TWO JOINTS. THEN THEY HAD THIS GUY, HE WAS LIKE SELLING THE DRUGS FROM HIS HOUSE, AND WHEN I FIRST BOUGHT THE TWO JOINTS, HE HAD A GUN AND HE ASKED ME DID I KNOW ANYBODY WANTED TO BUY A GUN, AND I TOLD HIM NO. SO I WENT AND SAT IN MY CAR AND SMOKED TWO JOINTS. WELL, I SMOKED ONE OF THEM RIGHT THEN. AND I GOT BACK OUT MY CAR AND I WENT

BACK, AND I WALKED UP TO HIM AND I ASKED HIM HOW MUCH DID HE WANT FOR THE GUN AND HE SAID TWENTY DOLLARS. SO, I GAVE HIM TWENTY DOLLARS AND I TOOK THE GUN, AND I WENT AND GOT BACK IN THE CAR. AND ON MY WAY LEAVING—

BONNIE JACKSON: WHERE WERE YOU GOING?

A: AT THAT TIME NOWHERE IN PARTICULAR. I WAS JUST FIXING TO LEAVE FROM AROUND THAT AREA, BECAUSE THE POLICE COME BY THERE PRETTY REGULAR. SO, ON MY WAY LEAVING I HAD TO TURN DOWN NORTH ACADIAN RIGHT ON THE SIDE OF CHURCH'S [Fried Chicken] PARKING LOT. SO, I STOPPED IN CHURCH'S PARKING LOT AND I SMOKED THE OTHER JOINT THAT I HAD. AND I WAS DEBATING WHETHER I OUGHT TO COMMIT SUICIDE OR NOT.

Q: HOW LONG DID YOU SIT THERE?

A: WELL, I REALLY DON'T KNOW WHAT TIME IT WAS THEN.

Q: WHAT KIND OF THOUGHTS WERE GOING THROUGH YOUR MIND?

A: THAT I HAD—I WAS LETTING PEOPLE DOWN. LIKE MY GRANDMOTHER HAD STARTED PRAISING ME FOR BEING ABLE TO GET OUT ON MY OWN AND HAVE TWO JOBS AND MAKE A MAN OUT OF MYSELF.

Q: AND SO, WHAT ELSE WERE YOU THINKING ABOUT?

A: WELL, I WAS THINKING ABOUT ALL OF THAT, AND I HAD BEEN LYING TO MY GRANDMOTHER FOR THE LAST WEEK OR SO, TELLING HER I WAS WORKING AND I WASN'T WORKING NOWHERE.

Q: WHY DID YOU LIE TO HER?

A: I DIDN'T WANT TO HURT HER. I DIDN'T WANT HER TO KNOW THAT, WELL, YOU KNOW, I HAD LOST MY JOBS, AND THE REASONS WHY I HAD LOST THEM.

Q: AT SOME POINT IN TIME DID YOU DECIDE TO GO TO THE RESTAURANT?

A: WELL, YEAH. I WAS SITTING IN CHURCH'S PARKING LOT, AND I WAS DEBATING WHETHER OR NOT SHOULD I SHOOT MYSELF IN THE HEAD, AND I SAID I WAS GOING TO WAIT AND SEE IF THAT JUST BE THE LAST THING THAT I DO. AND I THOUGHT ABOUT KEITH AND I SAID I WAS GOING TO GO BACK AND ASK KEITH COULD I GET MY JOB BACK. BECAUSE HE HAD GAVE IT TO ME BEFORE. AND HE HAD ALWAYS TOLD ME I WAS THE BEST WORKER HE HAD EVER HAD AT THE RESTAURANT. SO, I JUST FELT LIKE THAT IF I WENT AND TOLD HIM MY SITUATION THAT HE'LL HELP ME.

Q: SO, YOU WENT TO THE RESTAURANT?

A: YES, MA'AM.

—*Penalty Phase, Day 3: 53-4, January 25, 1992*

I drove right up in front. Keith came to the door after I knocked and smiled at me. He opened the door to let me in. We sat in the front at a table to talk. I asked him about getting my job back.

"I don't know, man," Keith said. "I've tried and tried, and you still won't come to work or do anything you should do, Feltus."

"Keith, you know that I've been going through a lot of changes with Marcia. Because we have talked about it before. It's been hard to get back to that spot that I was at before. But I know that I can do it if I had a little more time. Man, you know that I'm a good worker."

BONNIE JACKSON: WAS HE ABLE TO GIVE YOU YOUR JOB BACK?

FELTUS TAYLOR, JR.: NO. HE HAD A FULL CREW AT THE TIME, AND HE DIDN'T HAVE NO OPENINGS.

Q: AT SOME POINT IN TIME DID YOU CLEAN UP THE FRONT OF THE STORE?

A: WELL, WE HAD SAT DOWN AND LOOKED IN THE NEWSPAPER, AND THEY HAD AN OPENING AT A POPEYE'S DOWN THE STREET, AND HE CALLED THERE, BUT THE MANAGER OR WHOEVER WAS HIRING WASN'T THERE, SO HE ASKED ME COULD I WAIT TILL NINE O'CLOCK. HE ASKED ME DID I HAVE ANYWHERE TO GO, AND I TOLD HIM NO. SO HE ASKED ME DID I WANT HIM TO BUY ME BREAKFAST, AND I TOLD HIM YEAH. SO, HE TOLD ME IF I WANTED TO, I COULD HELP HIM OPEN UP LIKE I DID IF I HAD BEEN WORKING THERE EVERYDAY, LIKE I HAD BEEN KNOWN TO DO IN THE PAST.

—*Penalty Phase, Day 3: 55, January 25, 1992*

I went in the back of the store where the mop room was to get some rags to rub everything down and clean the windows.

On the way to the back, I passed a lady who was fixing food for the salad bar. I spoke to her, and she spoke back and asked me how I was doing. I said "okay," and I was just trying to get my job back, and she laughed and went on back to work. Donna was a cool person. She was always kind with a good heart. I guess you could say we were friends. We didn't talk a whole lot, but she knew that I was having problems with my old lady.

I went in the office to get some towels, and Keith had opened the safe. He was getting the money out to put cash in the register and count the rest to take to the bank. I stopped and all I could see was the money, and it was like that was the answer to all my problems. It was like being in a movie, like when someone sees a lot of money and says, *Damn, I'm going for it.* That was what it felt like to me. One big movie.

I turned around and walked out of that office with the towels in my hand. When I got to the front lobby, I threw the towels on a table and kept walking out to my car to get my gun from under the seat. I won't lie—the money seemed to be the way out of my problems.

BONNIE JACKSON: SO, WHAT DID YOU DO?

FELTUS TAYLOR, JR.: SO, THE GUN I HAD JUST BOUGHT, I HAD LEFT IT UNDER THE SEAT IN MY CAR. SO, I WENT BACK TO MY CAR AND I GOT THE GUN FROM UNDER THE SEAT. AND WHEN I RAISED UP, I SAW THE HANDCUFFS, BECAUSE I HAD KEPT HANDCUFFS OVER MY REAR-VIEW MIRROR. SO, I GRABBED THE HANDCUFFS AND I TOOK THE GUN AND PUT IT IN MY COAT POCKET AND I WENT BACK IN THE STORE.

Q: AND THEN WHAT DID YOU DO?

A: I TOOK THE MOP BUCKET BACK TO THE BACK AND DONNA WAS MAKING BISCUITS, AND KEITH WAS IN THE FREEZER DOING SOMETHING. I DON'T KNOW WHAT HE WAS DOING.

Q: AND THEN WHAT HAPPENED?

—Penalty Phase, Day 3: 56, January 25, 1992

I went back to cleaning up the front lobby. I mopped it and wiped everything down. Just as I was getting done, Keith walked out with a newspaper. He sat at a table next to the window. I walked over to the table and sat down. I was saying to myself, I just need to get this money and leave.

FELTUS TAYLOR, JR.: I THREW THE HANDCUFFS ON THE TABLE AND TOLD DONNA TO PUT THEM ON. AND SHE JUST LOOKED AT ME AT FIRST BECAUSE SHE WAS SHOCKED. SHE DIDN'T KNOW WHAT WAS GOING ON OR WHAT I WAS DOING IT FOR. BECAUSE THE LAST CONVERSATION I HAD HAD WITH HER BEFORE I QUIT WAS THE WEEKEND, THE SAME WEEKEND THAT I HAD LOST MY JOB. I ASKED HER BECAUSE SHE SAID SHE WAS HAVING SOME PROBLEMS WITH HER BOYFRIEND, THEY WAS ENGAGED, AND SHE TOLD ME THAT THEY HAVE PROBLEMS. AND I ASKED HER WHAT SHE THOUGHT I NEEDED TO DO TO TRY TO WIN MARCIA'S CONFIDENCE BACK. AND SHE GAVE ME AN EXAMPLE FROM AN ARGUMENT OR SOMETHING HER AND HER BOYFRIEND HAD HAD RECENTLY. SO THAT WAS THE LAST CONVERSATION I HAD HAD WITH

HER BEFORE THAT WEDNESDAY. AND SHE DIDN'T KNOW WHAT TO EXPECT. SHE WAS SCARED AND NERVOUS. AND WHEN I TOLD HER TO PUT THE HANDCUFFS ON, SHE JUST KIND OF LOOKED AT ME LIKE, WHAT I'M GOING TO DO THAT FOR? AND THAT'S WHEN I PULLED THE GUN OUT, AND SHE PUT THE HANDCUFF ON. THEN KEITH CAME OUT THE FREEZER, AND HE WASN'T LOOKING DIRECTLY AT ME AT THE TIME, BUT I HAD CALLED HIM. AND HE TURNED AROUND AND LOOKED AT ME AND HE GOT SCARED.

BONNIE JACKSON: WHAT HAPPENED NEXT, FELTUS?

—Penalty Phase, Day 3: 56–7, January 25, 1992

Keith pulled his arm away from me and tried to run out of the back door. He ran right into it and pushed it and fell back because it was locked. He must have forgotten that the door was locked. Normally, it would have been open so we could take the trash out and for the trucks to deliver food in the morning.

I ran over and grabbed his arm again. This time, I pulled him to where Donna was standing. I told them both to walk into the office to the right of us.

JIM BOREN: ALL RIGHT, TELL ME IN YOUR OWN WORDS, DIRECTING YOUR ATTENTION TO THE DATE OF THIS INCIDENT, APPROXIMATELY WHAT TIME—DID YOU GO TO WORK THAT DAY?

VIOLA KAGLEAR: YES, SIR, I DID.

Q: APPROXIMATELY WHAT TIME DID YOU GET THERE?

A: AROUND ABOUT 8:30 OR A LITTLE BIT BEFORE 8:00.

Q: OKAY.

A: BUT I HAD—

Q: OKAY, TELL ME WHAT HAPPENED WHEN YOU GOT THERE. DID YOU NOTICE ANYTHING UNUSUAL?

A: YES, I SEEN FELTUS'S CAR OUTSIDE AND THEN I WAS—WELL, I WAS KNOCKING ON THE DOOR FOR TO GO IN.

Q: NOW, WHY WAS IT UNUSUAL FOR FELTUS'S CAR TO BE THERE? WAS HE WORKING THERE?

A: NO, SIR, HE WAS FIRED.

Q: ALL RIGHT, GO AHEAD. TELL ME WHAT HAPPENED.

A: AND I PEEPED INSIDE AND I SEEN KEITH AND FELTUS, YOU KNOW, GOING INTO THE STORAGE ROOM BY THE—THE BAR WAS.

Q: WERE YOU LOOKING IN THE—WHERE WERE YOU LOOKING IN, WHICH DOOR?

A: IN THE FRONT, THE FRONT DOOR.

Q: AND THEN AFTER I BANGED AROUND ABOUT TWO TIMES I SEEN THE EXPRESSION ON KEITH'S FACE, SO I JUST SAY, WELL, LET ME WAIT A LITTLE WHILE.

—Guilt Phase, Day 1: 38, January 21, 1992

BONNIE JACKSON: WHAT WAS HE SAYING TO YOU?

FELTUS TAYLOR, JR.: WELL, HE WAS—HE WAS ASKING ME WHAT WAS WRONG AND WHY I WAS DOING IT. I DIDN'T HAVE TO DO THAT. AND HE ASKED ME WHAT WAS WRONG WITH ME. AND I TOLD HIM I JUST NEEDED THE MONEY. AND I TOLD HIM I HAD SOME BILLS AND I WAS HAVING SOME PROBLEMS; THAT I NEEDED THE MONEY TO TAKE CARE OF THEM. AND HE OFFERED—HE HAD LOANED ME MONEY IN THE PAST, AND HE OFFERED TO LOAN ME SOME MORE, BUT I TOLD HIM I KNOW HE DIDN'T HAVE THE KIND OF MONEY THAT—FOR WHAT I NEEDED AT THE TIME.

Q: AND THEN WHAT HAPPENED?

A: HE GOT NERVOUS AND HE COULDN'T OPEN THE SAFE, AND I TOLD HIM TO HURRY UP AND OPEN THE SAFE. AND I TOLD HIM, I SAID, WELL, I JUST WANT THE MONEY AND I'M GOING TO LEAVE. I SAID, I KNOW YOU'RE GOING TO CALL THE POLICE, BUT WAIT TILL AFTER I LEAVE BEFORE YOU CALL THEM. AND DONNA KEPT TELLING ME, WELL, THIS AIN'T LIKE YOU, FELTUS. YOU DON'T HAVE TO DO THIS. THERE'S OTHER THINGS YOU COULD DO TO TRY TO GET MONEY. BUT I DIDN'T LISTEN TO HER.

Q: WHAT HAPPENED NEXT?

A: WELL, THEY WAS TALKING TO ME TRYING TO GET ME TO PUT THE GUN. DOWN, BUT I WOULDN'T PUT IT DOWN.

Q: WHAT WERE YOU SAYING TO THEM?

A: I JUST WAS TELLING THEM I WAS HAVING PROBLEMS AND DIFFERENT THINGS, AND THAT I JUST NEEDED THIS MONEY REAL BAD.

—Penalty Phase, Day 3: 57-8, January 25, 1992

I was scared and nervous. While I was standing there looking at Keith, I started to cry and said, "Please, just let me get this money and go and everything will be okay for all of us. I don't have any job and nothing else right now. I told you that I have problems. Why can't you just understand that?"

BONNIE JACKSON: WERE YOU ANGRY?

FELTUS TAYLOR, JR.: NOT AT THAT PARTICULAR MOMENT I WASN'T. BUT I GOT ANGRY AFTER THAT.

Q: WHEN DID YOU GET ANGRY?

A: I REALLY DON'T KNOW WHEN.

Q: WHY WERE YOU ANGRY?

A: FOR A LOT OF DIFFERENT REASONS, BUT NONE OF THEM WOULD JUSTIFY WHAT HAPPENED.

Q: WHAT DID HAPPEN?

A: WELL, I THINK WHEN I ASKED KEITH FOR MY JOB AGAIN, AND HE TOLD ME NO, I THINK DONNA MIGHT HAVE SAID SOMETHING ABOUT, DON'T GIVE ME MY JOB, OR IS YOU GOING TO GIVE HIM HIS JOB BACK, OR SOMETHING TO THAT NATURE.

—*Penalty Phase, Day 3: 58, January 25, 1992*

Something went off inside of me.

FELTUS TAYLOR, JR.: AND I GUESS—I GUESS THAT'S WHEN I GOT REAL ANGRY. THAT WOULD BE ABOUT THE TIME I STARTED SHOOTING. AND I CLOSED MY EYES AND I JUST STARTED SHOOTING.

—*Penalty Phase, Day 3: 58-9, January 25, 1992*

I raised the gun and pulled the trigger. After shooting her, I turned the gun towards Keith and shot him, too.

VIOLA KAGLEAR: A FEW MINUTES LATER I HEARD SOME SHOTS AND I RAN OVER TO FROSTOP.

—*Guilt Phase, Day 1: 39, January 21, 1992*

He appeared to clearly dissociate during the stress of the robbery and when Donna Ponsano, a coworker, made the provocative remark to Mr. Clark, "You aren't going to give that nigger the job back, are you?," he described clearly like something snapped and he dissociated and stated it was like looking at Marcia, his ex-girlfriend, and feeling all the anger and hate that he had repressed come out and he just started shooting and later realized he had shot Donna Ponsano and Keith Clark.

—*Deposition from Or. Paul Ware, January 12, 1998*

Then I stood there, frozen in time. I was like a board. I didn't move at all. I looked at what I had done. I couldn't believe it myself. I looked at them down there on the floor.

It was like I was in a movie. I could not believe that I had just shot two people like that. Things were running through my head. Everything was going so fast. I wanted to go over and touch Keith or say something to him, but what could I say?

BONNIE JACKSON: WHAT HAPPENED AFTER THAT? WHAT'S THE NEXT THING YOU REMEMBER?

FELTUS TAYLOR, JR.: WELL, I STOOD UP FOR A MOMENT AND I JUST LOOKED AT THEM BECAUSE AT FIRST I COULDN'T BELIEVE WHAT I HAD JUST DID. AND THEY WASN'T NO ENEMY OF MINES OR NOTHING. I WASN'T REALLY ANGRY WITH THEM. ALL THEY EVER BEEN WAS A FRIEND TO ME, BOTH OF THEM. AND I REALLY DON'T KNOW WHAT HAPPENED EXACTLY AFTER THAT. I JUST PICKED UP THE MONEY OFF THE FLOOR AND I LEFT.

—*Penalty Phase, Day 3: 59, January 25, 1992*

FELTUS TAYLOR, JR.: AND I GOT IN MY CAR, AND I WAS DRIVING DOWN FLORIDA AND I STOPPED AT THIS RED LIGHT, AND I WAS THINKING ABOUT WHAT HAD JUST HAPPENED. SO, I KNEW—I KNEW WHAT WAS FIXING TO HAPPEN AFTER THAT, SO I STARTED TO, SINCE THIS HAD HAPPENED LIKE IT DID, I STARTED TO—I WAS ON MY WAY—I WAS GOING TO DRIVE TO MARCIA'S HOUSE.

BONNIE JACKSON: WHY WERE YOU GOING TO GO TO MARCIA'S HOUSE?

A: WELL, MARCIA—I KNOW SHE WASN'T DIRECTLY RESPONSIBLE, SHE WASN'T RESPONSIBLE AT ALL FOR WHAT HAPPENED, I JUST—I DON'T KNOW. AFTER I HAD GOT TO THAT POINT I JUST SAID, WELL—

Q: WHY WERE YOU GOING TO GO TO MARCIA'S HOUSE?

A: WELL, SINCE WHAT HAD HAPPENED HAD JUST HAPPENED, I SAID THAT I WAS GOING TO GO THERE AND I SAID I WAS GOING TO SHOOT HER AND THEN SHOOT MYSELF.

Q: WHAT STOPPED YOU FROM DOING THAT?

A: I WAS GOING DOWN FLORIDA [BLVD.], I WAS GOING TO HER HOUSE AND I HAPPENED TO SEE TWO POLICE CARS COMING UP THE STREET, AND I KNEW THEY WAS GOING TO CAJUN'S, SO I TURNED OFF FLORIDA, AND TURNED ON AIRLINE, AND WENT DOWN AIRLINE, AND I WENT ON THE STREET I LIVED ON AT THE TIME,

WHICH WAS PRESCOTT. AND I WENT AND PARKED MY CAR AT THE FIRST SET OF APARTMENTS THAT I PASSED WAS THE APARTMENTS WHERE A FRIEND OF MINES HAD STAYED AT, SO I WENT THERE AND I JUST SAT IN THE CAR AND LOOKED AT THE MONEY AND I LOOKED AT THE GUN, AND I DECIDED I DIDN'T—I LOOKED AT THE MONEY AND I JUST SAID I DIDN'T WANT IT. I DIDN'T WANT IT THE WAY I HAD GOT IT. AND I SAID I HAD JUST SHOT TWO PEOPLE THAT DIDN'T HAVE NOTHING TO DO WITH MY PROBLEMS, OR WITH WHAT WAS GOING ON IN MY LIFE, AND I JUST HAD SHOT THEM FOR NO REASON.

—Penalty Phase, Day 3: 59-60, January 25, 1992

I was scared. I smoked a joint in the car. Then I remembered that there was an empty field behind my cousin's apartment. I walked over to the field and put the money there.

Then I started walking down the street to my apartment.

Once I was there, I did not know what I should do. I kept thinking about those two people and what I had just done. I kept playing it over and over again in my head. I left my apartment and caught the city bus downtown, and I went to the levee. I still had the gun on me. Once I was at the levee, I threw the gun in the river.

I pulled out another joint and smoked it. Then I smoked a cigarette and left for the bus.

Tuesday, March 27, 1991—8:30 a.m.

I went over to Mae-Mae's house. She asked me where my car was. I told her that something was wrong with it, and I had to put it in the shop.

I asked Mae-Mae if I could use her phone, and she said to go ahead. I tried to call my cousin Raymond, but he was not home. I asked Mae-Mae if she would mind if I took a nap before I went to work. She said to go ahead. She didn't know what was going on with me at the time.

BONNIE JACKSON: NOW, ON THE DAY OF THE SHOOTING, DID FELTUS COME BY YOUR HOUSE?

WILLIE MAE BROWN: YES.

Q: TELL ME ABOUT THAT.

A: WELL, I HAD CALLED MY SISTER TO TAKE ME TO THE GROCERY STORE. AND WHEN I HEARD A KNOCK IT WAS HIM. I LET HIM IN. AND HE LOOKED ALL CRAZY AND WILD. AND HE JUST LAID ON THE FLOOR AND WENT TO SLEEP. AND I'D SAY ABOUT TWENTY

MINUTES AFTER HE WENT TO SLEEP, MAYBE MORE, MY SISTER CAME. AND, LIKE I SAID, I LOVE THE CHILD JUST LIKE MY OWN GRANDSON. AND I TRUSTED HIM IN MY HOME AND I JUST LOCKED THE DOOR AND LEFT HIM IN THERE. BECAUSE WHEN HE GOT UP ALL HE HAD TO DO WAS UNLOCK IT WITH THAT LITTLE KNOB AND GET OUT.

Q: WHEN HE CAME OVER THAT DAY WAS THERE ANYTHING UNUSUAL ABOUT HIM, SOMETHING ABOUT HIM YOU'D NEVER SEEN BEFORE?

A: YEAH. HE ALWAYS COME IN AND BE JOLLY. AND HE WAS GROGGY LIKE IN SLEEP, OR WAS DRUNK OR SOMETHING LIKE THAT.

Q: AND YOU SAY HE LAID DOWN ON THE FLOOR AND WENT TO SLEEP?

A: YES.

Q: AND YOU STAYED THERE ABOUT TWENTY MINUTES AND YOU LEFT AND WENT TO THE STORE?

A: RIGHT.

Q: WHEN YOU CAME BACK FROM THE STORE, WAS HE STILL THERE?

A: HE WAS STILL ASLEEP IN THE SAME SPOT.

Q: HOW WAS HE LAYING ON THE FLOOR?

A: A LITTLE BITTY FELLOW. JUST STRETCHED OUT WITH HIS FACE OUT. IT'S SOMETHING ABOUT HIM WHEN HE'S DISTRESSED OR DEPRESSED. HE WAS LAYING ON HIS FACE.

Q: YOU'VE SEEN HIM DO THAT BEFORE?

A: YEAH. A LOT OF TIMES WHEN HE GET UPSET. HE JUST FALL ON HIS FACE AND HOLD HIS HEAD. BUT BY HIM BEING SLEEP HE WASN'T HOLDING HIS HEAD. BUT HE WAS LYING ON THE FLOOR STILL IN THE SAME SPOT.

—*Penalty Phase, Day 2: 166-7, January 24, 1992*

I woke up two hours later and told her I had to go get my car, that they should be done with it by now. I took off walking down the street. I had on a pair of sunglasses and a baseball cap. For some reason, I went to a payphone and called the store. I just wanted to know how they were doing. Someone picked up the phone, and I asked if I could speak to Keith. The person said they just took him and the lady to the hospital because they had been shot.

I said, "Well, how are they doing?"

Whoever was on the other end asked me who I was, and I hung up the phone. I started hitting the phone on the little box and wondering what in the hell I was going to do. I kept saying, *What to do? What to do?*

I decided to go to my apartment and get some clothes. I did not know what to do, but I knew I needed to leave Baton Rouge. Every time I saw a police car pass, I jumped and was scared to death. I never wanted to shoot anyone, but I had, and I was really in it now. I thought about my grandmother and what that was going to do to her.

Tuesday, March 27, 1991—6:00 p.m.

I remembered Rosetta [my neighbor], saying she had some people up North. I went to Rosetta's apartment and told her I had to go out of state. I asked her if she wanted to go with me.

She said she had to think about it. Then she said, "You can hang out over here a while, if you want to."

We listened to some music, and she had the TV on with no volume.

She was keeping her friend's little baby boy. He was lying there on the sofa, and I was sitting next to him. I started looking at him and playing with him and thinking of a time when I was that small and started going back over my life. I said to myself, *If Marcia would have had a child for me, everything would have been so different.*

I laid him back down and starting looking at the TV. I asked Rosetta to turn down the music, and I turned up the news. Maybe that was a mistake because I never knew if Rosetta knew my full name. She used to call me by my nickname— Junior. The news people were talking about what had happened at the store and the two people getting shot. When they said my name, she looked at me, and I tried to act like nothing was wrong, that they were talking about someone else. When the news went off, I told her I had to go get my car because it was in the shop.

There was an old, empty house about two blocks from my apartment complex, so I went there to hang out until it was nighttime. Then I went back to my car to get my wallet and see if I could get my cousin to take me to the bus station. I ran the two blocks to that old house. Once I was inside, I just sat there on the floor and cried. I thought about what a mess I had put myself in and what could I do to be free of it all.

Once it was good and dark out, I headed down the street to my cousin's apartment on the other end of the street. I saw two or three police cars go past me—they were unmarked ones, but everyone knew that they were the cops. They slowed down, then went on down the street, and I stopped by a store on the way to try to get myself together and smoke another joint. I kept walking down the street like nothing was wrong.

When I got to the front of my cousin's apartment complex, I walked on into it. My cousin's apartment was right in the front, about three doors down. I walked to his door and knocked three times before he came. An unmarked car came past slowly and went all the way to the back. I thought to myself they must have found my car some way, but how? My cousin came to the door and opened it.

"Let me on in," I said. "I need to talk with you."

He just stood there. "You know that the police is looking for you. They say you shot two people."

I looked at him, and I did not say a thing. Another police car went to the back. I said, "Okay, man, I'm about to go." As soon as that car went by, I went down to the end of the building and jumped that six-foot-tall wood fence right into the empty lot behind the apartments. I hit the ground and started running to the old folks apartments on the other side of the field.

Tuesday, March 27, 1991 — 10:00 p.m.

It was about ten o'clock at night. I leaned out into the street to see if any police cars was coming or going down the street, and I saw none. I ran across it and went down by some cars in the parking lot. I just knew nobody had seen me come that way. I was on my knees with one hand on the ground and the other leaning on the side of a car, which I was using as a shield. I heard some noise, but I did not give it a second thought. Then from out of nowhere, I heard guns clicking. I turned and looked up, and there were about four or five cops behind me. Two were leaving from behind the building and two behind a car, and one looked to be out in the open. My high sure did leave in a hurry.

One of them told me to get flat on the ground, and if I even looked like I was reaching for something, he would blow my brains out like I had done those two people at that store. I did not say a word. I just did what he said.

One cop handcuffed me and then checked me for a gun. They did not find a gun, but they got two nice-size joints out of my pocket. They turned me around and led me to a car in the front of the building. They were trying to talk to me, but I would not answer them.

CHAPTER 18

Tuesday, March 27, 1991—10:30 p.m.

O N THE RIDE TO the police station, my mind was blank except for one thing. I was thinking of Marcia. She kept coming back into my head over and over again. All of the things we had done together, and all of that was now gone forever. When we got to the station, they led me to an office and handcuffed me to a chair. This guy started asking me what had happened and did I know what I had done. He said if he could, he would kill me right then.

About that time, Downing and Finch walked in and one of them said, "Boy, we had all of our rats out looking for you. You were lucky they found you and not us."

I had a baseball cap on my head that read *Please stop the violence*. Finch said, "Let me have that cap, there. We will keep it for a souvenir of you. I told you all you had to do was work for us, and you would have been okay. But now look at you. You are going back to prison for a long, long time."

Then they left out of the room. Officer Rice came in—he was a big Black man. He started talking to me about how much I would help myself if I just told him what had happened. "I know that you have been to prison for ten years, and the way things look, you will be going back that way again."

I just hung my head down because I knew he was right about that.

"Why did you shoot those two people?" he asked. "Where is the money?" He asked me all kinds of things, but he saw I did not want to talk. He left for a while.

I leaned down and rubbed a tear from my eye.

A little while later, Officer Rice and some other cop came back into the room and unhandcuffed me from the chair. The other guy cuffed me behind my back. They led me to the side doors into the night air and took me around the front of the building, where the news reporters were waiting. I put my head down and the cops walked me through them. A lot of people with cameras was taking pictures of me and wanting to know if I had anything to say. I kept my head down and didn't say a word. It was about two in the morning.

Then Rice and the other guy walked me back inside, like they were just bringing me there to the station. They led me back to the office and the chair I was in and handcuffed me back to the chair. Officer Rice started talking again about telling him what had happened and that he would talk to the judge for me to see if he would help me out some. Well, Rice left, and this other White guy came in to get me to sign a rights waiver, but I did not sign the first one he brought me. The rights waiver was at the bottom of a form where they read my Miranda rights to me and had to check that I understood what they said. The officer told me that it wouldn't be an admission of guilt if I signed it. But I asked for a lawyer and wanted one before I said anything.

Officer Rice came back in and said, "You know that those two people could die who you shot?"

"I don't want them to die. I never meant to shoot anyone. I don't know—it just happened. I wasn't planning on it to go that way." Then I started crying.

He uncuffed me from the chair and asked me if I wanted a cup of coffee. I took it because I knew it would be a long night. I told him what happened with Marcia and myself up to the shooting, but for some reason he did not write it down or have me on tape or videotape either. Officer Rice asked me again about the money, and I told him I would take him to it.

They took me to parish prison to book me.

On the way, I was just looking at everything like it was the last time I would ever see it again. I saw a few cars on the highway, some stores with the lights on in front. I thought, *This will be the last time I am on the outside world again.* They booked me with two counts of attempted first-degree murder and armed robbery.

They asked me if I wanted to make that one phone call, but I said no because I did not want to call my grandmother. I did not ever want to call her again. After this, what could I say to her? I had sent that lady through hell ever since I knew her. What could I say? I shot two people while trying to rob the place. I did not want to talk to anyone. I was mad at myself, and I was really mad at Marcia for helping to mess my mind up to the point that I did not care about what I was doing anymore.

I stayed in the booking area of the jail until about 10:00 a.m. They brought me a letter from this lawyer named Mrs. Jackson. I thought she might be the Mrs. Jackson that came on the end of my case right before I went to Wade. After that, a guard came to take me to another part of the prison. They took me to the old part of the jail, somewhere I had been before, a long time ago. The place had changed a lot since the last time I was there.

The guard led me to a cell in which they put people they thought may kill themselves.

The cell that I was in was big and had a window. There was a road right behind the prison that led out to Scenic Hwy. On the left-hand side of the corner was a Popeye's where a lot of the guards went to eat. There were some houses on that road, too. Whenever I looked out of it, I could always see people coming and going somewhere. I would look out of that window a lot and think about the bullshit I was in and how it got to that point. I hated myself and everything that had happened to me. I hated all the pain and hurt that I was putting others through. I asked God why in the hell he let me come into this world if all I was going to do was cause hurt and pain to others and to myself. I would sit on the floor in a corner of that cell and cry and cry until no more water could come out of me. I still had not called my grandmother, and I was not planning on calling her, either. I felt it would be best that way because there was nothing I could say or do that would change anything anyway.

Two days later, they put me in a holding cell where I waited for the officers to come see me. I saw them come through the door. Another guard came and unlocked the cell I was in and took me to them.

"Do you know why we are here?" one said.

When I said no, Officer Rice said the lady I shot had died.

It was like I was there listening to those words, but I was not really there. The words went right through me. Keith was still alive, but they did not know how he had survived. Man, what was happening to me now?

They dropped all three other charges and just charged me with one count of first-degree murder. I cried, and I was sorry that all of this had happened by my hand.

When I got back to my cell, I prayed for Donna and Keith's families. Keith had never been anything but good to me from the first day that I met him. He liked me as a person and thought I was a good worker. Keith had even loaned me money before until I got my check. Then I went and did something like that.

Later that week, Mrs. Jackson came to see me and to talk about the case. She was the same person who had my other case years ago. My other case put her on the spot because she did not know what was going on. All she had were the notes from the lawyer before her who had worked on the case. But I did not feel she would do any better this time. She told me the D. A. was going for the death penalty. When she said that, it really did not sink in at the time. I mean, I knew what she said, but it was hard, I guess, because this was happening to me. Then I said to myself, *So, what if they kill me? I will just be dead. That would be better anyway. Then everyone would have peace and go on with their lives.*

She told me they had found the money, and she asked me what I had told them. We talked about my case for a while. After I went back to my cell, I got in the corner of the floor next to my bunk and lay there until I went to sleep. One of the guards woke me up to see if I wanted to eat. I waved my hand and lay back down and went back to sleep. When I woke up later that night, they let me out on the first tier, which had been shut down, to shower and use the phone or just walk up and down the tier to talk. Most of the time, I showered and came back to my cell. Then one of the White guards asked me one night if I had a Bible. I said no, and he gave me one and told me to read it. I didn't read it right then and was not planning on it because it was over for me anyway.

The first two months, I would just sit and look out the window or at the walls in my cell. I finally called my grandmother during that time, and she came to visit me. She cried and asked me why I did such a thing. She wondered what was wrong with me and told me I hurt her very badly with all of this stuff. I also got a few visits from my cousins and the people I worked with from McDonald's.

This one young Black guard started talking to me at night when he worked. He would let me out of my cell to clean up for him after everyone had showered on the four tiers. I would mop out the showers and floor and clean the tables. He would let me hang on the tiers and talk to the guys or make phone calls for them. Other guards started talking to me and asking what happened with me. They said I did not seem like I should be there.

"Yeah, that makes two of us," I said.

Mrs. Jackson and my other lawyer, James Boren, started to come to see me more. Mrs. Jackson and I got past what happened with my case twelve years before. They were very friendly towards me, and I could see they were both kind and caring people. I started to trust them because I saw that they really was trying to help. They were talking to all kinds of people that I had been working with and trying to find out everything about me that they could. In prison, you hear stories about lawyers that don't do anything—just enough to get by. But these two wasn't like that at all.

As the days and months went by, the three of us became very close, and I knew I was in good hands. They only had so much to work with, but the two of them did their very best to make a good case for me. I remember once after Mrs. Jackson went to interview Marcia, she told me how it went and said that girl was such a bitch. She asked how I ever got involved with her. I could not help but laugh because I had never heard her talk like that before.

Mr. Boren was cool, too. I would tell him how I really felt about everything and how sorry I was that all of this had happened. I told him I wanted to write Keith a letter to tell him all of that. He told me to write it, and that he would hold it until it was a good time to give it to him. I said all right. It took me a while to write it because I really did not know what I wanted to say or how to say it. What could I really say, anyway? I had changed this man's whole life and the lives of his family and Donna's family forever.

How does a person deal with such a thing? It hurt to know that I had taken something I could never give back. Many times, I asked God to just kill me in my sleep and save everyone from going through all of the pain and hurt. If I would have had the courage to kill myself, I would have a long time ago, but I was scared to do it. I used to ask God why he let this happen. Why didn't he stop me or let me have car trouble or anything that would have kept me from going there that day? I had no answers for any of those questions.

It took close to a year before I went to trial. Every time I went to court for a hearing, it really hurt me down to my soul to see Keith there in that wheelchair. Knowing I was the reason for him being in it. Death would have been easier than going through that. It was hard for everyone involved, and I really did not want to see those good people go through it.

The days of my trial were long, hard, and struggling days. It was hard for both sides, and I hated every day of it. Mrs. Jackson got so caught up in it that she got sick from working so much. Mr. Boren had to handle things at the end. They both put up a very good fight for me, but the jury just did not want to hear anything they had to say. All they could see is what I had done. Even now, I do not blame them for that. I feel that it also had to do with the makeup of the jury. They were all White, and the two people that got shot were White.

I don't remember much of what happened during my trial because of the pills they were giving me. All through my trial, I was getting back to the jail late at night. I would be tired, my head would be hurting, and I could not think right. They would have my pills that helped me sleep waiting on me.

They was giving my pills to me at the wrong times. A few times, the med man would give me an extra one or two because he knew I was having a hard time.

Every morning, the guard came to get me from my cell at 6:00 a.m. and took me to a holding cell. There would always be a few guys in there from different parts of the prison that were going to court the same day. Then at 7:00 a.m., they would take us to a big van to go to the courthouse. They put us in holding cells, there in the basement. There was a TV outside of the cells we could look at.

While the trial was going on, I didn't get back to the jail until 10:00 p.m. sometimes and 11:30 p.m. other times. I should have been getting my medicine at 8:00 p.m. So, I would be really sleepy the next morning, and I had to get up at 5:00 a.m.

Those pills really would put me out on my butt. I would sleep in the holding cell during breaks from the trial. I would even fall asleep in court. I couldn't help it. Mr. Boren had to hit me on the arm or leg to wake me up. But I would still fade in and out on them.

My grandmother was there every day for me. No matter what, she always showed me that love and care that only God could give a person. I hated seeing her there like that because I knew her health was not good, and it was hard on her, but she was there anyway. I saw Keith and his family and Donna's family in the courtroom, too. I thought about how I had fucked their lives up—and mine also.

On **Tuesday, January 22, 1992**, I was convicted of first-degree murder.

The next part of my trial was the penalty phase. The jury would say if I got life in prison or death.

At the last part of my trial, a lot of people got up to talk about me. Donna's family said how much I hurt them with what I did. Some people I worked with said a few things, and Mae-Mae and Marcia's sister Karen talked. My lawyers got some experts, too—two social workers, a psychiatrist, and a psychologist.

Marcia got up on the stand. She did not know anything about the crime, but she talked about our relationship and how she said she wanted to have a child for me before I started acting crazy. She never said why I started acting that way. I guess the D. A. did not want to hear that part. Mrs. Jackson asked her a few things, but I felt she did not ask Marcia enough about our relationship. I do not know why, but I felt that the relationship was important for the jury to see the whole picture. Even though there was a lot that came out, there was a lot that did not, and I thought it was important for them to know. But they never did find out. It was really hard when my grandmother had to get on the stand. She was begging for my life and saying how much she loved me.

BONNIE JACKSON: MS. ROWAN, IN SPITE OF WHAT FELTUS HAS DONE, DO YOU STILL LOVE HIM?

HENRIETTA ROWAN: YES, MA'AM. WITH ALL MY HEART, I LOVE HIM. I HATE FOR WHAT HE DID. I MEAN, I FEEL SORRY WHEN I HEARD IT. AND I PRAYED TO THE LORD TO LET THEM LIVE. AND I HAVE ALL THE SYMPATHY FOR THEM. BUT STILL, I LOVE HIM.

Q: WHAT WOULD YOU LIKE TO SAY TO THE JURY ON HIS BEHALF?

A: WELL, I WOULD SAY TO THE JUDGE AND THE JURY, I PUT MYSELF ON THE MERCY OF THE COURT; I BEG Y'ALL, PLEASE DON'T TAKE HIM FROM ME, NOW. PLEASE, SPARE MY CHILD LIFE. GIVE HIM TO ME A LITTLE WHILE LONGER. I BEG Y'ALL, PLEASE. JUST SPARE HIS LIFE—

—Penalty Phase, Day 3: 174, January 25, 1992

I could not take seeing her up there doing that. I started crying. I got so mad at myself and my lawyers for having her up there that I grabbed the table that we were sitting at and picked it up and threw it over by where the judge and some other people were.

I just stood there crying and screaming.

They had to get some guards to take me into the back for a while. Mrs. Jackson had to get my grandmother and see about her. That was one of the worst times of my life.

MICHELE FOURNET: WERE YOU SITTING NEXT TO HIM?

JIM BOREN: I WAS RIGHT NEXT TO HIM.

Q: GO AHEAD.

A: IT WAS A VERY MOVING AND POWERFUL TESTIMONY FROM MS. ROWAN. FELTUS BEGAN MAKING SOME KIND OF NOISES. THAT'S WHAT BROUGHT MY ATTENTION BACK TO HIM. I PUT MY HAND ON HIS SHOULDER AND IT WAS LIKE TOUCHING A ROCK. I SAID SOMETHING LIKE, FELTUS, ARE YOU OKAY. I COULD—HE DIDN'T SAY ANYTHING. HE DIDN'T DO ANYTHING. THEN MY ATTENTION—I DON'T KNOW. IT ALL KIND OF HAPPENED FAST. THE NEXT THING I REMEMBER WITHIN MOMENTS OF THAT HAPPENING WAS THAT THE TABLE UPON WHICH ALL OF OUR STUFF WAS SITTING HAD BEEN PICKED UP AND THROWN AND FELTUS WAS KIND OF WANDERING, HAD STOOD UP AND I SAW THE DEPUTIES MOVING TOWARD HIM. FRANKLY, MY FIRST THOUGHT WAS THAT HE WAS GOING TO BE SHOT BY THE DEPUTIES. I MOVED TO FELTUS, PUT MY ARMS AROUND HIM AND SAID CALM DOWN OR SOMETHING LIKE THAT. AND THEN THE JUDGE—MY RECOLLECTION IS THE JUDGE, AT THAT POINT, DECLARED A RECESS. I REMEMBER LOOKING AT THE JURY AND THEIR EYES WERE THE SIZE OF SAUCERS.

—*Motion for Post-Conviction Relief, 61–2, November 24, 1997*

The judge called a recess for about an hour and a half.

JIM BOREN: WELL, WHAT I REMEMBER TELLING JUDGE PITCHER WAS THAT FELTUS WAS VERY UPSET, THAT HE SAID THAT HE WANTED TO GET ON THE WITNESS STAND AND THAT HE WANTED TO ASK FOR THE DEATH PENALTY. HE SAID—AND I SAID IN PARTICULAR HE WANTS TO HAVE THE DEATH PENALTY, HE WANTS TO BE EXECUTED TOMORROW BECAUSE HE DOES NOT WANT HIS GRANDMOTHER OR ANYONE ELSE TO GO THROUGH ANYMORE MISERY BECAUSE OF THIS.

—*Motion for Post-Conviction Relief, 64, November 24, 1997*

The judge called me back in first and said that he understood this was a hard thing to go through, but told me not to act like that again. They would have to keep me out of the courtroom or tied down if I did. I promised him that I would not, and the trial started back up. It went on for about another hour before they called it a night.

On Sunday, the lawyers said their closing arguments. The jury went in to decide what my outcome would be. I was in the holding cell, waiting and thinking about what had happened at the trial. The guard was watching the Super Bowl on a small TV. I sat in a chair by his desk and looked at the game with him.

My lawyers were saying it was a good sign that the jury was taking so long to decide and that he thought they would choose life and not death. It was after six when I got called back in to court. There wasn't anyone in there right then but my lawyers. I sat at the table, and they both said they were ready.

People started to come back into the courtroom. My grandmother and her friends and family, Keith and his family, and Donna's family and other people there to watch. The judge and then the jury came in. The judge asked them if they were ready, and they said yes.

Then the judge asked me and my lawyers to stand up. And after we did, he asked the jury to read their decision to the court. I did not look at them. I just looked down at the floor. I knew that it was hard for them, too. Then the words came that I would never forget, just like the shots that came from the gun that Keith would never forget. The shots that changed both our lives forever.

The jury foreman stood and said, "For the crime of first-degree murder, we sentence Feltus Taylor to death by lethal injection."

I just was holding my head down. It didn't surprise me, because I felt that they would do that anyway. My heart and everything else dropped to the floor, but I did not say a word or cry. Why? I did not want my grandmother to see me take it bad. It was hard enough on her. I heard her when she started crying. I looked back. Someone helped Mama Henrietta out of the courtroom. My friends were crying. Keith and his family and Donna's family was hugging each other. Bonnie and Jim was holding my hands.

The guards led me back to the holding cell, and both of my lawyers came to check on me. I told them I was okay and asked them to check on my grandmother. I just walked around in the holding cell, thinking about all of the pain I had caused everyone. I had a lot to think about and to work out within myself.

At the time of Feltus's conviction, the East Baton Rouge Parish District Attorney's office aggressively pursued death cases. Each new Assistant District Attorney who prosecuted homicides was encouraged to seek the death penalty. The D. A. at the time, Doug Moreau, a former LSU football player, promoted these practices in his office. The First Assistant D. A., John Sinquefield, was a huge supporter of the death penalty and zealously prosecuted Feltus.

PART FOUR

ON THE INSIDE
9 YEARS, 2 MONTHS,
10 DAYS

CHAPTER 19

A lot of times I am in a confused state of mind just from being in this cell so much! See, being on death row is harder in itself than not knowing what will happen from one day to the next. You go back over your life, looking at the mistakes you made that got you here. It can start to wear on your mind! If it wasn't for the people in the free world who I have become friends with, I don't know if I could hang on anymore ... When I first met them and we started to write each other, I thought to myself, "Why would they want to write to me? I am on death row for murder."

—FELTUS TAYLOR, ESSAYS, "GETTING IT TOGETHER"

May 1993

BEING ABLE TO TALK to someone on the phone or get mail is so important to a guy on the row, and it is hard for a lot of people out there to understand that. They mean well, but life goes on, and they are caught up in everyday life. That's why it was so special to me, when people took the time to write me. As the days turned into months and into years, Jane Officer, my pen pal, and I formed a very strong bond with each other.

She decided to visit me, all the way from England. That was very special to me. I had people sixty miles away in Baton Rouge who did not want to waste gas to drive up here. She had not been over here since Andrew Jones [the last execution by electric chair in 1991] had been killed, so I know that it was a bittersweet trip for her.

The first visit was good. We hit it off. I told her what Sister Helen [Prejean] had told me about writing down my thoughts and maybe turning them into a book.

Jane also thought it would be a good idea. We also talked about how I got to death row. I felt I could trust her with my feelings and thoughts because she would not judge me like most people had. If she did, she kept it to herself. Upon her leaving, she said that she was going to visit Andrew's family and his gravesite. I can only imagine how that was for her because they were very close friends, and it took a lot out of her when he died. I really didn't think she would get involved with me after all that, but she did. And she stayed involved.

Jane started to come visit me at least once a year. She and I looked forward to those visits. She also wrote me two or three times a month, and sent me pictures of some of the places that she went to on holidays.

Feltus had the ability, especially at that time, to bring out the mother in most women. He was very lost and his letters were quite childish. He also reminded me very much of some youngsters I have taught in the past in inner city schools. Very vulnerable and unable to foresee the results of their own actions till too late. His "typical" background I was familiar with through Andrew [Lee Jones] and I understood the effects of his early life on what happened later . . . Very early on Feltus started calling me Mom in his letters and as he was just 6 months older than my own son, David, it just seemed natural to call him my special son. He would sign himself as that or "your step son" . . . He always drew a set of smiley faces on his letters and referred to himself as "Mr. Smile."

—*Jane Officer, pen pal*

Jan Macdonald and I started writing to each other maybe a month after Jane and I did. Jan was younger than Jane Officer, and we found all kinds of things to talk about. I do not think she had ever written to a death row inmate before—I was the first. She acted like I was the same as anyone else she had met. We talked about sports, life, and some about God. We talked about me and how I got here to death row. We opened up to each other as time went by. Jan talked about herself, her family life, and her boyfriends. When her father died in the summer of 1993, I tried to be there for her and help her through it all I could. For a while, she had a lot of problems because she was always depressed and had low self-esteem. I understood that. We would talk about it, and I would try my best to help her with it. Sometimes I would help, and sometimes I did not do so well, but we both worked through some hard times together.

There were times she came from England to Los Angeles to visit her sister or friends, and she also wanted to visit with me. I could not understand it because there was nothing special about me. But Jan is one of those people that tries to find the good in everyone and everything.

Her first trip to Louisiana was okay. That was sometime in early 1993. She had a few friends that lived in New Orleans, and she went to stay with them a few days before coming to see me. It was her first time at Angola, and it was strange for her with the iron bar doors slamming all of the time. I knew she did not know what to make of it.

We both knew what the other one looked like because we had sent each other pictures, but she was a bit shorter than what I thought. She was smaller than I was, but she had a big old smile on her face and I had one also. We had a good visit, and we ate and talked and laughed together.

I remember looking forward to the [first] meeting. We had been corresponding for approximately 14 months at this stage. I had never been to Louisiana before, and whilst the surroundings were somewhat strange, felt that this was the most normal of things to be doing. It was a non-contact [visit], so I had difficulty seeing the exact expressions on his face, through the screen; however, he immediately struck me as very lovable and genuine. I had extreme difficulty equating the person standing in front of me, with the reason for him being on death row. To this day, it has always been a contradiction . . . At that stage, his level of guilt and self-recrimination was profoundly deep. We discussed the hours leading up to the shooting and he spoke about this state of mind when the incident occurred. He also seemed at a loss to be able to access that part of his character. At the end of one of the visits, he said, "Well, now that you know everything about me, I probably won't hear from you again." He also constantly questioned what my impression was, of him.

We also enjoyed each other's company and there was always a mutual affinity and humorous side to both of us. I know he felt loved, validated, and appreciated within the security of the friendship. I also feel that the friendship was mutually supportive. As profoundly aware as I was of the fact that Feltus was on death row fighting for his life, I believe that we treated each other as equals. In the beginning, he would joke that I wouldn't let him get away with anything. He also expressed that he liked the fact I wasn't always pitying him and lamenting over the dire circumstance, in which he found himself. I believe he felt comfortable with the balance I tried to strike between compassion/ sympathy and expectation, that he could and would always behave with dignity and be a human being who showed integrity. As importantly, he expected the same of me.

—Jan Macdonald, pen pal

Carol started to write me after she heard Sister Helen read my letter to the Life Lines group. Carol is cool—she says what is on her mind. I have been there when she has had problems, and she has been there for me. When she got married, she sent me pictures and cards to let me see what the wedding was like. It was like I was there with them. Even her husband would write me from time to time. They have never been to the United States. They have thought about it but haven't made the trip. Still, they have been there for me in spirit and in letters and a phone call now and then. When she writes me, she tells me about her life, at work, at home, when she gets pissed off about something or whatever is going on. She made me feel a part of her life.

From day one he was genuinely concerned about me, my family (especially my Grandad who was about 10 years older than Henrietta), and my friends, no matter what was going on in his own life. I could talk to him about anything and everything and knew I would get his honest reply. Feltus was so easy to talk to and had a great sense of humor. He always offered me help and advice on life without me asking. He was there for me of his own accord for 2 major setbacks in my life . . . But the main thing I like[d] about Feltus was quite simply "he was my friend."

[What he liked about me was] that I could tell him everything, even some things that I could not discuss with close family/friends. He knew he was my special friend, and he very quickly became my little brother (lii bro'), and I his big sister (big sis').

—Carol ____

It is funny how much just knowing these three people did for me. I started to feel like a real person again. I started to not be so angry with myself. They were doing more for me than anyone in Baton Rouge was, aside from Mrs. Jackson and Mr. Boren.

I was surprised when Mrs. Jackson and Mr. Boren told me that I was giving them a new outlook on a person facing the death penalty. Mr. Boren always said that by us becoming friends and really getting to know each other, he wanted to help others who faced the same thing as me. And I could tell Mrs. Jackson saw me for the real person that I was—my good sides and my bad—and how I got into this whole mess.

They believed me when I said I really was sorry and did not want things to happen the way they did. We talked about all kinds of things in the past, and I told them both about maybe wanting to write a book. They thought it was a good idea and said it would keep me busy, for sure.

I started to not care what other people thought about me because they did not really know me. They only knew what I did and judged me for that. I did not blame them, but there was more to me than the worst thing I have ever done. Most cannot see that far, but the ones that got to know me were usually surprised at the person I am. I was starting to see that there was more to me than my crime, but it was still clouded by a lot of junk I had inside.

I would lie in my bunk and listen to the guys talk at night about everything from love, to law, and God. A lot of times, they talked about death and the guys who were executed in the past.

What always got me was the different views everyone had about God. They would even try to use the Bible to prove their points to each other. They would always say what God should do but never what they had to do to be real with God. I saw a lot of people on the row who said that they were Christians—they went to church, but when they came back on the tier, gaming, smoking, drinking. Something was wrong with that picture.

I did not want to become like that—saying I was Christian, but not really being it.

But in everyone's life, there comes a time when a person has to sit down and really think about his life and the way that it is going. Usually, that time comes at a low point in a person's life. I was living in darkness. And I knew that the time to search for the light was coming for me. But I didn't know how to go about it. I knew I was looking for something, but I did not know what. I just wanted to do better than I was doing. I mean, there was something down inside of me that needed to come out that could change the meaning of life for me here on death row.

It was hard, though. I was so mad with myself. I still had not forgiven myself for what I had done. How could I? I had taken a life and left someone in a wheelchair for maybe the rest of his life. I mean, I thought about the victims that were involved in my crime a lot. I would think about how I have changed their lives and what they have to live with each and every day of their lives. It's not easy knowing that I have caused such grief, hurt, and hate.

No one in this world knows how to wake up every morning and look at those bars and think about why he is here. You wish that you could die right then, just to have all of it over with. To a guy on death row, death is easy. What is hard is living from day to day.

May 1995

The next person to be executed was Thomas Lee Ward, but people called him B. J. I came to know him some and was on the tier with him for a while. He was an older guy in his late fifties, and he had all kinds of health problems. He wasn't working on his case or anything. He always said he wanted to die because he had lived his life and was old. He didn't want a life sentence because he said he had too many health problems and wouldn't make it out there with the other inmates.

I went on the yard, and the tier he was on was facing the yard. He was on the hallway doing his hour, and he came to the window and called me.

"What's up? I heard that you have a bad date," I said.

"Yeah, I'll be waiting for you down in hell," he said.

I hollered back at him and said, "Well, you'll be lonely because I'm not trying to go down there."

He laughed at that, and I went back to running, but those words stuck with me. I mean, it was like he knew where he was going, and he didn't care. When I think about B. J., that is what I remember the most: *I'll be waiting for you in hell.*

When B. J. was put to death, he didn't let anyone come visit him.

The only person with him was his lawyer, and he didn't eat a last meal. He only drank Cokes and ate fruit. It was a low-key day for him, and I guess that is the way he wanted it.

That night, I looked at the news and started to think of myself up there on that TV and those news people talking about my death.

Sometimes you can listen to what others say about you, and you will really start to feel like it is true.

That is what happened to me in a lot of ways. I had done this horrible thing, and now everyone was saying how I wasn't anything and had never been anything. I listened to the D. A. talk about me during my trial. I guess it wasn't hard to start thinking of myself as really not fit to live. I had a lot to overcome and to understand about myself. Jan, Carol, and Jane got me to start seeing myself in a different way at times.

CHAPTER 20

March 1997

I N EARLY 1997, I was hit with the news that the Louisiana Supreme Court had turned down my first appeal, which they had kept for a year. That was really when I started thinking more about what I wanted to do before my time was up. My execution date was set for March 21, 1997.

It was a time of thinking and trying to get myself right with God, and with me. I couldn't get it out of my mind that God hated me for what I had done because he had given me the chance more than once to get my act together. I always ended up going another way that wasn't pleasing to him. Being on the tier where everyone had their own ideas about God was hard for me. We went to church, and the church people would talk about their relationships with God, and it was hard because I didn't know him like that. I felt like I was too dirty to pray. That I had messed up too many times.

I want to get this shit on over with! I mean I'm tired of going through this shit! I have hurt my grandmother and other people by getting into this shit and it is fucking with me, Jan. I wish that I was never born into this fucked up world. I didn't ask to come here then when I do I am a fucked up and I'm tired of it. I want to go on and get this matter over with. I just don't know how to tell my grandmother that I want this. She wants me to go on with all of my appeals but I don't really want two. But I told her that I would, but my life is so fuck up right how. I have no life I'm already dead, I'm just not in the ground yet!

My head hurts a lot now days, I can't have nothing that I want. I can't have my own family and can't have love or nothing else, so what am I living for then? I have fuck my life all the way up, and for what? So, what is life now for me? Not a damn thing. I'm ready to go, so other people can go on with their life and forget

all about me. I don't know if there is something on the other side or not. But I'm
ready to find out, you know?
        —Letter from Feltus Taylor, Jr. to Jan Macdonald, January 28, 1997

I got a stay of execution about two weeks before that date, so I was feeling a little better as far as my case. But when I went to another court to appeal, they also turned me down. They gave me another date.

In the **spring of 1997**, my case moved into appeals with the federal courts. That meant I got two new lawyers, though Mrs. Jackson and Mr. Boren would still help out here and there.

One of the new lawyers who was assigned to my case came to see me and to tell me what was going on. Her name was Jean Faria, and she told me she and Mrs. Jackson were good friends. She said she would work very hard on my case and that I could trust her. Well, I had my doubts about all of that at first. I did a little checking around with the inmates' lawyers, and they said she was a very good person to have on your side. She told me she had only lost one guy to an execution, so I felt a little better about her.

The other lawyer who would be helping her was Michele Fournet. I met her a little later. She seemed to be a real person and not fake. She seemed to care about her work and what she was doing, so I had no problem with her. I had heard things about her, too, and they were all good.

However, she and I didn't take to each other the way Jean and I did. I guess it was because I was in touch with Jean more, and I got to know her better through calling her a lot and talking about my case. Jean was just as cool to talk with as Mrs. Jackson was. She always wanted to know what I would be doing and how I spent my time. I told her that I was looking for another spiritual advisor and why. She said that she would also look around for me.

The days in my cell were becoming boring, and I really needed to get into something. I was tired of hearing all the same old bull from the guys, and I started feeling like I wanted to be around more people who were trying to do something with themselves—and more quietly, too. I found my way to A-tier, downstairs.

There was this White guy called Scooter who talked at church from time to time. He was into painting with watercolors, and I would stop in front of his cell every day to watch him paint. One day, he asked me if I would like to learn how to paint. I said yes, and he gave me a few books to read about painting. Then he started showing me what he was doing and how. He gave me a sheet of art paper and a brush and a little paint and showed me what to do. The first one didn't look like anything at all. It took a little time, but I got the hang of it. He gave me some paper and some of his paint, and I was on my way. I still had to go to him a lot until I really got it down and was doing better, but I was learning; and it felt good to be doing something on my own. I wasn't just lying around feeling sorry for myself. I sent some pictures I painted to my grandmother. She even put them up in her house, along with the family pictures and my diploma.

Scooter talked some about God, and he was into the study of religion, so we would talk about that, too. From time to time, I would pray when my head was really hurting me. Sometimes it would help, and sometimes it didn't seem to do anything. I was still confused, and I didn't like to talk about God because everyone would start arguing, trying to prove who was right about whatever they were talking about. I wasn't about that, so I would keep my thoughts to myself most of the time. But I would pick up on some things that sounded right to me and keep them to myself.

We started talking at length about God and life after death. At that stage, Feltus had already faced execution dates, however, I think the interest in spirituality and religion was part of a far wider search for life meaning for Feltus. He was not the kind of man who was simply clutching at a Bible, because he was contemplating his death. The "lost soul" who I had previously described moved to a much greater and serious spiritual depth.

—*Jan Macdonald*

The next guy up for execution was a White guy, who was a good friend of mine. His name was John Brown, but we called him J. B. He had been on the row, I think, ten or eleven years. He had had something like ten or so stays in the past. I first met J. B. at church. J. B. was from New Orleans. He didn't talk a whole lot, and he was mostly like the other guys around. I would laugh and talk with him on the yard, and we would share tapes with each other.

Before Antonio (another guy on death row) was put to death, we had a three-day church class going. Antonio was there for it, and we prayed for him all three days. During the breaks, J.B., a Black guy named Glenn, and I would talk. J.B. said something that stuck in my mind, and I remember it every time someone is put to death.

J.B. said, "Have you ever thought about what it will feel like to be lying on that table and all of that shit going up in you? They say it don't hurt and only puts you to sleep, but they are not the ones lying up there on that table. I mean, they relax your body, so you can't move, then they stop your breathing. So, you don't know if that person is in a lot of pain or not. That person could be laying up there in knots and struggling to get air."

"Well, you could be right about that part of it, J.B.," I said. "If you ever go over there, make sure to give me some type of sign if it hurts so Glenn and I will know."

The execution date that J.B. got in April 1997 looked really bad for him. He said he had a good appeal issue, but he didn't know how the courts were going to rule on it. J.B. was worried, and it showed in his voice and on his face. He said that he was ready, but he wasn't. Can anyone truly be ready for that?

When we went to church that Friday, I tried to laugh and joke with him, and he did for a while. Then he said, "If it's not like they say—about the execution not hurting—I'll give you a sign. But I'm hoping that won't happen, bro."

The day before his execution, J.B. went in front of the pardon board. I don't know why he did that. Everyone can go on the pardon board a day before the execution is set to go through, but they never do anything for a death row inmate. Even if they do, it has to be signed by Governor Mike Foster. And he isn't doing anything for anyone because he takes a hard line on crime.

The news that evening had something about the pardon hearing, and it was more of a show than anything else. J.B. looked bad on TV. There was worry lines all over his face.

The next morning, right after breakfast, Sergeant Henry opened my cell door, and I walked up to the front of the tier. There was a pair of tennis shoes, two sweatshirts, and some books J.B. wanted me to have. I picked it all up and took it to my cell. Then I walked back up to the front again.

I saw the major, colonel, and the warden coming out from B tier with J.B. to take him to Camp F, where he would wait until that evening. He stopped by the barred door of the B tier, the one across from mine. We just looked at each other. I saw it all over his face—the look of death, the look a person has when they know they are going to die. His head was down, but I could see his eyes. They was glazed over like he was in another world, spaced out and sad. I remembered that he had said he didn't want to go out looking like that.

I never wanted to see that look again. I watched as they led him out of the door and closed it. Sgt. Henry came back to put me back in my cell. I sat on the bunk and looked at what J.B. had left me. I prayed that the Lord would help him out in some way. I was down most of the day and thought about J.B. and what he must be feeling like over there with his sister, his son, and his girlfriend. J.B. was a pretty cool White guy, and I would miss him if it went through.

At the time, the state was still doing the executions at midnight. I asked a guard when he made his rounds down the tier if it had happened. He said it had. I thought to myself, at least it was all over with now.

The next day, I was surprised at what I heard. A few of the people who witnessed the execution said J.B. was struggling after they started the IV in his arm. Right before he died, his body kind of jumped, and he made a loud noise before he died. One person said it looked like a demon had come out of his body. I couldn't stop thinking about how he told Glenn and me that if it wasn't like those people had been saying, and you could feel yourself dying, he would let us know somehow.

I took the way he acted as the "somehow," and I still believe that was his way of letting me know that it was painful and not like those people say it was. It bothered me, that's for sure.

They say death is bad, but death is freedom to a guy on the row. The suffering is waiting and waiting for it to happen. I have had guys doing life sentences tell me they wish they were on death row waiting to die because a life sentence is just a slow death. A lot of them have already done thirty to forty years. Their families no longer come to see them or have died off, and they have no one and nothing to keep them going. They would much rather die. Who can blame them for thinking like that?

Sometimes, I think that would be worse—to have a life sentence and see my family and friends die out or stop visiting as time goes on. Other times, I'm more scared of death.

I wrote Mrs. Daggett, the lady my grandmother used to work for. It took me a long time to write to her because I knew I had let her down when I got into this trouble. She watched out for Mama Henrietta. Mrs. Daggett had planned to help me go to college. Instead, I ended up on death row. She would always tell my grandmother to tell me to write her. I finally did, even though I didn't want to do it at all. She wrote me this nice letter back and told me she still loved me and cared for me a lot. But I still felt unworthy of anyone's friendship. I would tell Jane, Jan, and Carol the same thing—why would they want to be my friend?

Jean and I were starting to become better friends. When Jean would come to see me, I could see it in her face and in her actions that she cared and was trying to do her best for me. I began to cherish her friendship so much. Plus, she said I am easy to work with. She gave of herself and I gave of myself, and that is why we came to have such a tight bond with each other. I gave her the nickname *the lawyer from hell* because, when she gets mad, she can out-curse any man around, and she is not scared to say what is on her mind to anyone. A lot of people don't like that, but she doesn't care. She is a rebel, and I love her for that.

What touched me the most with Jean and what made our friendship special was that she was trying to do some work that Mrs. Jackson and Mr. Boren had tried to do before my trial but couldn't. She was trying to find my birth mother. The most important thing to me was for them to find her because I always wanted to know what she was like and why she had left me. I told Jean what finding her would mean to me, and she understood. To be able to talk with her about my birth mother was really special to me, because it wasn't like you could share this with just anyone. It was difficult, and I had so many mixed feelings about her.

CHAPTER 21

THE DEATH ROW SEMINAR in the **summer of 1997** was an important one for me. Like always, I looked forward to that day. Everyone on death row got to visit with their families and lawyers and tried to look their best.

I was sitting at the table waiting on my grandmother and Jan Macdonald to come, and this tall, skinny guy came and sat next to me. I didn't know him at all. I guess he had asked someone who I was and they pointed me out to him.

He said his name was Charles deGravelles. He knew Mrs. Daggett from church, and she had asked him to talk to me. Charles had been coming to Angola with a prison ministry group, and he was their leader. He had been doing that for several years. We talked for a while, and he met my grandmother and Jan. I gave him my name and address, and he said he would write to me. There was something about him I liked, but I couldn't put my finger on it.

We started with writing off and on, just talking and getting to know each other a little better. I wrote Mrs. Daggett and told her I had met her friend. She wrote back and said he was a good guy.

Around this time, my case was in the post-conviction phase.

There were new people becoming involved in my case. Some of them were trying to get information about my life to use with the courts. Jane Smith was a social worker—a middle-aged, nice-looking White woman. She was very nice and knew what she was doing. She was a disciplined and balanced person. She had done her homework on my case.

Jane worked for Cecile Guin. Cecile worked on lots of death penalty cases and gave expert testimony on people's life histories during trials. She was also the director of the Office of Social Service Research and Development at Louisiana State University. When Cecile visited me once, I told her I was working on my autobiography. She encouraged me to keep working on my book because she felt it could really help the teens of today. A lot of the work she did had to do with at-risk youth and prisons. She said she would find someone to work with me to get the book done, which is what I had been needing all along—someone who would help me tell my story the way I wanted and had a passion for writing, too.

Even though I hadn't taken any writing classes, I wrote what I felt. I developed a passion for writing I didn't even know I had. As time went on, I felt it grow and grow inside of me. It's a passion I feel God gave me to use for a reason. I would sit in my cell and watch the news on TV and see the kids and teens getting into more and more trouble out there. It seemed like they were all getting killed, coming to prison for the rest of their lives, or ending up on death row. I would wonder what could be done to help stop all of this madness.

Around this time, I got a call from Feltus' lawyer, Jean Faria. Jean's son, Gabe, was at Trinity Day School and she and her husband, Joe, had been attending Trinity (my church). She wanted Feltus to have a spiritual advisor and had heard of my work. She was floored when she found out I was already in touch with Feltus. I was floored by her call and took this as a sign that I should be pursuing this path.

—Charles deGravelles

In one of our first visits, I told Charles I wanted to do something for young people that would get them to think about their lives and where they are headed. He thought that it was a good idea, but I needed to pinpoint what I wanted to do.

Charles always wanted to build me up spiritually. He would read to me out of the Bible and tell me what it meant to him, and I would tell him what it meant to me, and we would just talk it out until I had a good understanding of what was going on. We would pray together for my grandmother, his family, the victims' families, and just everyone in the world.

Charles did something that really touched me. He bought me a study Bible that cost sixty-four dollars and had my name put on it. I know how much it cost because anything sent to a prisoner had to have a receipt with it from the store it came from. It was really special to me. He also sent me some good church tapes to listen to.

Charles just seemed to really care about me as a person. I mean, you could see that in the way he talked and acted. He wanted to get to know the person that I was on the inside. From the start, he was a laid-back kind of guy, and it was easy for me to talk with him. I felt like I could trust him—he had that way about him. We built our relationship from Bible readings, prayer, and getting to know each other, and getting to know each other's families. Even though he worked and had his own family to see about, he would check on my grandmother for me.

We were two seemingly different people, from two different worlds, but the Bible seemed to bring us together. I told him about my world, and he told me about his. Every time that we studied the Bible together, I always came away with something to think about. He planted seeds that took root as time went on. He put in time with me that no one else had. I started to find myself not wanting to let him down. Just the idea would hurt me to my very soul.

My change really came after meeting Charles. He helped me from a spiritual standpoint. He opened me to a new side of me, which was way deep down inside and covered with a lot of junk. He saw my bad sides and my good, and he stuck around.

I found myself really not wanting any of the people in my life to think they wasted their time on me. I wanted to make them proud of me. For some reason, I didn't want to let these people down like I had done in the past. Now that I think about it, I had been let down so much in my own life that I had a habit of doing the same thing to other people who cared for me, even when I really tried to do the right thing.

In **August 1997**, I had to get up at 5:00 a.m. to get ready to leave Angola to be in Judge Ralph Tyson's courtroom. After breakfast, a guard gave me a bright orange jumpsuit to put on, so in case I tried to run, they would have no trouble seeing me from far off. They made me take off all of my clothes and turn around to show them I wasn't hiding anything on me. Then I put on the jumpsuit. One of the guards put the leg irons and some handcuffs on me.

It was a nice, cool morning out, and the sun was just coming up. It looked so good out there. It reminded me of the times I would drive to work on days like that. The trip to Baton Rouge was so wonderful to me. Getting to see all the cars and people going to work was so nice. I missed looking at the trees and old buildings. It was as if I hadn't left, but I had and had been gone a long time. But it was home, and it looked good to me anyway.

When we drove downtown, it looked the same. We went along some streets I'd been down many times before. But I wasn't enjoying it like I used to because after I saw the courthouse, I started thinking about how the day would be for me, and about Keith and his family. I knew they would more than likely be there. Every time I have to relive it, they do also, and it's hard on everyone.

When we got upstairs to the courtroom, I had to wait in a holding cell by myself. It was a room with four chairs and a window cut into the door with a screen over it. I could see the people coming into work and going here and there. Michele and Jean came in first to talk with me. Jean wasn't going to be able to stay because she was due back at the office, but she wanted to assure me that Michele could do what needed to be done in court that day. She gave me a big hug. About that time, Charles came in to listen in and to say a prayer with us all. Jane Smith was just there for support and to make sure I was doing okay, which meant a lot to me.

About thirty minutes later, it was showtime. The two guards led me down the hallway to Judge Tyson's courtroom. One of the guards opened the door behind the bench where I had to walk in, and I was facing the front. The D.A.'s table was to the left, and the defense table was to the right. Right behind that was where everyone else who wanted to come would be sitting. I went and sat at the table with Michele. I didn't say much to her—I just listened to what she and the D. A. had to say to Judge Tyson. He listened some and didn't at other times. I heard he was a hard judge to deal with.

Keith and his mom and dad were sitting behind the D. A.'s table, about three rows down, looking and listening to what was being said. I looked back at them once, and Keith was looking at me. I turned back around and looked down at the table. Judge Tyson called a recess for about twenty minutes. I didn't have to leave the courtroom, but I did because I had to use the bathroom.

When the guard brought me back in, Keith was sitting by himself. His mom and dad had stepped out for a second, I guess. I looked at him, and he looked at me and said hello. I nodded my head back at him. He didn't look mad or anything right then, but when his mom and dad came back in, he changed.

I hate to say this, but I feel that it's true, though. If his mom and dad didn't hate me so much for what I did, I feel we could have talked in some type of meeting set up by my lawyers. I had started praying every day and every night for Keith and his family—I wished and prayed so much that I could talk with him and tell him how I feel about what I've done to his life. I knew I was the only one who could answer any questions he may have about what happened so he could put that part of his life to rest. I had tried to get in touch with him, but all my attempts failed, mostly because of his parents. They hate me so much, but I can't blame them. They are old themselves, and now they have to take care of their son, too. Thinking that I brought this upon them for no good reason and have forever changed their lives is enough to make me mad as hell. However, I don't want their hate for me to eat them up on the inside.

That day I wanted more than anything for God to help them overcome their hate for me and let me talk to him. Even if it wouldn't be anything more than for him to let out his hate, madness, or whatever on me. If that would help him, then I was more than willing to do that—it would be the only right thing to do.

Judge Tyson didn't want to hear too much of what Michele had to say. She seemed to be doing a good job at talking, then the D. A. would cut her off, they would go at it, and the judge would have to stop them. Everything Michele tried to say that day Judge Tyson shot down, so it wasn't a good day for us at all. The judge gave Michele another court date to come back and try to settle some other issues she was working on.

When it was time to go back to Judge Tyson's Court for my hearings, Jean, Charles, Michele, and Jane Smith were there again to support me. Jean was talking to Michele about working something into my case to make the judge hear it.

It turned into a long, unsuccessful day. Michele did try her best, and I have to thank her for all that she tried to do. I'm not mad at Michele about anything. She did her job and did it well, but she only had so much to work with. That time was much like the first—the judge didn't really want to do anything that would help me. Michele tried, but the D. A. was just too good.

At the end of that day, everything went wrong. The judge set another execution date for me, and everyone was sad except the D. A. and the victims' families.

Now, Jean would really come into play because she was the one who would have to get my appeal ready for Judge Frank Polozola at the first Federal Court of Appeals. I was a little down, but I already knew it was unlikely that Judge Tyson would do anything for me, anyway.

Jean was working her butt off on my case and trying to find my birth family as well. My execution date was coming up fast—May 22, 1998—and she didn't really know if the Fifth Circuit would look at my case or not.

At that time, she had Jane Smith and a guy named Roger Phillips—a private investigator—try to find my birth family. Roger was able to track my birth mother down in New York. Her name was Shirley Wiggins. Roger got on a plane and went up to see her. She was in jail waiting to go to court for some charges of trying to use phony prescriptions. The first visit he had didn't go that well because she didn't want to open up to him. She felt it would hurt her case, but where she got that from, I'll never know. She wasn't all there in the head anyway because she had some mental problems. Roger didn't get much out of her that time, but he said that she was beautiful—kept herself up—and educated. He went back a second time to try to find out more about me and my other family members.

I wondered how she really felt about my situation. Not that it was her fault that I am where I am, but I wondered if she cared at all. He said when he told her I was on death row, she was shocked, as I guess any mother would be. I was a bit mad about what she did with me, but I felt something in my heart for her. I don't know what it was, though, maybe a little love. I really don't know.

Roger learned that my birth mother didn't know who my birth father was. Now, that is cold when a woman doesn't know who the father of her child is. I won't lie, I hated her for that, and I hated her for just giving me away the way that she did. But I wanted to know more about her and her life. I really wanted to understand why she had given me up. She left me with two old ladies who took care of me for a while. Then, they had to give me up because they couldn't take care of me.

Roger also found out that she had more children besides me. So, I had three brothers and two sisters out there somewhere. My youngest sister was living with my birth mother before she went to jail. Roger wanted to go see her, but my birth mother didn't want him to tell her about me for some reason.

I got a letter back from my birth mother in late May. I was shocked, happy, and mad all at the same time. It was a very special letter to me.

May 13, 1998

Dear Feltus:

I am so sorry for what happened to you. I feel that it is my fault, if only I would have been old enough to keep you and raise you the way I should have maybe life would have been different for both of us. I am still trying to get out so that I can see you. If it is the Lord's will, I will make it to see you. I pray every day that your life be spared. You are a part of me, I gave birth to you of course I love you. I have made such a mess of my life. I am praying that I can hold up long enough, to walk out these prison gates one day to live a normal life.

I am finish with the past life. I became addicted to prescription medication a decade ago and I would do anything to get them including steal, so that's why I am here, I am not a violent person nor have I ever been. There is so much I would like to say but so little time. Whatever happens to the both of us, always remember I did love you and still love you now. No matter what. Continue to pray, miracles do happen.

Love and peace

Your mother

P.S. I pray every day for the both of us.

Then she had another page that she added which said this.

Feltus, never ever feel that you weren't loved, as I begin to get older, I often wondered what happened to you and what you were doing. I haven't been to Louisiana in so many years. I won't know where to start looking for what little family that is down there. I hope and pray that your life will be spared if not look for me because, I will join you one day and we will be forgiven for all of our sins. And if it must be, die with your head up high and with the knowledge that you are worthy of the kingdom of God. Oh, I hope for something from God to change and we might meet before either of us dies. I will always love you.

Your natural mother

P.S. I don't know what will happen, but if I get out, I will see you.

Now, this letter from her really, really touched my soul. I cried for a while after reading it. I could really get a feel for her and what she had been through. My heart went out to her.

Not long after that, Jane Smith and Roger found my great-aunt, a lady by the name of Annie Collins, who was in her seventies. She was the sister of my birth mother's mother. She was able to give them information on a lot of my family members, including a sister and brother I had living in Baton Rouge. The first thing that came to my mind was that I wondered if I had ever passed him or her in a store or on the street somewhere. I wondered if I had even talked to them and didn't know who they were. Maybe I went to school with them. Annie even told them where my sister lived, and they were able to go see her and get some pictures to send me. Jane said that she sounded very happy, even after telling them I was on death row.

My brother and sister said they wanted to come visit me. I won't lie—I was very happy about it. I had always wondered what that day would be like when we met for the first time. I mean, I thought it would be like those talk shows where they find long-lost loved ones. The people on the shows hug and kiss and cry together. For some reason, that is the idea I had built up in my mind of our meeting, but I would get a rude awaking about that.

One night, the lieutenant told me I had a special visit approved by the warden. I thought nothing of it. I figured it must be Roger or Jane Smith coming to see me. But, boy, was I surprised. I was the first one in the visiting shed. As I was looking through the door to see who it was coming to see me, I saw Roger, a woman, and a guy. I didn't know who they were. As Roger came through the door, I said hello and shook his hand. He turned to the other two and said, "This is your brother and sister, Feltus." It was Leo and Sheila.

I hugged them both, and we sat down to start talking. The only thing that I picked up on right away was that Leo hugged me, and Sheila only shook my hand. Right off, I was hurt. You would think she would have hugged me also. I understand that this was all new to her, and it was her first time coming to a prison, but, damn, I am her brother.

I guess she didn't feel the same way that I did about it. I learned that she and Leo were very close, and that my birth grandmother had raised Sheila and someone else had raised Leo. Leo was the oldest, thirty-nine years old, and Sheila was thirty-four. We were the first three kids. Our mother had done the same thing with all three of us—given us up.

Sheila was really mad with our mother for doing such a thing to us. She and Leo had only seen her once or twice in the past years. I told them she had written to me twice and that even though I was hurt at what she done, it was in the past, and we needed to try to overcome that and be a family again. But my words were in vain, and it hurt me. I was trying to show them that if I could forgive her, then they could, too. We needed to work through all of this, along with me being on death row.

I guess it was too much for Sheila to deal with. She was doing well for herself. She was married and had two kids and a good husband. She was a schoolteacher, and her husband worked at a plant. She was living a good life. Now, my brother, on the other hand, was a different story. He lived the street life and didn't own a car and had just gotten a job. He had been to jail a few times, but Sheila had been there to get him out. I said to myself, *Now, if she can do this for him, why can't she get to know me?*

We took two pictures together. I kept one, and they kept one. I would guess Leo kept that. Sheila said she would write and would come back to see me again. But after they left, I didn't hear from either one of them. I guess our meeting was a bittersweet one. It was nothing like what I had been seeing on those talk shows, nothing at all like that.

CHAPTER 22

CHARLES HAD A FRIEND in the Department of Corrections. Richard Thompson was involved with the juvenile institutions in the state. He wanted me to do a video talking about myself and how I got to death row. When Charles came to me and told me about that program, I told him I really wanted to be a part of it because it would be a good thing to do for at-risk kids. I was glad the guy wanted to use me, but I knew the real reason they wanted to use me was that I had an execution date scheduled that would be my last.

They came for a visit to explain what he wanted to do. If the program worked with the juvenile correction centers, he wanted to try to get it into the inner-city schools, which is what I was hoping for. For the video, I wanted to present one essay per day with questions at the bottom of the screen to do in class. Charles and Richard thought that was a good idea.

I was very pleased with how well it went. I did a clip for the victims' families because it didn't seem like I was ever going to get to meet with them. I read one of my essays, and they even shot some of my artwork. I gave Richard's wife a painting that she liked. They also took some tape of me walking out on the yard to put in with the parts with me talking. After it was over, Charles said I had done really well. He had a big smile on his face.

Most of all, I wanted to give something back that could really help young people. I wasn't the person everyone thought I was. Those people could just see me on the outside of myself. I feel God wanted to show me that, even from death row, he can use whoever he wants to do a job. He used Saul from a prison cell, also. I didn't always see it, but people say they saw it in me. When I look at how I was when I came to prison the first time and eventually went to death row, I can see the change that took place in me. It's not by my own doing that I was able to change, either.

The change came from the people God placed in my life at a rough time to show me that he was still there and still loved me, even if I thought he hated me and I hated myself. I got down on my knees and asked God if he saw any hate in me for another, to please take it away. I want him to help me to be more of the person he wants me to be. That wasn't an easy prayer for me, but it's one I pray every night. I'm not perfect, and I still have my times when I fight with myself. But I just ask him to forgive me and help me to be the person that he wants.

As it started to get closer to the execution date, I started getting more and more mail from Trinity Episcopal, from people who cared and were praying for me. Plus, Cecile, Jane, Michele, Jean, and Charles were coming to see about me. I was really reading my Bible and praying, and I felt a great peace come over me. I was all right with whatever came my way. I wasn't scared of death, and I wasn't scared about what was happening to me at that time. I was surrounded by more love at that time than I had ever felt in my life before. It was from God, I know it was, I felt it in my heart. I had never felt anything like that before.

I had total peace. I can't explain it, but it was there. Boy, God was really good to me. I was really, really ready to go meet him. Charles was right there with me through it all. The man never left my side. I know it was hard on him, I could tell, but he was happy and smiling and making jokes all the way through.

Jan Macdonald and Jane Officer came to be with me. I called my grandmother a lot, to make sure she was doing okay with all of this going on. I know it was hard on her, and she would feel it more than anyone. It was my job to help her to look at it in another way, that I was ready and God had given me the peace and strength I needed to get through this. She told me that she wouldn't cry because I had asked her not to, but she would be happy because she knew I would be with the Lord.

Three days before my execution, Jean had it set up with the warden for me to call my birth mother in the jail she was in, but the people brought the wrong lady to the phone. I think that my birth mother just didn't want to talk with me. I didn't get to talk with her at all. I was angry and sad over that. It just hurt me more than anything else.

Two days before my execution, Jan Macdonald and Jane Officer brought my grandmother up to visit me. Early that morning, Jean called the prison and told them to let me call her. When I called her, it was about 8:20 a.m.

When I answered the phone, she said, "Feltus, the Fifth Circuit gave you a stay!"

Now, I should have been happy about that, but I wasn't. She picked up on it in my tone because I was really ready to go.

My grandmother, Jane, and Jan were on their way up to visit me. Jean hadn't gotten in touch with them yet. I told Jean that I would tell them the news when they got here. I told her thanks for working so hard on my case.

When the guard said that my visit was here, I got ready and was happy they were out there. I was glad for them and for my grandmother, but I was still unhappy about the stay. I mean, when a person gets ready and gets in that mindset to die, and then the courts play with you and say, "I'm not going to kill today, we'll do it later," that messes with your mind for a while. I think that is what happened to me.

I was confused. I felt that that was the suffering part—not dying. When I got to the shed, they were all there waiting for me. I hugged and kissed all three of them.

Then Jan said, "Feltus, you got a stay this morning!"

"Yeah, I know," I said. "Jean called up here to tell me right before you all got here. But how did you all find out?"

Jan had a cell phone in the car, and she had called to check in with Jean on the way up. Jan said that they cheered in the car. They were happy, and my grandmother was, too.

"Feltus, you don't sound happy about it," Jane Officer said.

She was right. I didn't know what to feel anymore. I told them that and tried to get them to see where I was coming from. I feel they all understood what I was saying, but my grandmother wanted me to see it through. At one point, I was ready to give up my appeals, but I let Jean and Charles talk me into going on. They just don't know what this does to you. It's hard to deal with day in and day out, but I felt that I had to do it for them. Not just because we all were friends, but because they had put so much of themselves into me and my case. I just didn't want to let them down by giving up like that. I owed them all that much. I asked God to help me to deal with all of the madness I had caused.

One of the most outstanding memories was when Jan, Jean Faria and I were with him in May 1998 the day after he had the stay then. He had been very upset the day before but we had Henrietta with us and she is always guaranteed to bring a smile. But the next day he was beside himself with anger and shock and said he really wished he had died as he felt so bad about all the hurt for us all. He was worried that Jan and I had spent money and holiday time for "no good purpose"; that he had, in some way, let us down. He said . . . you could all go away and feel sad for 6 weeks and then get on with your lives and forget me . . . We all looked shocked but I said, quite angrily . . . "Do you really think I've forgotten Andrew, that I don't think of him in some way every day of my life 7 years later?" By the look on Feltus' face I don't think it had really truly got through to him till that moment that we all really loved and cared about him . . . especially when Jan and Jean said something similar. From then he knew that we would always be there when he needed us . . . no matter what.

—Jane Officer

I remember Feltus' demeanor during this week. I sensed a real level of depression with him, especially on the Thursday (after he had got the stay). Jane, Jean and I visited with him that day. He was absolutely shocked at the stay, and we spent most of the visit attempting to encourage him to continue with his appeals. He would joke with us that he would make the prosecutors day by writing him a letter saying he was dropping his appeals. Despite the joke, there was a sense of seriousness with the statement. I think that day was the closest I had ever seen him, to giving up his appeals. He suggested to us several times that even if he were to get a new trial and life sentence, all his friends would soon forget him and stop visiting.

One other point stands out about this visit was the fact that, Dobie Williams was also in the same visiting room. At the beginning of the week Feltus' date had been the most serious; however, with his stay, the day before, Dobie's new date of—I think mid-June—became even more serious. I remember when visiting time ended. We all stood up and can still see Dobie and Feltus standing together. I felt so fearful at that moment.

—Jan Macdonald

I took a rest break for about two to three weeks and just tried to get myself back together. But something else put that fire for writing back under my butt. I was watching the news one evening, and there was another shooting at a high school. A boy named Kip Kinkel killed his parents then hurt twenty-two students and killed two at his school in Springfield, Oregon. I just felt so bad at what these teens were doing to their lives that I had to start writing things to go into the workbook again. Plus, I wrote [an essay] for the *The Angolite*, and they printed it. I got a few letters letting me know that I had done a good job. That would help give me the power to go on with it.

In **June 1998**, Dobie Gillis Williams had an execution date. This happened when I was really working hard on my book and on my essays. I wrote down everything that was going on and what I was feeling.

Dobie and I talked from time to time, and we shared tapes with each other. When he was out of coffee, he would send over to see if I had any, and I would do the same thing. I would see him on visits or at church sometimes when he went or out getting a haircut. He was pretty cool with me. Some of the guys didn't like him, but that's how it is on the row. You can't please everyone.

He had been on death row for more than twelve years. Dobie had arthritis really bad in his hands and feet. Sometimes, he could hardly walk or hold things in his hands. And sometimes, he told people, he was ready to get this bull over with. I never talked to him about God, so I didn't really know how he felt about that subject.

The night before his execution date, the guards moved him from the cell he was in to the first cell in the front so they could watch him to make sure he would not hurt himself before they could kill him. That one makes a lot of sense, doesn't it? What is the difference if he does it to himself or they do it? Well, the difference is they want to make a show out of it for people. The news media will play it into the ground, and you would be surprised at the people—besides the family of the victims—who will come to see a person die. It's like they are going to a party or something. Jean told me that, because she remembered what it was like when the guy she represented was executed.

I found out that the party list to watch me die in May was kind of big. I made a joke about it with Jean. I said I should pull my pants down and moon everyone before I go. Well, we got a laugh from that. I got that idea from the cartoon character Bart Simpson. I would really like to see the newspapers the next day if I did that. I bet they would have a lot to say about that one for sure.

When I was out for my hour on the hallway, I saw all of the big rank people, like majors, assistant wardens, and a few other people who you would normally not see at night. They all wanted to make sure that Dobie was okay and didn't need anything. I went to the gate at the front tier. I asked the freeman how Dobie was doing because we were not on the same tier. He said he was holding up okay and was in bed listening to the radio. Music calms the soul, that's for sure.

When my hour was up, I went into my cell and sat down and just tried to feel and think like he must have been doing over there. I felt that he must have been listening to music and going back over his life and where he went wrong. And the crime he committed must have replayed a thousand times in his mind.

When I woke up the next morning, the only thing that was on my mind was what Dobie would be facing that day. I got up and looked out my window, and it was cloudy. Then I turned to go to the front of my cell to watch TV since the morning news was on, and they were talking about Dobie and the plan of execution. I got on my knees and said a prayer for Dobie and his family.

My cell was at the front of the tier, so I could see when the warden and major and guards came to get him to take him to Camp F. That is where the execution chamber is. I watched them pass with Dobie in handcuffs and leg irons. I waved, and he waved back. He looked as he always did, but there was some stress on his face.

I knew he would have a day of visits to help him make it through. I wondered if he was hoping for a stay of execution. I thought that once you got all the way to Camp F, you didn't want it to be stopped because that would be so hard on people's friends and family. The victim's family must have been through a lot, too, reliving it all.

I watched the five o'clock news that night. They said Dobie was to be put to death at 8:30 that night if the US Supreme Court didn't step in and stop it. I wondered what was going through his mind, knowing that death was on its way for him. And that he really didn't have to go this way—if only he had talked with someone or tried to get some type of help before it got to this point. Now, there was no return back for him. I wondered if I may have to walk that very same road one day.

The six o'clock news said that Dobie had eaten his last meal. He had fried catfish, shrimp, and chocolate ice cream with the warden and his spiritual advisor, Sister Helen.

Around 7:00 p.m., I was standing at the front of my cell looking at the TV when I saw Dobie going back to his cell. He got a stay. Someone's prayers was answered, but for how long? Death had to turn back around, but what about the next time?

I found out that he got a stay because his lawyers wanted to get a blood test. They said it could prove that he didn't do the crime. But the test came back with the same type, and a new date was set. Dobie had no more courts to go through, and the governor wasn't going to stop it.

Right after my stay, I put some of the members of my [biological] family on my visiting list. They came to see me a few times, but then they kinda fell off. They said they would write to me and send me a few dollars. I never asked them for any money or anything, but they said they would. Sorry to say, they never wrote or said anything about any money. I called them, and they said they were going to write to me again.

They never wrote, and they didn't show up when they said that they were coming to see me. So, I was let down by them. I decided I would give them another month, and if they didn't show up, I was just going to take them off my visiting list. I took them off because if they didn't care or couldn't make the time, they should have said so at first and not make promises they knew they weren't going to keep.

I had to pray a lot and ask God to take away the anger I felt toward them. I wanted so much for them to be a part of my life. I didn't think that that was so wrong. I said if my death would have brought them together, then it was all worth it. I wanted to try to put my birth family back together.

But after a while I saw it didn't matter so much. I started to think that in a lot of ways, I already had a real family—my grandmother and all my friends who have taken me into their hearts and homes and cared for me as a person.

Dobie got another date for January 8, 1999. Everybody knew that this date would be it. For a while, he seemed mad with everyone about what was going to happen. Then, as time went on, he seemed more at peace and together about it.

Just as I had seen that look of death on J.B.'s face, I saw it again on Dobie's. I hated that sight. It always did something to me on the inside, and I would think about it for days and nights.

Dobie was ready to get this over with. His arthritis was really bad, and he couldn't hardly walk or get up out of bed. It was just getting worse and worse as time went on. He really didn't want a life sentence because he wouldn't be able to do anything out there with all of the other guys. So, in a lot of ways, death came as a friend to Dobie, a friend that would set him free from all of the suffering and pain he had living on death row.

Right before I went to bed that night, I went and looked out of my window and just thought about how it must feel to know that this would be your last night on this earth. You have to have God just to keep yourself together, knowing such a thing. God is the only one who can give you that peace, so it won't matter because you know that you're going to be with him. That is all that matters, nothing else.

I awoke at 5:30 a.m., about ten minutes before breakfast was brought down the tiers to us. I washed my face and, at the same time, looked at the TV. As I was watching the early morning news, the reporters mentioned this was the day of Dobie's execution. Then they showed his picture. It was like I just couldn't take my eyes off of it. He had got by death twelve times before, but this time everyone was feeling that this was it. I didn't really eat. I just kind of picked at it and thought to myself, *What's going through his mind right now?*

As I put my tray back at the front of my cell, I saw the major, captain, and lieutenant going over to the tier that he was on to get him ready to go to Camp F, where he would be the whole day with family and friends until they got word from the courts. Then another guard went over to the tier with the chains and leg irons that would be put on him before coming out of his cell. As they walked by where I could see them, the major was holding his belt from behind as he walked. I remember saying to myself, *Now why is he holding it? It's not like he can run anywhere.*

Dobie had on a black baseball cap, a blue shirt, blue jeans, and tennis shoes. He smiled at the lady guard in the booth who worked the doors. I didn't see that same look I had seen a few weeks ago, and I was glad. Then I heard someone say, "Dobie, I'll be praying for you." I wonder what went through his mind then? After they left, I walked over to my window and looked outside. The sun was out, and there was not a cloud in sight. It was a nice day, around seventy degrees. My mood was up and down that day. In some ways, I was happy for him because all of his troubles would soon be over with.

Then his family could start to go on with their lives again. Yes, they would hurt, but anyone who loses a loved one hurts for a long time. Then they move on with life. And I really felt that was what he wanted.

But I know that he didn't want to die and not by the state. That evening, when the five o'clock news came on, they said that he had about an hour left before his death. At 6:30 p.m., they would kill him. I remember, at six o'clock, I went to my window again and thought about how Dobie must have been feeling and thinking in that cell waiting for them to get him. He had visited all day with his family. I know it was hard to say goodbye at the end of that visit. His family was waiting outside of the gates in the front of the prison to hear the word.

It was almost as if I was there with him, seeing the look on his face when the warden came to say, "It's time, Dobie." With Sister Helen reading from the Bible for him. I could see him taking those steps to that bed; then seeing it and knowing that when he jumped up on it that he wouldn't be getting back off it, not by his own power anyway. I know that right then, his whole life must have flashed before him. Then lying down must have felt really cold at that point. Then his body dancing around within him as the drug started working and shutting his system down. But the people watching couldn't tell from just looking at him.

Later that night, it rained, and I said to myself, *This is to wash away his footprints from the earth forever.*

A few days later, I found out from a freeman that they couldn't find a vein in one of Dobie's arms so they had to put it in the side of his neck. Damn, that must have been hurting him.

Sister Helen wrote a little letter to the guys on the row and said how well Dobie took the whole thing. And that he smiled at her right before he faded out never to come back. I was glad in a lot of ways because I knew that all of Dobie's troubles was all over with. But I was also sad in a way, because I would miss him a lot.

Dobie was gone, and who would be next? It was just a matter of time before we found out.

I stopped working on my book so I could write some more essays. I wanted to put more into the workbook that would go out to at-risk youth. Although it was very hard work, I got it done—the very first book of any type that I wrote by myself. I was happy and pleased with the way it came out. Charles was pleased, too.

The Fifth Circuit had already been holding my case thirteen months, and you never knew what they would do. Jean and all the other lawyers I knew felt it was a good sign that the Fifth Circuit was holding it so long. But I didn't know what the hell was going on.

I had to call Jean a few times to talk with her about how I was feeling. She understood, which is what I liked about her the most. She always had a way to make me feel better and have a better outlook on things. I love her very much for that, too.

We also had a talk about my birth mother. I told her I cared about the woman, but it just didn't seem to be working out because I hadn't heard from her in months. Jean just laid it on the line like it was. She told me that Roger had checked, and my birth mother had gotten out of prison. She wasn't at the last address she had given. So, they were lost right now at trying to find her.

My birth mother said that once she was out, she would get in touch with my lawyer because she wanted to come down here to see me. She had the number to Jean's and Roger's offices, but they had no word from her yet. She had been out of prison for about a month. Jean told me to just let it go because she wasn't what she had claimed to be. It wasn't doing me any good to keep thinking about her. I tried to just put it out of my mind, but it's hard as hell to do because I really wanted to talk with her and even see her face to face. Why would a mother do that?

It was like that letter she wrote me didn't mean a damn thing to her. If it had, she would have gotten her ass down here. It made me mad as hell with her, and I even started to feel that hate come back inside of me.

I started to hate myself all over again and wanted to just be dead and have all of this bull behind me and over with because my life had never been anything and it sure wasn't anything now. I asked God why he brought me into this world because I didn't ask to come. All I have done since being here is cause hurt and pain to other people. I felt all of that old stuff coming back on my shoulders. It was very hard to deal with.

CHAPTER 23

THE DAYS JUST SEEMED to get hotter and hotter in those cells. I couldn't do nothing but lay around and drink Cokes all day, trying to cool off, listening to the fools on the tier talk about everything but the right thing. It was starting to get to me, and I was thinking about moving to another tier. I guess that I was just a little mad with myself and the heat.

During the last part of **July 1999**, I got the bad news. Jean said the Fifth Circuit turned my case down. We talked for a few, but there really wasn't much to say at that point. She said, "Don't give up yet, but it looks bad right now." She was right to tell me that because I only had one court left to go to—the U.S. Supreme Court—and they didn't have to look at it if they didn't want to.

So, that was it for me. The Saturday newspaper said the D. A. had gone to the judge that Friday to get him to sign my death warrant for September 9, 1999. My date was set.

Two weeks before my execution date, I finished my book. I was on such a high. But then I had time on my hands to think about what was really going on. The same way that I was up on a high, I came down just as hard. The last two weeks were wild. The first week I mainly caught up on my rest and wrote letters.

The warden had all kinds of church people coming by my cell to talk and pray with me. Sometimes, I enjoyed talking with them, and other times, it was a pain in the butt. I mean, they'd all come because I had a bad date. It's not like they ever came before. And some were coming for the wrong reasons. See, some of those people just wanted to visit me to see a man facing death—to see what I look like and how I am dealing with it. They asked a lot of questions. Most of the time, I would tell them I'm doing good and whatever God wanted to happen would happen. And that I was okay with that. Then they would look at me funny, as if to say, *How can this be when he is about to die?* They didn't understand that I was at peace with everything. I was not looking at the storm or what was going on around me. I was just looking at God and making the best of it.

But that wasn't the answer that they were looking for. They would start to tell me if there was something that I needed to confess that I could and then we could pray about it together. They felt a person that was facing death should be all upset, worrying, crying, and begging.

But it wasn't like that for me. They couldn't help me at all. The help that I needed and wanted, I felt that I already had in God and the people that I already had around me. I do believe they all meant well, but they didn't really know what to say to me.

What could they say? I had found peace on death row. It was hard, at times, but I found if I just sat back, got off to myself, and forgot about where I am, I would find some of the things that quiet can bring. I could feel the junk leaving my mind and I could get a clear picture of the Lord's love for me. That peace just came into my body and I felt good about everything. No matter what was going on around me.

People need peace. It's like having to keep oil in a car to keep it running right.

You have to get the oil changed every so often, to keep it in shape. If you didn't, that car would give you all kinds of trouble and the motor would lock up on you. Then it wouldn't be good anymore. Peace for us is like *oil for a car*. If we don't get that peace in our lives, then we run the risk of our motors freezing up.

And most of them church groups had a different idea than me on what God is really about. After an hour or two of listening to these people, I would get really confused about what I believed, myself. And that didn't do me any good. So, I was really tired of seeing them every few days.

Every church group that came to death row had to come by my cell to see me. To see the animal that would be put to death soon, like I was in a zoo or something. But they couldn't save me. I had to do that for myself.

For two weeks, not only did I have to put up with all those church groups, but I also had to put up with the crap that Warden Burl Cain was giving me and my lawyer. Don't get me wrong; in a lot of ways, he was good to death row. But in others, it seemed that he was all about the power.

It was during the week of the pending execution date when Jean came to see me about my case. She told me how bad it was really looking for me at that point. There was only like a one in a hundred chance that the U.S. Supreme Court would review my case. I had never been through that court before—and it was the last one possible.

Jean had bought us something to eat, so we ate and drank Cokes together while we talked about how I would want my funeral to be if the execution went through. About three hours after she came to see me, we met with Warden Cain, Assistant Warden Vonnoy, and the lawyer for the warden standing nearby. Once the lady guard let them through the gate between us, he told Jean and his lawyer to wait outside of the door for a minute. Before he closed the door, he told one of the guards to take off my handcuffs, and he did.

Warden Cain sat behind the desk and Warden Vonnoy sat next to him. I was on the other side.

"Do you know who you want to come and visit with you on the last day?" Warden Cain asked.

"Yeah," I told him, and I started to write their names down.

He looked at it and started to ask me questions about the people. Then he signed for the two lawyers to come in. Once inside, Jean sat next to me and the guy went over by the wardens.

Warden Cain told me what Thursday, September 9th would be like so I could prepare myself. He told me that he would come get me that morning before 7:00 a.m. and take me over to Camp F where the execution would take place. I would get to eat whatever I wanted throughout the whole day. I could visit with my family and friends from 8:00 a.m. to 3:30 p.m. Then, they would all have to wait outside the front gates of the prison to find out what happened.

Around 4:30 p.m., they would set things up for my last meal. I would eat with Jean, Michele, Charles, the warden, and the guards that would be on the strap-down team. I would get to talk on the phone to family and friends while I waited for that time to roll around. After the meal, they would put me in a holding cell and have me put on a diaper. (Now, come on. I know that I've outgrown those things).

At 6:30 p.m., about six people would lead me to the room where it will happen. I got to pick three people, and the prison picked the other ones. No one would tell me who would be on the strap-down team—the people who would actually put me on the table and tie me down. From what I've heard, they're mostly assholes.

There would be about thirteen people on the other side of the glass window who would watch me die. They would be people from the victims' families, some news people, guests of the warden, Charles—because he was my spiritual advisor—and one of my lawyers.

I kept thinking of J.B. and how his body had jumped at the end—wondering if that was the sign he had promised to give if it hurt. My fear was that they wouldn't give me enough of the first drug, and I'd be wide awake when the second drug froze my muscles. I was scared, that's for sure. I didn't want to be awake and struggling for air.

Plus, there were all the people the warden was going to let come to the execution. People that didn't know me—only what I have done—and wanted to see what an execution was like. The warden would have coffee, Cokes, and sandwiches for his guests to eat where they waited. I mean, it's like they were going to a football game or something.

The reason that I knew this was, a few days before the execution date, this Black guy came to see me. His name was Johnson, and I had gone to school with his nephew.

He and Warden Cain were very good friends. The warden let him come down the tiers whenever he wanted, to talk to the guys that he knew from Baton Rouge.

When he came up to my cell, he asked, "How are you doing? Do you think this is it?"

I just looked at him and said, "I'm okay. Whatever God wants to happen will happen."

"You know, me and Burl is good friends, and he asked me if I wanted to come to the execution to see what it's like. How do you feel about me doing that?"

At first, I looked at him and said to myself, *What in the hell do you want to come to an execution for?* But I said, "It doesn't matter to me if you come or not. If that is what you want to do, then do it, okay? It don't matter to me."

"I'll come, then," he said.

We talked for a few more minutes, then he left.

I have to say that it was really wild. I didn't like it at all, but there was nothing that I could do about it. I knew that I couldn't let that news get the best of me. I tried to put it out of my mind and think about God.

On **Tuesday, September 7,** Warden Cain and Assistant Warden Vannoy came into the visiting shed, where I was meeting with Jane, Jan, and Michele. They wanted to talk with me—again. We went over to another table and Michele came over with me.

He said that he just wanted to see how I was doing. He told me that he had decided he wasn't going to let me have the visits with the people that weren't on my regular visiting list. The reason he used was this: since those people hadn't been coming before, he saw no reason to let them come now.

I said it was to say our goodbyes to each other.

But he said I could call or write them for that. So, the warden had gone back on his promise to let in all those people but one. And he said it in front of everyone. But what could I say?

Then he went on to something else. "Well, you know that Stone Cold Steve Austin wrestling shirt that you wanted? I told one of my workers to go out and buy it for you. I will send it to you this evening. If you get a stay, you can keep it, but if the execution goes through, I want it back."

"Why?" I asked.

He said that he was going to take it off me after I was dead, frame it, and put it in the prison museum so his guests could see it.

Now, that was some shit. Michele thought so, too. Jane and Jan couldn't believe it at all. We laughed because it was so funny, but it was very real at the same time. My execution seemed to be a big show, more than anything. We took a few pictures, and then we hugged and kissed goodbye. Jan and Jane were coming back the next day to bring my grandmother to visit me.

After I got back to my cell, I lay down to get some rest. The whole thing was taking a lot out of me because I was wearing a mask on the outside. Trying to be happy and smiling in front of everyone so they wouldn't be worrying about me so much. I would pray and ask God to give me the strength that I needed to get through all of this and not to fall weak or break down in front of everyone.

I was scared and worried about the people that I cared about and what they were going through, not so much about myself. I was thinking about what it must have been doing to the victims' families, also.

That evening, I looked at the TV for a while, then I went back to sleep because the next day would be a hard one. I would have to look in my grandmother's eyes and see the pain and hurt that I had caused her by being in this mess.

Just thinking about it made me crazy on the inside. When I was doing all the dumb things that got me into trouble, I never thought about how it would have hurt the people who really cared about me. If only I would've thought first, I wouldn't have done it. I never would have done it. I never meant to hurt anyone.

On **Wednesday, September 8**, I woke up about 6:00 a.m., about five or ten minutes before breakfast came. I ate and then told the guard that I needed a shower because I had a visit coming that morning. After the trustees picked up the breakfast trays, the guard let me out of my cell to go shower. Boy, that water felt good running down my body like that, and I had to wonder if I would be around after tomorrow to feel that water again. I finished my shower, put on my underwear, and walked down the tier to see if anyone else was up and needed something, like water or ice or the phone. Everyone except a guy named M.C. had gone back to sleep. He gave me instant coffee. I got some water out of the hot water pot and then told the guard to let me into my cell.

I read my Bible and said a prayer. I looked at the early morning news on TV, and they did a part on me saying that I had an execution date coming up for the next day. This date that I had was a serious one. The U.S. Supreme Court had never looked at my case. They didn't have to look at it either. They could just turn it down. It looked bad. But I would worry about tomorrow, tomorrow.

Today, I had to get through with my grandmother.

I fell asleep for about an hour. The guard woke me up and said that my visit was here. I washed my face again, put my clothes on, and told the guard I was ready. About five minutes later, I was on my way downstairs to the shed. I was the first one down there. The freeman took off my handcuffs and went back out. A woman guard came in the room who would be there for the whole visit. She was cool—a good person, friendly and easy to talk to. That was good. I didn't want to have to deal with an ass at a time like this.

I kept looking out of the window in the door to see them coming. Jan Macdonald came into view first, then my grandmother in her wheelchair pushed by Jane Officer. I opened the door for them to come in. I hugged and kissed my grandmother, then I did the same to Jane and Jan. We all went over to a table at the far side of the room. The lady guard was sitting in a chair across the room from us. My grandmother sat right next to me.

I asked Mama Henrietta how she had been doing.

She looked at me and said, "I've been better, but God is with me and will help me through this." She still had that strong, low voice that she always had. "I just say my same prayer to God, and I ask him not to let nothing happen to you. But if that's not his will, I ask him to do what is best for you."

I just looked at her because I know that it was from the heart. That was all that mattered to me. My grandmother had gotten so small and fragile and feeble-looking. She was eighty-six years old. She had a number of health problems. She had a bad heart and diabetes. She couldn't go through a lot without it really taking a toll on her. I could see the wrinkles in her face and on her hands. She had her glasses on. They were round in shape, and they were a little big for her face. She had lost a lot of weight and was much smaller than I last remembered her.

I love her so much—she is my heart—and just the thought that I wasn't out there to help her as I should have been was enough to make me want to go in a corner and die somewhere. Looking into her eyes, I could see the pain and hurt that I was putting her through, and I really hated myself for that. What could I do at that point besides try to comfort her? I had to let her know that I was okay and try to get her not to worry about me—no matter what happened the next day. Just let her know that my love for her would always be no matter what. That it was up to God as to what happened.

She seemed to be enjoying her visit, but she also seemed to be getting tired. I didn't look for her to be staying too much longer. After we were done eating, we took pictures with each other. I took a few with my grandmother, with me making funny faces, and she seemed to enjoy those very much. I was glad to be able to make her smile.

Jan and Jane moved to another table to give my grandmother and me a little time together before they left. I hugged her again and sat down next to her and just held her hand while I looked into her eyes and told her how much I loved and cared for her. No matter what happened the next day, God would always be there for us both.

"No matter what, you are my grandson, and I love you very much," she said.

"I know that for sure," I said, "I'm sorry to be hurting you in this way. I didn't really mean for it to turn out this way." Then I had to stop talking because I felt myself wanting to cry, and I didn't want my grandmother to see me break down in front of her. I wanted to be strong for her and for everyone else. So, we just sat there holding hands and kinda looking away from each other.

Jan looked over at me. I moved my head to let her know that they could come on back over. My grandmother had to go to the bathroom, so I helped her up from the wheelchair and led her to the restroom door. We had to walk slow. She couldn't walk fast because she was weak and sickly. While my grandmother was in the bathroom, Jane and Jan said not to worry because they would take care of my grandmother for me.

All of us could tell that she was ready to go because she had nodded off to sleep once or twice while we were talking throughout the visit. When she came out, she said she couldn't stay much longer because she was getting tired.

She had stayed longer than we had planned and that was good. I was very thankful to God for just letting her be able to feel good enough to come up here. It was really a blessing just to see her. Because she just usually was able to come once a year.

I kissed and hugged them each goodbye. I told my grandmother I would call her later that night.

She said, "Okay, I'll be looking for your call."

As they were leaving out of the door, we all hugged each other one last time and Jan and Jane said they would see me tomorrow.

I was . . . very surprised at how much he obeyed her [his grandmother]. During the last visits, when Feltus, Henrietta, Jane Officer and I, visited together, Feltus would play around and stick his tongue out at Jane or pull a rude face at me. A few times his grandmother would catch him doing it and would slap his wrist and correct him. He always stopped immediately, and would bow his head. There was no mistaking who was in charge!

—Jan Macdonald

Once I was back in my cell, after visiting my grandmother, Jane, and Jan, I put on a pair of shorts and just lay down thinking and hurting on the inside. It was a very hard day, and it took a lot out of me. I took a nap for a few hours. I woke up about 8:30 p.m., and I told the guy on the hallway to bring me the phone so I could call a few people. There was still no word from the court. This was serious, but it seemed like a dream to me.

After talking with a few people, I was feeling a little low. So, I started to talk with the guy in Cell 1. His name is Jimmy Williams, and we are good friends. Jimmy came to death row from Baton Rouge in August 1995. He is my homeboy. I didn't know him from the streets, but I had seen him on TV when he was going to trial. When Jimmy first came, he was kinda wild and still had that I-don't-care attitude within him. But over the years, somewhere within his self, he found a need for

God. He started to read all kinds of books. He started to pray and read the Bible also. We would stand at the bars and talk for hours on end about God and where we both went wrong out on the streets. We talked about the young people that was out there, not caring and doing the same things that we had been doing and worse. And about how something needed to be done to help them. We talked about this a lot and how we both wished that we could in some way help them from where we were. I saw a real change come over Jimmy, and I'm glad to know him and to be able to call him a friend. I am closer to Jimmy than I am to anyone on death row. He has become like my little brother. I was glad that he was next to me at a time when I really needed him around.

One of the main things I learned from Feltus is that a person can't live alone, that we all will need someone to lean on at one time or another. Thought I could be a shoulder to others by listening and counseling them in their time of need, at times I felt down I wouldn't allow no one to listen to and counsel me because I didn't want to get attached to anyone here.

I recall one night I was in a depressed mood and didn't care to talk to anyone. Feltus beckon for me to come up to the bars so we could talk, but I refused to talk to him. He persisted and I lashed out at him that he had problems of his own and couldn't help me with mine, and that I would rather be left alone to deal with my problems my own way. Feltus left me alone.

Later that night, after I had calm down, Feltus reached his mirror over in front of my cell to see what I was doing. I tried to ignore him. He held his mirror in front of my cell for maybe a minute and stared without saying anything until I allowed him to catch my attention. Again, he beckons with his mirror for me to come to the bars.

Relenting, I got up to hear what he had to say. "What's wrong?" he asked. "Nothing," I answered.

He paused a minute, I assume to get his thoughts in order . . . "You can't keep all that stuff bottled up inside of you," he said. "The only way you'll feel better is if you talk about it."

"I don't need to talk to nobody 'bout my problems. I can deal with them myself."

Feltus scoffed at my statement. "Don't say you don't need nobody, because everybody needs somebody. They got dudes here who ain't even got no family or people to write to them or come see them. We blessed to have people who care something 'bout us."

—Jimmy R. Williams, Death Row Inmate

Jimmy and I had already said that we were going to stay up all night and just talk to each other because I felt that if this was my last night on earth, I may as well stay up.

I would have enough time for sleep, after I was dead.

The closer that time got, the more unreal the whole thing seemed to me. I told this to Jimmy and Ricky. He was on the other side of me in Cell 3. A small White guy with a face like a mouse. He wears glasses, and he was a pain in the butt at times because he talked loud, and would say some of the craziest things. But he always kept us laughing around here. I really think that he has a good heart even if he is a little weird, you know. He cared about me, and he was worried also. He always went to bed at 8:00 p.m. and got up early in the morning. But that night, he stayed up until midnight, talking and laughing with Jimmy and myself. We talked about everything, from the first time that Jimmy and I met until the time I met Ricky. It was good to laugh like that for a while and not really think about the next day and what it would bring.

Well, around midnight, Ricky said, "I'm going to bed, but I'll be up in the morning, Felt."

I said, "Good, little buddy. Thanks for staying up this long with me."

Everyone that came out of their cell that night to do their hour stopped in front of my cell to talk with me and say how they were praying for me. I thought that it was nice of them. Some of the guys that I didn't even talk to and even the ones that were asses said, "I'm praying for you, man." Now who on earth would think that these guys—who are called the worst of the worst—would be praying and talking kind words to each other?

When Kevan Brumfield came out for his hour on the hallway, he came right in front of Jimmy's and my cell to talk and laugh with us. Brumfield was from Baton Rouge also. Him, myself, and Jimmy was right next to each other for about a year and a half. Brumfield liked to play and make jokes about everything. That guy would lie in a second. Him and Jimmy knew each other from the parish prison. Jimmy would always bust him in a lie. But would that stop him? Hell no, he would keep right on going. He would tell Jimmy, "Yeah, I'm lying, but it sounds good, right? So let me go. I'm on a roll."

So that night, all three of us just talked and laughed with each other. I could tell that Brumfield was scared, and he even said it to us. I know he was also thinking about himself and what it would be like for him if he had to face such a thing.

Yeah, I was scared, and I was thinking what it would be like to have to face all of those people the next day. I was hurting for the people that I was putting through this and wondering why they wanted to go through such hurt and pain. I also had to think about Keith and his family and the Ponsano family. I didn't blame them for wanting to see me dead. But just like I had asked God to forgive me for what I had done, I asked Him to forgive them for wanting to see me dead. Because after it is over, the next day they would still be faced with the same problems that they had been having.

Once I was done praying, I lay down in my bed and wandered off to sleep for about an hour or two. Then the guard woke me up and asked me what time I wanted to take my shower.

I told him around 4:00 a.m. I looked over at the time, and it was 2:30 a.m. I took my mirror and put it around the bars to look into Jimmy's cell to see what he was doing. He was sitting on his bed reading his Bible. Jimmy—my good and faithful friend—was right there. I called him up to the bars, and we started talking about God and praying together. I could see that this was hurting him. We talked about all the different outlooks on God and our real reason for being here on this earth.

Brumfield was still up in his cell. After I was done showering, I went down to talk with him for a while. The guard had told me that I could just hang out. So, I talked to Brumfield, then went and stood in front of Jimmy's and we prayed and talked.

I went back to my cell at 4:30 a.m. The guard made his rounds and let Brumfield back in the tier. I guess Brumfield had begged the man to let him back out so he could come down and talk with Jimmy and me again. We started to laugh before he even got down here to us. I knew that Brumfield was scared and troubled about what was going to happen to me.

I really don't feel that death is that big of a deal. It's just the waiting. Because no matter where we are in life or how much money we have or don't have, death will come to see each one of us, and there is nothing that we can do about it. It really don't matter how one dies. It's more about what kind of life you lived and what you did for others.

At 5:00 a.m., the guard was ready to put Brumfield back into his cell, but right before that, we said a prayer with each other.

We laughed again, and Brumfield shook my hand and said, "I'm going to miss you, Feltus."

I said "Yeah, I'll miss you also—and those way-out lies of yours." He walked down to his cell.

Jimmy was talking, and I stopped him and told him how I was glad that we were friends and that I thought of him as a brother. I said, "If this happens, I will miss you very much, bro. Just try to always keep that good outlook on everything and learn all you can about God. He will help you, even if no one else cares. In the end, God is all that matters, you know."

When they brought breakfast at 6:00 a.m., I didn't want anything to eat. I started getting dressed. Ricky was up and talking to me, and Jimmy had gotten pretty quiet. I guess he had things running through his mind. I put my pants and shirt on.

Death row Warden Kalone came, and the major came with him to strip search me to make sure that I didn't have a weapon on me to try to hurt one of them. I gave them my pants, shirt, and tennis shoes to check out, and I took off my underwear and T-shirt.

I couldn't believe how low I had fallen to be treated like that. But could I cry and say anything? No. I had brought all this on myself. I asked myself, *Am I that evil?* But I knew that no matter what man said, only God could really judge me and my life. In a lot of ways, I was only getting what was due to me for what I had done. But only God knew for sure what was in my heart.

Never would I have believed that I would end up on death row for killing someone. I was about to go to Camp F where I would later be put to death—if the U.S. Supreme Court didn't do anything for me. I didn't know what to think. I did still have some hope, but it would be a very hard day, I knew. Just like all of the guys before me and the ones that will be after me. It would be the hardest day of all our sorry lives.

"You can go on and get dressed now, Feltus," Warden Kalone said. "I think you check out okay."

After I got dressed again, they put the leg irons and the handcuffs on me and then opened my door. As I came out of my cell, I turned to the right and shook Ricky's hand and told him that I would see him around. Then I walked past my cell and to Cell 1 where Jimmy was standing at the door looking at me. I stopped and told him that I cared about him just like he was my real brother. I shook his hand, and I told him to be cool and take care of himself. When I was leaving, he was just looking on at me going through the door. I had my head up. I was determined not to let this beat me down. I was going to go with dignity. And I think that I did a damn good job of it, too.

They led me down the stairs and into the lobby. As I was walking through each gate, the Black woman guard looked at me like, *There goes another young brother that made a mess of his life.* And she was right.

She let us out of the side door where the van and truck were. We walked around to the van's side doors and the warden for death row opened it. I got in, then he closed and locked the door. He got in the front seat and some other guy was driving the van. The major got in the truck and followed behind us. We went out of the back gate. The Black woman at the back gate looked into the van and the guard driving said, "Feltus Taylor." She wrote my name down and then she opened the gate for us to go through.

The drive to Camp F was about a mile and a half. Along the way, we passed a lot of different camps and the main prison. We passed fields with cows and horses. We passed fields of corn and soybeans and some old buildings that wasn't in use anymore. That was the first time I saw all of that, and the road snaked around here and there. They pulled into the front parking lot and backed up close to the door.

I could see the prison guards standing at each end of the building with their M16s. I mean, come on. Like someone was going to fly in and pick me up. I was tripping that they had all of this for me. It was a little over the top, I think. But it was Burl's show, and he did things the way he wanted them to be done.

The guard opened the front door to Camp F's visiting shed. We went through the visiting room and turned to the right. We passed a shower to the right, then a phone, then three sets of cells. I went into the first cell. Right in front of the cell that I was in was a table with a TV set and a VCR on it. They brought two movies with them that I had seen the night before. I will say one thing for the deathwatch cells. They were very clean and had a lot more room in them than the normal cells did.

Sgt. Lee Henry was already over there waiting for me. I had asked for him to be there because him and I are cool. Sgt. Henry is a short Black guy. He has short hair, and he is dark in color. He likes to laugh and tell jokes a lot so I wanted him around. When things started looking hard, I knew he would get the laughs rolling in, and that was what we all needed that day.

About five minutes later, Warden Vannoy came in front of my cell and asked me did I need anything. He said that I could get whatever I wanted to eat for breakfast.

I told him that I wanted eggs, bacon, and toast.

About fifteen minutes later, I had my food and a cup of coffee. I sat on the end of the bed and ate the food and it was really good. *Damn, it's a shame*, I thought. *You have to be about to die before they will treat you okay around this place.*

I turned on the TV to look at the early morning news, and there I was again. News people were talking about me dying. I knew it would hurt the other people who cared for me. I started looking for something else to watch.

I knew that Charles would be coming early so he could be here the whole day with me. I was going to keep him in a good mood all day. That was my job—to keep everyone else okay.

At about 8:00 a.m., Charles was here. He came down the small hallway and sat at the open chair right at the corner of the table.

Sgt. Henry was at the other end, writing down in the little book what I was doing every fifteen minutes. They do that for about one week before the execution. I really don't know why because you can kill yourself in less time than fifteen minutes, that's for sure.

Charles asked me how I was doing.

I said, "I'm good," and smiled. But I could see the worried look on his face.

We didn't have a chance to get started talking good before the guard said that I had another visit coming. Charles went on into the visiting area. Sgt. Henry put on the leg irons and handcuffs.

"Sgt. Henry, you know to take off the handcuffs, right?" I said.

He said yeah.

But after we went into the visiting shed, he didn't take them off. I don't know why. Maybe he was waiting for Warden Vonnoy to tell him that it was okay. I had to sit down with them on for about an hour, and I was mad because I couldn't move around with them on. Jane and Jan was my next visitors. Charles talked to them about England because he and his wife had been there before.

Warden Vannoy came through the door, and I got up and asked him about the handcuffs. He told Sgt. Henry to take them off. I looked at him and said he could have done that before. He just smiled at me. I went back to the table feeling a lot better, at least somewhat human, anyway.

One wall of the room had been painted by an inmate. It was a guy looking up at another coming to get him in a chariot with two horses pulling it. It seemed to be coming from heaven to earth to get him.

It was a shock to me to see where the execution room was. I didn't know it until I had to go to the bathroom, when I asked Sgt. Henry where it was. He told me that it was on the other side of the visiting shed. There was a smaller hallway leading down the outside of the shed. At the end of the hall was a door and on the other side was the bed. I said, *Damn, that is too close for me.* From time to time throughout the day, I looked back to think if I would be going that way. I tried to imagine what it would feel like, but I couldn't. It was too much for me to even think of at the time.

About an hour and a half later, I was sitting in my chair and looking into the parking lot when I saw a van pulling up with Raymond and Rodney in it. I was very glad to see them show up. We had always said we were cousins, because we had been close when I was on the outside.

When they came into the room, I got up and hugged the both of them. They sat down with Charles, Jane, and Jan. I felt right then that I was on the outside with them all. It was good that we were all together in that way, but I was sorry that it had to be the way it was. We didn't know what would happen at the end of the day.

By nightfall, I could very well be dead. I tried really hard not to be down and to keep a smile on everyone's face that was in the room.

Jean and Michele came about 10:30 a.m. Jean said still no word yet from the court. She said to keep praying and to keep our fingers crossed. They sat next to Charles and started talking to him.

Raymond and Rodney started talking to me. We talked about a lot of different things, and things we had did when I was home—like all of us going out together with our women and having a good time. Raymond brought up about the fight that Marcia and I had at his house one night. Marcia ran out to my car and locked herself in it. I was on the outside of the car, begging her to open the door so we could talk. Raymond thought it was so funny, and I had to laugh myself.

Then I wondered what Marcia was thinking. I know she knew what was going on with me because it had been on the news and in the newspaper, and Mae-Mae, her godmother, knew. I wondered if she was even thinking about me at all.

A little later, Cecile showed up. She has one problem—she can talk on and on. In a lot of ways, I was glad because when everyone else had run out of things to say, I knew that she would find something to talk about.

Another van came, and I could see the faces of my grandmother's sister Nig and her daughter Ruby, and Ruby's son C.G. I was very surprised because I didn't know if they would come or not. When they came into the room, I walked over to meet them. They looked the same but older. It had been so long since I'd seen them. I hugged each one of them, and I kissed Lil' Ruby and Aunt Nig. C.G. was now a grown man, and the last time I saw him he had to have been around twelve years old. We hadn't been in touch for a long, long time.

For a while, it was nice, but every now and then I would see Aunt Nig looking over at me, and we would just look at each other. I could almost think the very same thing that she was thinking. *How in the world did you let yourself get into this mess? Now you are hurting everyone around you by these people killing you like this.* She was so right. I really had made such an ass out of myself.

A few times, I went back to my cell area to make a few phone calls to some people that wasn't able to come and visit. I didn't talk that long because I wanted to get back to the visiting area where everyone was. I was thankful that they had taken the time to come by and wanted to be with me. It was a blessing from God. Even if the worst happened, I was surrounded by the people that did care about me.

I wondered what time the victims' families were coming along with the D. A. to the prison. I knew somewhat what they would be doing. They would go to the warden's ranch house, where they would eat and talk and wait to see what will happen, just like the other side.

On one side, you got some people that want you to live, and on the other side, you got some people that want to see you dead. No matter what happens, one side would be happy and cheering, and another would be sad. It don't make any sense, and I'm not just saying that because I'm the one sitting in the hot seat. Everyone loses in this war here. I killed, and they will kill me.

Around 3:00 p.m., Warden Cain and Assistant Warden Vonnoy came by. I guess they wanted to see how things were going with everyone. They talked to the other guards and hung around for a while. At 3:30 p.m., Warden Cain came into the room and said that it was time for us all to say our goodbyes. But no one moved. Everyone just kinda turned and looked at me with water in their eyes.

Ruby was already kinda mad because Cain didn't let us take any pictures. I don't know why, really. But Warden Cain fed me some bullshit line about people sending pictures here and there to show what the person was like before they killed him. But he just didn't want to do it because my people that wanted to take pictures with me was from out of state.

About ten minutes passed by, and Warden Cain said that it really was time to go, and that we all needed to wrap up our goodbyes.

This time, I got up and hugged Raymond and told him that I loved him and kissed him on the side of his face. I did the same to Rodney. Rodney started crying openly, and Raymond had a few tears also. Then, I went to Aunt Nig and Lil' Ruby and C.G., and on until I got to everyone that was leaving. That was the hardest thing that I had to do in my life.

When I hugged and kissed Jan, she didn't want to let go of me. I looked into her eyes, and she had tears running down both sides of her face. I told her that I would be okay and that she could do this for me. She let go, and the hurt and pain of losing me was all in her face. I hugged and kissed Jane. She done better than Jan, but she also had tears in her eyes.

Aunt Nig and Ruby told me that they loved me no matter what, and I thanked them for that love that they gave to me. I hugged C.G. He just couldn't understand the whole thing, and it was hard for him to deal with. He called Burl a redneck motherfucker, but Burl didn't hear him. I told C.G. to just chill before someone heard him. I watched all of them leave and get into two vans that were parked outside of the building.

I looked through the window as they left, and I wondered if I would even see them again. Now, the only people left was Jean, Michele, Cecile, and Charles. Four people that I really, really cared for a lot. We just sat down and kept on talking about the day.

Michele went to call her office to see what they had heard, and it was still no word. A guard came back with a camera and took pictures of me and the rest. We took a lot of pictures—even a few funny ones. *All in all*, I said to myself, *if I die today, it will be okay*. It was a good day to die.

Around 4:00 p.m., we were sitting in a little group, talking to each other. Everyone was getting nervous and stuff. I had a pack of cigarettes on the table, and I got one out to smoke and then Jean got one. It was strange because Jean had stopped smoking a year before. Then Michele got one, and she hadn't smoked like in fifteen years. Then Charles got one, and he didn't smoke at all. I thought that to be really funny. We all smoked about half of that pack together. I played with them about that for a while.

I went to my cell to use the bathroom, and while I was there, Burl and Warden Vonnoy came in my cell to talk to me. They wanted to know how I was, if I needed anything and all that bullshit. Burl told me what time that they would come to get me, and he asked me did I want to eat in my cell or in the visiting shed. I told him in the shed. They were already fixing the food up in the room.

Then Warden Cain said that he was sorry about the pictures with my family. I don't really know if he was or not. Sometimes, he seemed to care and others he just seemed not to. I hope that God will one day change his heart for the better.

I made one last call to my grandmother. Her house was full of people. Ruby, C.G, and Aunt Nig, Jane, Jan, and Roger Phillips were there, too, and I said goodbye again to them.

When I went back into the visiting room, I saw all of the food, and it looked really good. It was like what I wanted—all seafood. But I wasn't that much up for a full meal. Then I thought, *What the hell. I'm about to die, anyway!* But I don't think that none of us was really hungry.

I think that Jean wanted to hit Cecile because Cecile never—and I mean never—wanted to shut up from talking. She was in high gear right then. But she was scared and didn't know what to do, and you couldn't blame her for that. We all had our own way of dealing with this. Jean had been running to the phone back and forth throughout the day. I know that she was worrying, and I could see it on Charles's and Michele's face too.

I had walked over to get my food, and there was a lot to choose from. Jean and I went back to the table to sit down, and Michele and Charles was up getting theirs. Warden Vannoy and a few guards on the strap-down team wanted to eat also.

Jean didn't like them being there. I guess it was strange for them to eat with the guy that they would be putting to death. But a lot of things in prison are funny like that. It don't always make sense.

Jean was sitting next to me, and we had started to eat when a lady guard told Jean that she had a phone call.

I couldn't help but look at her going into the office, and it was like everything went into slow motion. I had my eyes fixed on that doorway, watching, looking, and waiting for her to come out with the good or bad news. I couldn't think about nothing else. As I was looking at the door, I saw her coming out of the office with a smile on her face and both of her thumbs up. I had my spoon in my hand, and I dropped it onto my plate and said in a loud voice, "Thank you, Lord!"

She came straight to me and hugged me, and I hugged her. Then I just started to cry and cry. Jean told my other friends, and they came to hug and kiss me.

As I looked around the room, even Assistant Warden Vonnoy was smiling. The room seemed to get in a lighter mood.

Warden Cain came back in the room and said, "I bet that food will taste a lot better now, right?"

I just smiled at him. He told one of the cooks to fix me up some of whatever I wanted to take back with me to the cell. I would take a lot back so I could give it to the guys back on the tier.

I went and sat down by the window to look out on the pretty prison grounds where they kept the cows. The sun was so beautiful to look at this time of day. I thanked God again and again for what He had just done for me and for the people that were standing by me and my grandmother. The Lord really did answer my prayers and everyone else's that day. But why? Was there still something that I needed to do? Something that I hadn't got right yet? Only God knows.

My visitors and me got about another hour together before they had to leave. Just like me, they needed some time off to regroup and put this behind them. We all hugged again, and they all told me to call them later.

The ride back to death row was really good because I didn't think that I would ever see the light of day again.

Sgt. Henry said, "Didn't I tell you that you would get a stay?"

God was with me that day, but just like Dobie and the ones before him, how many more times would I go through it? I prayed none, but it was possible. Only God knew the answer to that one.

The guards brought me back to death row. I was standing in front of the tier that I lived on, and everyone started to holler and make noise. A lot of them said, "Damn, we are all glad to see you back, man."

But it was already starting to seem like a small victory for me because I didn't know what would happen in the months to come. When I got back into my cell, it was empty. The freemen had cleaned it out because they didn't think that I was coming back. They had to go get me some lockers, sheets, blankets, and a pillow. Everyone wanted to talk to me. When I came out for my hour at 9:00 p.m., I brought the food out with me. I started giving it to different people up and down the hallway. They were glad to get it, because they hadn't had food like that since they left the streets. I kept enough for Jimmy and myself to have whole meals.

When my hour was over, it was 10:00 p.m. I put the TV on the news to see what they had to say about me. The D. A. was mad because I had gotten the stay. Keith was there, too. He was sitting in that wheelchair, and I was standing at the bars of my cell door looking at the TV. It was as if we were standing face to face, looking at each other. His words to me was loud and clear and ringing in my ears.

He said, "Feltus, tell your lawyers to stop fighting for you, and let's get this over with. Enough time has gone by. It's time to bring this to an end."

All of the other guys were cursing and talking shit about what he had just said. But not me. I didn't see it that way. I had messed up his life, and he had every right to be mad and hurt that I didn't die. If I only could have talked with him to try to heal him and his family . . . I would gladly give up my appeals for that.

I couldn't eat anything after seeing the news. I gave the food to Jimmy, and I went to bed because I was tired.

I lay down and replayed in my mind the things that had happened that day. I was burnt out. But I was still alive.

The next day when I woke up, I was still very tired, and I didn't want to do a thing. I didn't want to talk or write anyone.

It took me three weeks to recover and get myself back together, but one thing was for sure. I would never be the same again after going through September 9th.

CHAPTER 24

There were five legal issues highlighted in the appeals that Feltus' lawyers made. They were: (1) Jury composition and possible racial bias—It was an all-White jury, and his lawyers raised the issue that the jury could not expect to render a verdict free from bias. The LA Supreme Court found no evidence of bias in sentencing; (2) Mental health and medication concerns— Feltus was not given the psychotropic drugs in the Baton Rouge City Jail, near the courthouse, which he had been routinely given at the Baton Rouge Parish Prison in the months before the trial. The Court rejected this argument; (3) Exclusion of jurors opposed to the death penalty—any potential juror who said they did not support the death penalty was not allowed to sit on the jury. While this issue was cited as an appealable issue, the Court ruled there was not sufficient evidence to overturn the verdict; (4) Volume of alleged errors—there were 339 assignments of error during the trial. Many of these errors were not objected to at the trial. The Court rejected this claim, citing the fact that no reversible errors would have altered the outcome; (5) International Human Rights—Amnesty International used Feltus' case to exemplify violations of fair trial standards, especially the medication and mental health issues. The court found that the trial met constitutional standards. There is little doubt that racism and medication/mental issues were significant factors in Feltus' death penalty conviction.

THE U.S. SUPREME COURT held my case for about seven months. In April 2000, Jean called.

She said, "Feltus, they turned you down, and I don't understand why."

Yes, I was hurt and let down, but I didn't show it while I was on the phone with Jean. "Well, you gave it your best, and that is all that you could do. So don't feel bad about that. You can't win them all."

"Are you sure that you're alright?"

I said, "I'm not alright because I may die now. But we did our best, and there is nothing to be mad about. I can handle it."

"Feltus, you're a strong person," she said. "I'm not that strong at all."

I told her that we would be okay no matter what happened. She said to let her go to work because she had a lot to do.

"Yeah, go give them hell," I said. I knew she was working just as hard for others as she was for me.

After that, we hung up. All I could do after that was walk around in my cell and think about what would happen now.

Not long after the court refused my case, the D. A. got an execution date set for June 6, 2000. I had forty-one days left to live.

It's been wild, wild in the field. But through it all, I have learned so much. If I had known what I know now when I was on the streets, I wouldn't have ended up on death row. The reason that I'm here on death row is because I was blind to the real world. I was blind to love and when I thought that I had found true love, it wasn't. It turned out to be a fake.

As I sit here now in my cell, waiting to die, I think about all the things I have done in my past. It hurts like hell to know that I've wasted my life. Going back to prison was my worst nightmare come true, and to think that I will die here makes it even worse. Sometimes I dream that I'm back home, then I wake up in the middle of the night and see those bars staring back at me, letting me know that this is for real. It really hurts. These cells are cold as ice in the winter, and hot as hell in the summer. I feel like I'm less than human, like an animal in a cage.

It took me a while before I could even begin to write, before I could even begin to see that my life could have meaning. And I have God and my friends to thank for that. I wasn't aware at the time, but each of these people brought something new to the table that I needed in order to help make me into a much better person. They gave me something that has helped me to become the person I am now. I hold a very special place in my heart for each one of them.

Now I have more than a lot of people do on the streets, even though I'm locked up on death row. When you stop to think about that, you can't help but say that I am blessed. Jan, Jane, Jean, Charles, Cecile, and everyone else I have named so far have become my family—one I wouldn't trade for anything in this world. They are my angels, sent by God to pick me up when I was bowed down.

I would really like to say something to the readers of this book, something to make you think. I have never before told my past in detail. And I'm not doing it now because I'm proud of how bad, how evil I was. I'm doing it because people are always speculating about why I am as I am. And to understand that about a person, why they do the things that they do, you have to know the whole story of their past. You have to know all their experiences, all the pain that's been a part of their life. Plus, this book has a meaning for me. I would not spend one hour on this book if it didn't have some meaning.

I wrote this book to get you to stop and look at your own lives, to get you to take stock of yourselves. See what you need to change within yourself. I'm not saying that your life has been anything like mine, or that you are making the very same mistakes I have. I just want you to see that anyone—no matter how good the intent—can fall and not really see that it's happening until it's too late to stop it. When you finally do realize what's happening, it's too late. You've hit bottom.

It was difficult for me to tell this story because it hurts me inside to think that I have done all the things I did. But if I want my life to have meaning I have to tell my story. If one person learns something from this, it was worth it. Please think about the story I told you.

I never even knew that I had a talent within me for writing. So, it is a real blessing that I found it, and I thank God for that. Writing means so much to me. It's a way for me to be free in my mind, and I'm helping people at the same time. I know that God put this in my heart to do.

In my very last days, I have visited with friends and family. I added more to my book, and I wrote letters and made phone calls. All kinds of people have been coming to talk and pray with me. It's good, and I know that they care, but talking about death so much only makes me depressed.

I do believe, though, that the Lord will see me through this. I really am okay with it. I know God is real in my heart and that is all that matters. Whatever happens on **June 6th**, I, Feltus Taylor, will be ready.

On the night of June 5th, Feltus and I stayed awake all night up until the early morning hours of June 6th. Around 4 a.m., he withdrew to himself and read his favorite passage from the Bible (Psalms 139:13–18), prayed, and meditated. Sometime after 5 a.m., the guard let him out of his cell to shower. After showering, he stood in front of my cell and read his favorite passage for the last time, then we exchanged prayers. Feltus was determined to keep everyone else's spirits up so there would be no sad memories of his final days. Here is something he told me on May 30th, eight days before his execution:

"Ain't no use in feeling all depressed and sorry for myself now. I'mma try to stay in good spirits and keep on laughing and joking. Even if my jokes are corny sometimes, I'mma try to keep everybody else involved with me, in good spirits also and laugh and joke with them."

Feltus often joked about dying, jokes that made most of us nervous. Even as he was chained up and leaving off the tier, he joked about it.

That night at about 8:30 p.m., I sang softly the chorus to the song "Crossroads" by Bone Thugs N Harmony. It's sort of a melancholy rap song expressing of being united with a friend or a loved one in heaven. When I looked at my watch again the time was 8:42 p.m. I thought to myself, Yeah, ol' boy probably dead now. Where my cell is, I am able to see the front entrance of the prison. At 8:53 p.m. I saw a hearst enter the prison. When I saw the hearst is when the impact hit me that Feltus was gone and would not be back. I shared with others that it is a dizzying experience watching a perfectly healthy person leave to go get killed. At 9:25 p.m. the hearst left out of the prison.

—Jimmy R. Williams, Letter to Cecile Guin, June 15, 2000

I must tell you, I don't usually have much trouble expressing my feelings, but it's difficult to describe what I've been walking around with for a over week now—a combination of shame, grief, anger, pity, pride and awe. It was a powerful day—very hard, as you might imagine, but also filled with God's presence, his mercy and grace. I do think it's going to be a while before I get a good night's rest.

The day was somewhat breathless. We'd only just made it to Camp F and begun to visit with Feltus when we found ourselves traveling back to Baton Rouge for a hearing in State District Court before Judge Don Johnson. I've been told such a hearing on the day of an execution was unprecedented.

Michelle Fournet, one of Feltus' attorneys, argued that because certain funds, unavailable at an earlier stage of Feltus' case, were now available, the defense should now be able to access those monies to hire expert witnesses to testify about the effects of misadministration of prescription drugs to Feltus during his sentencing phase. The misadministration of these medications, they argued, led to his angry outburst in court, which prejudiced the jury. Prosecutor John Sinquefield argued that all issues, including funding, had been heard and adjudicated at the various levels of the legal process, all the way up to the U.S. Supreme Court. Although Judge Johnson was clearly annoyed at Sinquefield's bulldog tactics, the defense pleadings were denied, and sometime around noon we were in the car headed back for Angola.

I felt sorry for Feltus and for the Clark and Ponsano families as the crime was dredged up and recounted yet again. I marveled that the victims' pain and emotions were still so intense, so raw and on the surface, since the crime took place over nine years ago. I was praying for them even as I was praying for Feltus and a favorable outcome for Feltus in this last-ditch legal gambit. During the hearing, Feltus was composed and didn't show any emotion, but those of us who knew him, knew how difficult this was for him too. Warden Cain and Secretary Stalder as well as other wardens and corrections officials attended the hearing.

We returned to Angola after our pleadings were denied. The afternoon was a bittersweet time. Feltus spent some time working with Ronlyn Domingue, the young woman from LSU who has been helping him to edit his autobiography, and he was able to meet with each of the rest of us separately and together in smaller groupings. At least three times, we gathered as a group for prayer. Several times during the afternoon and early evening, Feltus excused himself to make phone calls to other friends and family members who were not with us. With Feltus at Camp F were family members: his great-aunt, Mrs. Maggie O'Neal and her daughter, Ruby, from Memphis; his boyhood friends, Raymond and Rodney Jones; his long time "pen friends" Jan Macdonald from Los Angeles and Jane Officer from Birmingham, England; friends from Trinity Episcopal Church in Baton Rouge who were on his visiting list: Ann Gonzales and Tim Spruill; an old friend of Feltus' family, Mrs. Katherine Daggett; Ronlyn Domingue (mentioned above); his social worker, Cecile Guin; his attorneys Michelle Fournet and Jean Faria, and myself. Staff Chaplains Roger Mitchell, Robert Toney, a staff psychologist whose name I have forgotten, and various security officers were present most of the day. Staff Chaplain William Simon led us in prayer early in the afternoon, but didn't stay at Camp F.

Here's one telling event that will give you a glimpse into Feltus' faith. Sometime in the afternoon, one of his friends offered him a cross to wear around his neck during the execution. It was a pretty cross that had been made in Jerusalem. Feltus smiled and politely refused. "I don't need that," he said, "'cause before long I'm going to have the real thing."

Around 4:30 p.m., Feltus gathered his friends and family and we stood together in a circle holding hands. He led us in prayer, beginning, as he often did, "I want first to give the praise and the glory to God." He thanked the Lord for each one of us individually. Each of us, in turn, had the opportunity to pray, give thanks, and reflect on how much he had meant to us. It was a truly blessed and beautiful moment.

At 5 p.m., Warden Cain and others came in, and all of Feltus' party left but Jean, Michelle, Cecile, and myself. As you might imagine, it was a difficult time for both Feltus and those who had to leave.

Afterwards, the five of us—Jean, Michelle, Cecile, Feltus and I—talked quietly, laughed, kidded; Feltus remained composed throughout. Chaplains Mitchell and

Toney joined us from time to time to give words of support and encouragement. I know how important it was for Feltus to stay strong for us because he loved us so much, and of course we felt the same way. His final meal was brought in— barbecued pork ribs and shrimp, fried onion rings, grilled cheese sandwiches, and I forget what else all. Feltus ate and the rest of us picked at the food, but all of us, I think, even Feltus, were just going through the motions, struggling to maintain a sense of normalcy.

Around 7 p.m., the four of us were moved to the holding cell area where we sat in folding chairs in the presence of a security officer, Sgt. Henry. About 7:30 p.m. Jean and I were summoned by Warden McFatter to the building next door to Camp F (where they do security training, I think). We joined the other witnesses Keith Clark, John Sinquefield, Donna Ponsano's sister, other family members, three reporters, and others who were already there. Warden Cain gave us a briefing on what would take place all too soon. Secretary Stalder was there as were two medical doctors (one a coroner for W. Feliciana Parish) who would certify Feltus' death.

After the briefing, Jean and I were able to go back into the holding cell area to exchange with Feltus our final goodbyes. This was very hard for me and I know it must have been for Jean and Feltus as well. But I was so very proud of him: he was filled with the strength and grace and peace that comes from God. He was beautiful. I knew he would be okay. We had had a long visit the night before back at death row and had more time then to talk and pray together, so this was a time of very few words. As I hugged him, I recited the first few lines of the 23rd Psalm.

Jean and I and the other witnesses were led into the witness room. Jean and I sat close to one another, held hands and prayed silently. A little before 8:30 p.m., Feltus came into the execution chamber and was led directly to the microphone. He looked directly at those to whom he spoke—Keith Clark, the man he shot and paralyzed, and the sister and other family members of Donna Ponsano, the woman he shot and killed. This is what he said: "I want to tell you, Keith, and the Ponsano family, that I've always regretted what I've done, it was my own doing. After this is over with, I hope you find the peace to move on." His words to them were totally heartfelt and sincere. In the three and a half years of our meetings together, Feltus and I never failed to pray for these people, for their healing and restoration. Being able to face the people he'd hurt and to say he was sorry was something he had long wanted to do.

As he was led to the gurney, he looked at Jean and I with the deep love we shared. He smiled. I thought my heart would burst. He was dignified and *peaceful and carried himself proudly. They can kill him, I thought, but they cannot touch him.*

After he was strapped down, the curtain between the witness room and the execution chamber was closed while he was connected to the IVs. Shortly after the curtain was opened, the lethal injection began, and he and Warden Cain exchanged a few words. In a moment he closed his eyes. After a few moments, the Warden motioned to the doctors who came into the chamber and carefully examined Feltus. He was declared dead at 8:40 p.m.

In the Advocate the following (Wednesday) morning, Keith Clark, the man Feltus shot and paralyzed, was quoted as saying, "I saw a man go to heaven tonight, I do believe." This is what I saw too.

—Charles deGravelles, Episcopal Chapel of the Transfiguration,
Letter to Lane Nelson, The Angolite
June 14, 2000

AFTERWORD

Cecile Guin PHD, LCSW

ELTUS' FUNERAL WAS EVERYTHING he told me it would be. It was not like my middle-class upbringing in the Presbyterian Church. It was not quiet and dignified. It was, as he had explained to me, going to be "rockin' and rollin.'" As I got to know Feltus in the years leading up to this, we talked a lot about our different backgrounds—mine, one of opportunity; his, an all-too-familiar story of growing up poor and Black in Louisiana. I always tried to explain to the people whose cases I developed life histories on how their life trajectory had propelled them into a death penalty trial or life on death row. Feltus' story was different and it transcended my past experiences with the criminalization of the poor.

Death row stories are not usually inspiring. *Waiting to Die* presents a different perspective—one of human redemption and transformation.

By the time I met Feltus, he was already on death row. His attorney called my office to ask if we could develop a life history on her client and work with the legal defense team to prepare Feltus' story for a jury, hoping he would get a second trial. Another social worker and I began working on the case, not knowing that our lives would forever be changed.

And yet, here we were, leaving a crowded funeral at an old church where Feltus' life was celebrated. It was Feltus' elderly grandmother, Miss Henrietta's church and her church family that provided the proper homecoming for her beloved grandson.

The choir and the accompanying music were loud and boisterous, compelling everyone to join in the singing. The eulogy was provided by a local district judge who had served as co-counsel in Feltus' trial many years before. We were all in the church pews—his legal team and many of their family members, the social workers who had worked with Feltus to develop his life story, the students who helped get his writings transcribed in the computer, and the most significant people in Feltus' life, his grandmother, spiritual advisor, and two attorneys. His great-aunt and cousins had come from Memphis and his longtime pen friends from England were there. The devoted young writer who had worked with Feltus to develop his original manuscript was among the mourners.

The small church held all of us that day—we were from different worlds, yet we came together to celebrate a life that we shared. We went from the church to the cemetery where Feltus was buried. It was so difficult. I was physically exhausted and emotional from the days leading up to the execution. I really had believed I was so psychologically strong and so well prepared for whatever life would bring my way that I could bear anything. Well, I was wrong. To this day, Feltus was the only death penalty mitigation case I worked on who was executed.

The day of the execution and the last hours we spent with Feltus were the most difficult times I have ever had in my life—still twenty-five years later, I remain humbled by my inability to emotionally bear what was taking place. I had bruises up and down my legs from pinching myself to prevent uncontrollable tears and I babbled incessantly, thinking that talking was better than the silence and sadness. I openly wept when I kissed him on his bald head as he was led to the execution room. He told me everything would be ok. Later on, I thought about the absurdity of the situation with the condemned man comforting the social worker.

One of Feltus' attorneys told me in the days after the funeral that my life would be forever changed and she was right. It was not an immediate effect; it was a slow realization that our experiences in life may be more than we can bear, leaving us vulnerable, questioning the point of continuing and/or developing the fortitude to continue if faced with critical challenges. I certainly thought about this from my past, from the last twenty-five years of my life, and the years going forward.

We all survived, some better than others, and I eventually developed a renewed commitment to help those individuals and families facing the death penalty. A large part of my emotional survival can be attributed to a return to my busy and supportive university office and continuing work with the death penalty, but more importantly, my ability to develop research dollars to prevent children and youth from becoming violent offenders.

I endured Feltus' execution by continuing the work with the students and employees who would help me get Feltus' manuscript completed. We wanted the world to know what loving support and spiritual transformation could do to bring a killer, in the eyes of the community, to a place where he felt his life was blessed and he could face death, truly believing he was going to a better place. Feltus was able to communicate his deep sense of remorse to the surviving victim and the victim's family members left behind.

He gave me hope. To think that someone with Feltus' background could be restored is remarkable. His personal transformation is the ultimate example of a person who turned himself around under dire circumstances, and became the best he could be—maybe the best anybody can be—what we all aspire to. Feltus helped me mature, he pushed me to continue my doctoral research on pathways into crime, and that also gave me respite. I needed proper boundaries, and Feltus helped me deal with some of the problems I'd had separating the sadness I felt with some clients through the years with the need to empower them. He made my work more bearable. After Feltus, I felt there was nothing else in life that could go wrong that I wouldn't be able to handle.

The years came and went—the students who had worked tirelessly to transfer Feltus' handwritten manuscript into the computer graduated and moved on with their lives. The young writer who worked closely with Feltus to edit his manuscript graduated and became a successful author in her own right. I remained friends with the lawyers and spiritual advisor. My youngest sister "adopted" Jimmy, Feltus' young neighbor on death row, as Feltus had asked that we help him. Jimmy is now off death row and is in general population, now working on a master's degree in Divinity, having taken the pathway that Feltus took to redeem himself.

I remained in touch with one particular student, Monique Morrison, who never knew Feltus. As she graduated and made arrangements to move to Los Angeles to begin her career in the film industry, I handed her a copy of Feltus' manuscript, and said, "Here is a story of a very dear client of mine. Please do whatever you can to tell his story." I, in a way, handed her the torch, and, thank God I did, because she took the manuscript with her and spent the next two decades devoted to getting Feltus' story told.

Over the years, I would wake up in the middle of the night—either dreaming about Feltus, or having nightmares about my promise I made to him. As I aged, I often thought about the deep sense of failure I would feel if I could not get Feltus' story out to the world before I died.

Monique called me several times a year or came to visit me when she was in Louisiana and told me what she was working on with the manuscript. I provided her all of my interview and case notes and I believe she got to know Feltus better than most of the other people involved. We ordered the trial transcripts and she developed an understanding about how the conviction happened. She was involved in a great deal of "follow-up" with people in the book that could help her understand everything that was going on in Feltus' life and the years leading up to his death.

She met with Feltus' living victim and found him to be at peace. She questioned me extensively about my career path, early life influences, traumatic experiences, and how these characteristics had contributed to my relationship with Feltus and my plight to get his manuscript published. She got to know my family and my close companion, who remains committed with me to fulfill Feltus' dying wish.

More importantly, Monique worked through so many conflicts with ownership of Feltus' intellectual property, and there were many over a period of fourteen years. She developed a relationship with two Louisiana State University officials who figured out how to obtain intellectual property clearances and a copyright. I had spent years trying to find someone at the university who could help us get through the legal barriers we faced. When I finally met Andrew Maas, and he showed me the file of paperwork from the years of begging for help from the university, I was able to see that it wasn't that no one wanted to help me—they just did not know what to do. With a background in engineering and law, Andy figured it out and supported another university lawyer, Robert J. Brown, in working with Monique to make it happen.

How did we get from that horrible day in early June 2000, to the day in 2024 when I received a call from Monique, saying that Feltus' book is finally going to be published? It has been a long, tough journey. Getting *Waiting to Die* to the public is a story within a story.

The second story has a positive ending. We are able to tell Feltus' story, and the world will get to experience the making of a meaningful life and the power of forgiveness. For me, I would not have passed this up for anything. It has been a part of me for twenty-five years and has defined my outlook on life. I will not miss the nightmares and cold sweats evoked by fear of failing Feltus, and I look forward to knowing how *Waiting to Die* transforms the lives of others.

INDEX

ABOUT THE AUTHORS

Feltus Taylor, Jr. was raised in South Louisiana, and struggled with severe mental and developmental disabilities most of his life. He ultimately faced execution at Louisiana State Penitentiary's Angola Prison for his involvement in a violent crime.

Taylor spent less than a decade on death row at Angola Prison, a period marked by appeals and significant personal reflection. During this time, Taylor began to make peace with his situation and aimed to deter others, especially young people, from following a similar path. His story was later documented in his autobiography, *Waiting to Die: One Man's Journey on Death Row*, detailing his life's journey, the events that led to his crimes, and a close look at the "inside" and "outside" of Louisiana's harsh penal system. He was executed by lethal injection in 2000.

Taylor's life story highlights profound themes about the impacts of socioeconomic factors on crime and the potential for personal redemption, even under unlikely circumstances. It is an intimate and heartbreaking portrait of a young man struggling with identity and self-worth.

Monique Morrison was born and raised in South Louisiana, and is a proud graduate of Louisiana State University. A passionate storyteller with a deep love for true, compelling narratives, she brings over two decades of professional experience in the film and television industry, along with five years in publishing. Monique now splits her time between Bend, Oregon, and Los Angeles, where she resides with her beloved family - her spouse, children, and dogs.